Animal, Mineral, Vegetable:
Ethics and Objects

Animal, Vegetable, Mineral

Ethics and Objects

Edited by

Jeffrey Jerome Cohen

Oliphaunt Books | Washington, DC

ANIMAL, VEGETABLE, MINERAL: ETHICS AND OBJECTS
© Jeffrey Jerome Cohen, 2012.

This work is licensed under the Creative Commons Attribution-NonCommerical-NoDerivs 3.0 Unported License. To view a copy of this license, visit: http://creativecommons.org/licenses/by-nc-nd/3.0, or send a letter to Creative Commons, 444 Castro Street, Suite 900, Mountain View, California, 94041, USA.

This work is Open Access, which means that you are free to copy, distribute, display, and perform the work as long as you clearly attribute the work to the authors, that you do not use this work for commercial gain in any form whatsoever, and that you in no way alter, transform, or build upon the work outside of its normal use in academic scholarship without express permission of the author and the publisher of this volume. For any reuse or distribution, you must make clear to others the license terms of this work.

First published in 2012 by
Oliphaunt Books | Washington, DC
an imprint of punctum books
http://oliphauntbooks.com

ISBN-13: 978-0615625355
ISBN-10: 0615625355

Library of Congress Cataloging Data is available from the Library of Congress.

Cover Image: Mandrake, from *Tacuinum Sanitatis in Medicina* manuscript (Österreichischen Nationalbibliothek, Codex Vindobonensis, series nova 2644, ca. 1390)

Facing-page drawing by Heather Masciandaro.

for you who read this book, inter alia

Acknowledgments

This volume would not have been possible without the hard work required to conceptualize and then mount the two day conference "Animal, Vegetable, Mineral: Ethics and Objects in the Early Modern and Medieval Periods" in March 2011. The conference team of Lowell Duckert, Gil Harris, and Nedda Mehdizadeh have my deepest gratitude. Not only did they shape the conference, they were the best of all possible respondents for the plenaries. I am also indebted to every student and faculty member of the GW Medieval and Early Modern Studies Institute for dreaming the event and assisting in its coming into being. The eleven keynote speakers, ten of whom were able to transform their remarks into the essays collected in this volume, were models of collegiality and engaged intellectualism. The presenters at the numerous sessions and the lively audience ensured that "AVMEO" (as we called it) will always be seen as high water mark for the work of the Institute. The power of the Venetian Room at the Hotel Lombardy to sustain our fellowship into the night also deserves note.

GW MEMSI is funded by the George Washington University's Office of the Vice President for Research. I would like to thank Vice President Leo Chalupa for his unfailing support of our work, and for his willingness to send the repeated message that *humanities research matters*. Our dean, Peg Barratt, has likewise been steadfast in her advocacy on our behalf as well as her support for the Institute. We also owe a vast debt of gratitude to the alumni and friends whose philanthropy help to sustain our mission. The day to day functioning of the Institute and the execution of the conference would not have been possible without the assistance of the queen of the English Department, Connie Kibler.

Last, I would like to thank Eileen Joy for her camaraderie, her brilliance, and her inspirational ability to get things done. Working with her in her role at punctum has been a delight. Having her as a friend I treasure beyond words.

TABLE OF CONTENTS

INTRODUCTION: ALL THINGS *Jeffrey Jerome Cohen*	1
WITH THE WORLD, OR BOUND TO FACE THE SKY: THE POSTURES OF THE WOLF-CHILD OF HESSE *Karl Steel*	9
ANIMALS AND THE MEDIEVAL CULTURE OF EMPIRE *Sharon Kinoshita*	35
THE FLORAL AND THE HUMAN *Peggy McCracken*	65
EXEMPLARY ROCKS *Kellie Robertson*	91
MINERAL VIRTUE *Valerie Allen*	123
YOU ARE HERE: A MANIFESTO *Eileen A. Joy*	153

SHEEP TRACKS: A MULTI-SPECIES IMPRESSION   173
Julian Yates

THE RENAISSANCE *RES PUBLICA* OF FURNITURE   211
Julia Reinhard Lupton

POWERS OF THE HOARD: FURTHER NOTES ON MATERIAL AGENCY   237
Jane Bennett

🙢 RESPONSE ESSAYS 🙠

SPEAKING STONES, JOHN MUIR, AND A SLOWER (NON)HUMANITIES   273
Lowell Duckert

'RUINOUS MONUMENT': TRANSPORTING OBJECTS IN HERBERT'S PERSEPOLIS   281
Nedda Mehdizadeh

ANIMAL, VEGETABLE, MINERAL: TWENTY QUESTIONS   289
Jonathan Gil Harris

INTRODUCTION: ALL THINGS

Jeffrey J. Cohen

Though superseded by a newer translation, Denton Fox and Hermann Pálsson's version of *Grettir's Saga* is a text to which I feel a considerable attachment.[1] Its rendering of the Old Norse narrative is crisp and lucid, capturing the austere yet wry style of the original prose.

---

[1] *Grettir's Saga*, trans. Denton Fox and Hermann Pálsson (Toronto: University of Toronto Press, 1974). Further references by page number. The newer translation is by Jesse Byock (Oxford: Oxford University Press, 2009). For the saga in Icelandic, see *Grettis saga*, ed. Örnólfur Thorsson (Reykjavík: Mál og menning, 1994).

Even more than its artistry, though, what compels me about the Fox and Pálsson translation is the series of photographs with which the book begins. Between the introduction and the story's instigation have been inserted twelve poorly reproduced black and white pictures depicting locales mentioned in the saga. Unattributed and unpaginated, this interlude of images captures the multiplicity of histories, real and imagined, that animate the Icelandic narrative and its English reworking: a seeming timelessness in which the landscape is ever as it has been; the ninth through eleventh centuries, when Grettir and his ancestors were supposed to have journeyed these frigid expanses; the early fourteenth century, when the saga's unknown author dreamt a past that never was and placed its unfolding action at familiar fjords, glaciers, and vales; and the 1970s, when Fox and Pálsson published their English translation of *Grettir's Saga*, the first in sixty years. The initial photograph, for example, is labeled "Bjarg in Midfjord, site of Grettir's birth." The image depicts an undulation of grass, a lone rock, and a distant mountain—presumably Kaldbak, the chilly ridge that Grettir's great-grandfather Onund darkly spoke of having traded his Norwegian grain fields to possess. Yet the picture also contains a farmhouse that if not exactly modern is in no way medieval, with its bright paint, three expansive levels, and chimney. The telephone poles and curve of road quietly argue against placing a young Grettir within that home. Yet the story radiates such a keen sense of domestic vitality that it is difficult to resist thinking of this boy destined for a life no farm could contain, creating his particular brand of chaos within that pastoral space. Every time I look at the photo I expect to see geese and a horse, futilely fleeing his juvenile rage; or his beleaguered dad, storming out of the farmhouse after telling a young Grettir one more time that he has made a *very* bad choice.

Other photographs in the sequence are less anchored in time and narrative. "Arnarwater Moor, where Grettir supported himself by fishing" has no human content, just rocks and grass and mountains. It's easy to imagine that nothing has changed here in a millennium. The white snow and dark stone of "Eiriks Glacier" could be as full of half-trolls now as it was when Grettir dwelled in an ice cave, learning for the first time compassion for animals (a grieving ewe rebukes him for the devouring of her lamb) as well as the boredom that comes from a life of monstrous solitude. My favorite image, however, is captioned simply "Bjarg, a rock known as Grettir's Lift." A boulder dominates the photograph, looming perhaps nine feet high and twice that wide. A young man stands on either side, each with one hand upon the stone: on the left, a bearded fellow in jeans, a t-shirt, and a jacket holding what looks like a small shovel; on the right a man with much shorter hair, glasses, and a wool sweater with a distracting pattern. The exposure for the picture was not well executed, so the image is too bright. It's difficult to make out details. The first man actually could be holding a camera or a bicycle pump, and the second figure could be a woman. But my best guess is that we have here depicted the two translators of the saga. Having traveled to Iceland together, Denton and Hermann had themselves photographed touching a narrative landmark, *Grettishaf*, a stone so heavy that Grettir alone could raise it.

A boulder christened "Grettir's Lift" appears twice in the saga. Shortly after his first Althing ends with condemnation to three years of outlawry abroad, Grettir is journeying with some distinguished men and impresses them with his ability to heft the rock: "everyone thought it remarkable indeed that so young a man could lift the stone" (31). The landmark reappears briefly as Grettir fights haughty Gisli, stripping him slowly of his clothing so that he is reduced to streaking across the landscape in his breeches (125). The stone becomes an immediate and lasting sign of Grettir's remarkable powers, a piece of the landscape that "still lies there in the grass and is now called Grettir's Lift" (31). The picture reassures us that to this day we can see and lay hand upon the historical marker. Its endurance confirms for us that the saga's power abides. Denton and Hermann, I imagine, had themselves photographed touching Grettir's Lift in acknowledgement of *Grettir's saga* own impress upon them. The rock takes the place of the narrative, and promises that some things will never vanish into history, that stories possess an enduring materiality, weighing heavily even when they may have very little that is historical behind them.

The picture of the translators with hands upon the boulder well emblematizes a recurring theme of the saga. Unembellished as its prose may be, the narrative could not progress without a world enmeshed in densely expressive material objects. No matter how firmly anchored they may seem, these objects may, like Grettir's Lift, suddenly begin to move. Though their power sometimes becomes most evident just at the moment of a human touch, they possess an uncanny agency all their own. Fire, ice, and water are actors in the text: they consume, convey, renew, destroy. So is wood. Grettir's great-grandfather and the man most similar to him sports a timber leg, attached after his limb is severed in battle. The trunk is quite literally Onund Tree Foot's support, the bestower of his full name. The disability also makes him stronger, more renowned. Only some of the characters in the saga are people. Early in life Grettir is cruel to animals; toward the end of his days he befriends a lonely ram. The short sword that Grettir snatches from the undead Kar the Old becomes his most treasured possession, his constant companion. Kar resided in a dark burial mound, where he sat upon a throne in silent and perpetual surveillance of his silver and gold. Grettir severs the barrow-dweller's head to end his haunting. He knows that the life of objects is in their circulation, that their consignment to subterranean stasis deprives them of story. Kar's liberated sword therefore serves him well until his last moments of life. Even in death it cannot be loosened from his hands.

Yet Grettir is also undone by an agential object. Whereas a tree had been the source of Onund's continued life, Grettir dies when a log on which a curse has been inscribed arrives at his island hideout. His axe rebounds off its trunk and gashes his leg, infecting him incurably. Grettir's downfall is engineered by a sorceress, a woman who knows how to place the world's materiality into movement: the enchanted driftwood floats to Grettir's hideaway against the current, and each time it is tossed into the ocean the log returns. Things matter in this text. And why should they not? *Thing* comes from a medieval Germanic word denoting a judicial assembly. Thus Grettir's life revolves around periodic meetings of the Althing, a national convocation of Iceland's powerful men at which law cases are decided, officials elected, and momentous decisions ratified. This contentious annual assembly held at a place called the Thingvellir was a two-week struggle for power. Its participants vied over how best to be heard, how to have an enduring impress, how to bring about a desired future. Here Grettir's outlawry—his being outside the protection of the law—is twice pronounced. Grettir dies just before he is admitted back into the society that employed the mechanism of the Althing to exile him.

What if at this contest for agency some of those who spoke were not priest-chieftains or influential landholders? What if short swords, enchanted tree trunks, and hefted boulders were allowed a voice? Shouldn't an Althing include all things? Isn't a republic a *res publica*, a public thing? At a parliament (from

French *parler*), who gets to speak? In his book *Statues* Michel Serres explores the place of things like stones or statues, objects condemned to silent roles in human dramas.[2] Because Germanic and Latinate terms for "thing" are etymologically related to the words for cause (*causa, cosa, chose, Ding*), Serres observes that things tend to be admitted to reality only by legal tribunals and assemblies—as if reality were a human fabrication.[3] Yet things, especially things that appear to hold themselves in silence, must possess a power indifferent to language: something that comes from themselves, not via human allowance. Silent things must be able to speak, exert agency, propel narrative. The philosopher of science Bruno Latour has famously imagined just such a Parliament of Things, where

> Natures are present, but with their representatives, scientists who speak in their name. Societies are present, but with the objects that have long been serving as their ballast from time immemorial . . . . The imbroglios and networks that had no place now have the whole place to themselves. They are the ones that have to be represented; it is around them that the Parliament of Things gathers henceforth. 'It was the stone rejected by the builders that became the keystone' (Mark 12:10).[4]

Or the stone hefted by the Icelandic warrior doomed to a life of bad luck and unhappiness, a stormy life that proceeded through his dependence upon objects: rocks to lift, swords to keep him company, last days with a

---

[2] Michel Serres, *Statues* (Paris: François Bourin, 1987).
[3] Serres, *Statues*, 294, 307.
[4] Bruno Latour, *We Have Never Been Modern*, trans. Catherine Porter (Cambridge: Harvard University Press, 1993), 144.

fire and a ram and an island and a shepherd's hut that became his best home.

Like *Grettir's saga*, the essays collected in this volume make a cogent, collective argument that *things matter* in a double sense: the study of animals, plants, stones, tracks, stools, and other objects can lead us to important new insights about the past and present; and that they possess integrity, power, independence and vibrancy. In an acknowledgement that a politics inheres in our relations with objects (relations not necessarily premised upon human supremacy and matter's mere utility) can found a politically and ecologically engaged ethics in which the human is not the world's sole meaning-maker, and never has been. Karl Steel analyzes the world of things that undergirds the story of a feral child, and argues that these objects in the narrative are also subjects that exist for themselves, enacting violence as well as being violently consumed. Through the exchange of animals Sharon Kinoshita traces the complicated relations between Latin Christendom and the Islamic world, finding in these creatures on the move mediators as well as symbols. Peggy McCracken explores what hospitality might mean when it invites an emperor to the gendered crossing of the line between the human and the vegetal. Kellie Robertson uses the striking example of the "Chaucer Pebble" to explore a profound cultural change in the efficacy and agency of rocks, from objects possessed of animate virtue to inert matter with little place in human ethics. In medieval mineralogy Valerie Allen discerns a narrative power that invites us to rethink modern conceptions of scientific method and the creation of truth. In her manifesto Eileen Joy vigorously argues for an ethical slowing down, an attentiveness to people, texts and objects that discerns liveliness even in the literary and the supposedly inanimate. Julian Yates follows in the tracks of some sheep as they wander a terrain of philosophy, ethics, and cross-species companionship. By giving place to stools and chairs, objects typically below notice, Julia Reinhard Lupton traces the social orders they structure and the biopolitics they sustain. In the piles of toys, clothes, papers and refuse accumulated by hoarders Jane Bennett finds not a pathology so much as an awareness of the potential vibrancy of all objects.

A series of response essays closes the book. Following in the tracks of the naturalist John Muir, Lowell Duckert argues for a slow mode of tracing human and nonhuman interrelation. Nedda Mehdizadeh explores Thomas Herbert's encounter with stone ruins to examine the thickness of history and the intimacies of inhuman agency. Jonathan Gil Harris offers in closing a series of questions about human and nonhuman lives that open future paths of inquiry. Together these essays and responses encourage readers to imagine a world that does not revolve around humans, but a multiply centered expanse where we are one of many entities possessing agency, narrative power, philosophical weight, and dignity.

WITH THE WORLD, OR BOUND TO FACE THE SKY: THE POSTURES OF THE WOLF-CHILD OF HESSE

Karl Steel

The Chronicle of the Benedictine monastery of Saint Peter of Erfurt, in Thuringia, includes two records of boys raised by wolves:

> 1304 Anno Domini MCCCIIII. Quidam puer in partibus Hassie est deprehensus. Hic, sicut postea cognitum est, et sicut ipse retulit, cum trium esset annorum, a lupis est captus et mirabiliter educatus. Nam, quamcumque predam lupi pro cibo rapuerant, semper meliorem partem sumentes et arbori circumiacientes ipsi ad vorandum tribuebant. Tempore vero hiemis et frigoris foveam facientes, folia arborum et alias herbas imponentes, puerum superponebant, et se circumponentes, sic eum a frigore defendebant;

ipsum eciam manibus et pedibus repere cogebant et secum currere tamdiu, quod ex use eorum velocitatem imitabatur et saltus maximos faciebat. Hic deprehensus lignis circumligatis erectus ire ad humanam similitudinem cogebatur. Idem vero puer sepius dicebat se multo carius cum lupis, si in se esset, quam cum hominibus diligere conversari. Hic puer in curiam Heinrici principis Hassie pro spectaculo est allatus.[1]

[A certain boy in the region of Hesse was seized. This boy, as was known afterwards, and just as the boy told it himself, was taken by wolves when he was three years old and raised up wondrously. For, whatever prey the wolves snatched for food, they would take the better part and allot it to him to eat while they lay around a tree. In the time of winter and cold, they made a pit, and they put the leaves of trees and other plants in it, and placed them on the boy, surrounding him to protect him from the cold; they also compelled him to creep on hands and feet and to run with them for a long time, from which practice he imitated their speed and was able to make the greatest leaps. When he was seized, he was bound with wood to compel him to go erect in

---

[1] Oswald Holder-Egger, ed., "Chronica S. Petri Erfordensis Moderna," in *Monumenta Erphesfurtensia saec. XII, XIII, XIV*, ed. Oswald Holder-Egger, MGH SS. re. Germ. 42 (Hanover: Impensis Bibliopolii Hahniani, 1899), 326 [117–442]. All translations are my own unless otherwise noted. This paper has benefited greatly from conversations with several people, including Beth Bonnette, Brantley L. Bryant, Alison Kinney (as always), Sarah Laseke, Josh Reynolds, Robert Stanton, and Will Stockton.

a human likeness. However, this boy often said that if it were up to him he much preferred to live among wolves than among men. This boy was conveyed to the court of Henry, Prince of Hesse, for a spectacle.]

The other episode, perhaps a version of the same story, runs as follows:

> quidam puer a lupis deportatus in Wederavia in una villa nobilium, que dicitur Eczol, qui puer XII annis cum lupis erat in magna silva, que dicitur vulgariter dy Hart. Hic puer isto anno tempore hyemis in nive in vanacione captus [fuerat] a nobilibus ibidem morantibus, et vixit forte ad LXXX annos.[2]

[In 1344, a certain boy, taken by wolves in Wetterau in an estate named Eczol, who was with the wolves for twelve years in a great

---

[2] Holder-Egger, "Chronica S. Petri Erfordensis Moderna," 376. From very early on, the dates of these episodes become confused. Philipp Camerarius, *Operae Horarum Subcisivarum Sive Meditationes Historice* (Nuremberg: Christopher Lochner and Johannis Hofmann, 1591), 362–63, which otherwise exactly copies the *Chronica Moderna*, places both events in 1344; John Molle's translation of Camerarius, *The Living Librarie, or Meditations and Observations Historical, Natural, Moral, Political, and Poetical* (London: Adam Islip, 1625), 239–40, dates both to 1543. Later sources use still other years. I know of only one other medievalist who has written about this material: Gherardo Ortalli, "Animal exemplaire et culture de l'environnement: permanences et changements," in *L'Animal exemplaire au Moyen Âge (Ve - XVe siècle)*, ed. Jacques Berlioz and Marie Anne Polo de Beaulieu (Rennes: Rennes University Press, 1999), 41–50, who cites the Hesse story as an index of changing medieval attitudes towards wolves and the natural world more generally.

forest called the Hart. This boy was captured during winter in the snow by nobles who were in the area for hunting, and he lived for 80 years.]

There is nothing else like this in the Erfurt chronicle material, which tends not to list marvels, but rather to record catastrophic weather, political and papal conflicts, and a depressing number of pogroms, forced conversions and mass suicides, and accusations of ritual murder and Host desecration.[3] Barring its date, neither story seems to have any particular reason for being where it is: for example, depending on the manuscript, on either side of the Hesse event the chronicle speaks of a bridge-destroying flood, the Battle of the Golden Spurs, an archbishop's death, a severe winter, or a poisoned noblewoman.

So far as I have been able to discover, the two Erfurt accounts of animal-nurtured children are just as much outliers in medieval texuality as a whole. The many other medieval stories of animal-fostered children differ from the Erfurt material in their subjects' illustriousness. The other accounts borrow from the animal what the genealogies of the Melusina stories borrow from fairy, a way to free noble or sacred foundations from the mundane interdependence of a merely human lineage.[4] The Erfurt chronicle's stories

---

[3] For ritual murder accusations, see 289–90 (in Mainz in 1285 and 1287) and 323 (in Weißensee, Thuringia in 1303); and for mass suicides, 318–19 (Würzburg and Röttingen in 1298, during the Rintfleisch pogrom).

[4] See Jacques le Goff, "Melusina: Mother and Pioneer," in *Time, Work, and Culture in the Middle Ages*, trans. Arthur Goldhammer (Chicago: University of Chicago Press, 1980), 221–22 [205–22]. Space does not permit me to treat these figures in any detail, but they include Romulus and Remus and Cyrus (all known to the Middle Ages); several figures from chivalric narrative, including Isumbras, Octavian, Sigurðr (in

more closely resemble one in Procopius of Caesarea's sixth-century *Wars of Justinian*, where a she-goat raises an otherwise unexceptional child abandoned during wartime;[5] just as wavering a line might be drawn between the Erfurt stories and an eleventh-century schooltext by Egbert of Liège in which wolf cubs caress rather than eat a little girl protected by a blessed, red cloak.[6] The Erfurt chronicle's children, who, from the perspective of nobility, come from and come to nothing, superficially resemble the many feral children stories told from the early modern period to the present day: most famously, Amala and Kamala, two wolf-raised girls discovered in 1920 near Calcutta; Oxana Malaya, the so-called dog girl of the Ukraine, taken from the animals 20 years ago and recently featured in a BBC documentary; and a five-year-old girl from the Siberian city of Chita, never allowed outside her apartment but—per the 2009 police report—conversant

---

Þiðrekssaga), and Wolfdietrich; a widespread exemplum on the infant adventures of the illegitimate grandson of the King of Crete (Frederic C. Tubach, *Index exemplorum: A Handbook of Medieval Religious Tales* [Helsinki: Suomalainen Tiedeakatemia, 1969], #647); and several figures from early medieval Ireland: Cormac; Armengenus, father to Saint Bairre; and Saint Ailbe of Emly, all raised by wolves (Kim McCone, *Pagan Past and Christian Present in Early Irish Literature* (Maynooth: An Sagart, 1990), 191–92, 214–18; Charles Plummer, ed., *Vitae sanctorum Hiberniae*, 2 vols. (Oxford: Clarendon Press, 1910), 1:65; and William Watts Heist, ed., *Vitae sanctorum Hiberniae ex codice olim Salmanticensi nunc Bruxellensi* (Brussels: Bollandist Society, 1965), 118, 130.

[5] Procopius, *History of the Wars*, trans. Henry B. Dewing, 7 vols., Loeb Classical Library (Cambridge: Harvard University Press, 1916), VI.17, 2:11–15.

[6] Jan M. Ziolkowski, *Fairy Tales from Before Fairy Tales: The Medieval Latin Past of Wonderful Lies* (Ann Arbor: University of Michigan Press, 2009), 93–124.

in the language of the dogs and cats who raised her.[7] These and other modern accounts of feral children

---

[7] For the last two examples, see Tyson Lewis and Richard V. Kahn, *Education Out of Bounds: Reimagining Cultural Studies for a Posthuman Age* (New York: Palgrave Macmillan, 2010), 41–42. Studies of feral children are common (and modern fictional and poetic engagements perhaps inexhaustible). For lists of ancient, medieval, and folkloric stories of feral children, see Charles W. Dunn, *The Foundling and the Werwolf: A Literary-Historical Study of Guillaume de Palerne* (Toronto: University of Toronto Press, 1960), 92–106, whose twenty cases range from ancient Mesopotamia and China to the Amazon forest; Eugene S. McCartney, "Greek and Roman Lore of Animal-Nursed Infants," *Papers of the Michicgan Academy of Science, Arts, and Letters* 4 (1924): 16–28 [15–40]; and Michael P. Carroll, "The Folkloric Origins of Modern 'Animal-Parented Children' Stories," *Journal of Folklore Research* 21.1 (1984): 66, 70–73 [63–85]. Barring the brief list in Aelien's third-century *Varia historia* 12.42, the earliest catalog I know appears in Alexander Ross, *Arcana micro-cosmi, or, The Hid Secrets of Man's Body Discovered* (London: Thomas Newcomb, 1652), IV.2 (available online at http://penelope.uchicago.edu/ross/index.html). Ross, who cites the Hesse story, remarks that, "it is no more incredible for a Wolf to nurse a child, then [sic] for a Raven every day to feed *Elijah*." Representative recent studies, which tend not to differentiate sharply between animal-raised and isolated children, include: Douglas K. Candland, *Feral Children and Clever Animals: Reflections on Human Nature* (New York: Oxford University Press, 1993); Julia V. Douthwaite, *The Wild Girl, Natural Man, and the Monster: Dangerous Experiments in the Age of Enlightenment* (Chicago: University of Chicago Press, 2002), 11–69; Michael Newton, *Savage Girls and Wild Boys: A History of Feral Children* (New York: Thomas Dunne Books, 2003); Kenneth B. Kidd, *Making American Boys: Boyology and the Feral Tale* (Minneapolis: University of Minnesota Press, 2004), 3–7; Lucienne Strivay, *Enfants sauvages: approches anthropologiques* (Paris: Gallimard, 2006); and Adriana Silva Benzaquen, *Encounters with Wild Children: Temptation and Disappointment in the Study of Human Nature* (Montreal:

differ from the Erfurt material, however, by tending to speak of a child at least initially unable to talk, reluctant to eat anything but raw meat, cringing from human contact, and not long surviving reentry into the human community. Perhaps the earliest such case appears in an early seventeenth-century Hessian chronicle: the child, caught by hunters and brought to the local lord, went about on all fours, jumped unusually high, but, once taken to the castle, hid under benches, and died soon afterwards because of his intolerance for human food.[8]

Unsurprisingly, modern engagements with feral children utilize this data to consider human limits. They raise questions about the minimal socialization humans require, about the transition from human prehistory to history, and the leaps from animality to *homo infans*—speechless man—and then finally to speaking, rational humanity. Other engagements think about colonial encounters—the nineteenth-century English had a flair for turning up such stories in India— or judge their believability. Perhaps unwittingly drawing on medieval characterizations of human madness as animalization (as in the stories about

---

McGill-Queen's University Press, 2006). Only Strivay and Benzaquén give much attention to the Middle Ages or the Erfurt chronicle; most concentrate on Peter of Hanover, Victor of Aveyron, Kasper Hauser, and the many cases that follow, for, as Nancy Yousef observes, the "Enlightenment invented the wild child," so to speak, in that a widespread interest in the topic appears only in the early eighteenth century ("From the Wild Side," *History Workshop Journal* 65.1 [2008]: 215 [213–20]). For a treatment of feral children in sympathy with mine, see H. Peter Steeves, *The Things Themselves: Phenomenology and the Return to the Everyday* (Albany: State University of New York Press, 2006), 17–47.

[8] As Wilhelm Dilich, *Hessische Chronica* (Cassel: Wessel, 1605), 173, sets this event in 1341, the account may be just an early modern development of the medieval story.

Nebuchadnezzar, Yvain, and other humiliated nobles), many modern scholars have argued that so-called wolf children were in fact abandoned to the wilderness because of autism.[9]

The Hesse story lends itself easily to such analyses of human limits, as it is not so much about a boy altered by being raised incorrectly as about a pliable substance, contingently lupine or human. The boy is notably passive: *deprehensus* by either wolves or humans; *captus* by wolves; then *deprehensus*, most of what the boy experiences are things that happen *to* him. The wolves *cogebant* him to go on hands and feet, just as he *cogebatur* to walk upright in the likeness of a human. It seems that the boy's only activity is to imitate, to recount what has happened to him, and to wish the humans had let him be. This story, therefore, suggests nurture's superiority to or dominance over nature; or of the absence of any such thing as "human nature." Per Jean Itard, educator of Victor of Aveyron, perhaps most famous now as Truffaut's "Wild Child"—

> that moral superiority which has been said to be natural to man, is merely the result of

---

[9] For a representative diagnosis, see Carroll, "Folkloric Origins," 67–68, or for a related, much earlier assessment, which identifies as melancholics those who believe themselves to have been transformed into animals, see Camerarius, *Operae horarum*, 343–46. A study of the interconnections between discourses of animality and disability might begin with Heidegger (see Jacques Derrida, "'Eating Well,' or The Calculation of the Subject," in *Points: Interviews, 1974-1994*, ed. Elisabeth Weber, trans. Avital Ronell (Stanford: Stanford University Press, 1995), 277 [255–87]) or, perhaps more directly, with Temple Grandin and Catherine Johnson, *Animals in Translation: Using the Mysteries of Autism to Decode Animal Behavior* (New York: Scribner, 2005).

civilization, which raises him above other animals by a great and powerful stimulus,[10]

which, in the case of the pedagogy of Itard, meant a refinement and multiplication of the child's desires. The story of the child of Hesse finds its apotheosis in Itard's good revolutionary argument for the improvement of even the meanest sort of humankind.

This interpretation can be improved upon by noting, first, that the Hesse child, unlike the feral children of later centuries, loses nothing because of his peculiar upbringing except his ability, or desire, to walk upright. Since he can still talk, this is not a story about the complete exposure of the human child to its relations and thus of the non-existence of anything human at all. There is something there. But neither is it the story of an authentic self lost by misfortune or rescued by reintegration into its proper, human community. The child has no problem with language, nor does the tale suggest he ever lost it; he assimilates poorly to human society not because he became irreparably animalized, but because he would prefer to be among the wolves. He is therefore no more dispossesed than the boy in Caesarius of Heisterbach's thirteenth-century *Dialogus Miraculorum*. In this work, a moral and doctrinal guide and wonder collection staged as a pedagogic conversation, the master speaks of a girl temporarily kidnapped by a wolf to pluck a branch from the teeth of another; the student responds with his own story, which runs:

> Ego quendam iuvenem vidi, qui in infantia a lupis fuerat raptus, et usque ad adolescentiam

---

[10] Jean-Marc-Gaspard Itard, *An Historical Account of the Discovery and Education of a Savage man* [anon. trans. from French] (London: Printed for R. Phillips, 1802), 144.

educatus, ita ut more luporum supra manus
et pedes currere sciret, atque ululare.[11]

[I saw a certain youth who was snatched up
by wolves as an infant and was raised by them
into adolescence, and he knew how to run on
hands and feet in the manner of wolves, and
how to howl.]

This child has acquired a certain lupine knack but has apparently lost nothing worth remembering, while he has gained the quality of being a wonder or inspiration to young students who perhaps wish that they too could howl.

Here as elsewhere, disability is situational. The Hesse child becomes disabled only when the adult humans capture him and compel him to assume what they dictate as the proper human posture. An exemplum from Jacques de Vitry's popular *Sermones ad status* or *vulgares* tells of a similar effort, but this time from the perspective of the wolf. Jacques writes,

Dicitur autem quod lupa aliquando infantes
rapit et nutrit. Quando autem infans se nititur
erigere ut super pedes incedat, lupa pede
percutit eum in capite nec permittit ut se

---

[11] Caesarius of Heisterbach, *Dialogus Miraculorum*, ed. Joseph Strange, 2 vols. (Cologne: H. Lempertz & Co., 1851), 1:261. Judging from the early manuscript evidence, the student may have been named Apollonius, and he may have actually told this story; see Brian Patrick McGuire, "Friends and Tales in the Cloister: Oral Sources in Caesarius of Heisterbach's *Dialogus Miraculorum*," *Analecta Cisterciensia* 36 (1980): 242 [167–247], conveniently reprinted along with another article on the oral sources of the *Dialogus Miraculorum* in a variorum collection, Brian Patrick McGuire, *Friendship and Faith: Cistercian Men, Women, and Their Stories, 1100-1250* (Aldershot: Ashgate, 2002).

erigat sed cum pedibus ac manibus bestialiter eat.[12]

[A she-wolf stole and suckled some children; when, however, one of the children attempted to stand upright and walk, the wolf struck him on the head with her paw, and would not allow him to walk otherwise than like the beasts, on his hands and feet.]

Albert the Great's monumental treatise on animals offers another such story about a pair of wild humanoids caught in the forests of Saxony; the female died from wounds inflicted by hunters and their dogs, while the man learned to speak badly (*imperfecte valde*) and to walk upright on his two feet.[13] These various bodily

---

[12] Jacques de Vitry, *The Exempla or Illustrative Stories from the Sermones vulgares of Jacques de Vitry*, ed. and trans. Thomas Frederick Crane (London: David Nutt, 1890), 78. These early thirteenth-century sermons belong to a four-part collection including sermons *de tempore, sanctis,* and *communes*. For a list of the fourteen extant manuscripts of the *Sermones vulgares*, see Johannes Baptist Schneyer, *Repertorium der lateinischen Sermones des Mittelalters für die Zeit von 1150-1350*, 11 vols. (Aschendorff: Munster, 1969-1990), 3:220–21. For a similar modern case, see the many (contradictory and evidently apocryphal) accounts of the gazelle-boy of the Mideast, captured in 1946 in Iraq or Syria or some other nearby country, capable of great leaps, and tamed only when his captors cut his tendons; for a brief and highly skeptical treatment, see Serge Aroles, *L'enigme des enfants-loups: une certitude biologique mais un deni des archives, 1304-1954* (Paris: Publibook, 2007), 266–68.

[13] Albert the Great, *On Animals: A Medieval Summa Zoologica*, trans. Irven Michael Resnick and Kenneth F. Kitchell, Jr. (Baltimore: John Hopkins University Press, 1999), Vol. 1, 308–9. For the Latin, see Albertus Magnus, *De animalibus libri XXVI*, ed. Hermann Stadler, 2 vols. (Munich: Aschendorff, 1916), II.4, 1:244.

corrections furnish the materials for what Derrida called a "limitrophic" investigation of the human/animal boundary, among others, a study of "what abuts onto limits but also what feeds, is fed, is cared for, raised, and trained, what is cultivated on the edges of a limit."[14] Belonging to a tradition stretching back to Plato and forward to Freud, medieval scholars frequently argue that the stereotypical upright human form allows, reminds, and enables humans to direct their eyes away from mundane desires and toward heaven, while the bestial form—which this tradition presents as quadrupedal and prone to the ground—confines animals to merely terrestrial appetites.[15] The medieval corporeal tradition frequently cites either Psalms 48:21 ("Man when he was in honor did not understand," etc.) or Ovid's description of Prometheus's creation of humans in the *Metamorphoses*, where he makes humans

> ... into a shape not unlike that of the gods.
> But one way or another, man arose—erect,
> standing tall as the other beasts do not, with our faces
> set not to gaze down at the dirt beneath our feet
> but upward toward the sky....[16]

---

[14] Jacques Derrida, *The Animal That Therefore I Am*, ed. Marie-Louise Mallet, trans. David Wills (New York: Fordham University Press, 2008), 29.

[15] For an extended discussion of the "homo erectus" topos, see Karl Steel, *How to Make a Human: Animals and Violence in the Middle Ages* (Columbus: Ohio State University Press, 2011), 44–57.

[16] Ovid, *The Metamorphoses*, trans. David Slavitt (Baltimore: Johns Hopkins University, 1994), I.79–83.

In a typical formulation, the encyclopedia of Bartholomew the Englishman cites the Ovidian maxim and then explains that the upright human posture means that "homo itaque coelum quaerat, & non tanquam pecus ventri obediens, mentum in terra figat"[17] ["and so man strives for heaven, and is not like livestock obeying its stomach, with a mind fixed on the earth"], while, in another usual interpretation, the twelfth-century *Sentences* commentary of Robert of Melun observes that human bipedality shows that humankind "praeter cetera animantia rectum habet"[18] ["has rulership over other living things"]. Two incarnations of two *teloi*: the human, a subject oriented towards the immutable, looking down on the mutable only to dominate it; and the animal, ever-changing, a dominated object concerned only with mutable, temporary things like itself.

Such interpretations of the human form seek to rescue humans from worldly entanglement. For Freud, standing means smell gives way to sight as the dominant sense: "the fateful process of civilization would thus have set in with man's adoption of an erect posture. From that point the chain of events would have proceeded through the devaluation of olfactory stimuli and the isolation of the menstrual period to the time when visual stimuli were paramount and the genitals became visible."[19] Sight pretends to be the least tactile of sensations, the one most removed from what

---

[17] Bartholomaeus Anglicus, *De rerum proprietatibus* (1601; repr. Frankfurt: Minerva, 1964), 48.
[18] Edited in Richard Heinzmann, *Die Unsterblichkeit der Seele und die Auferstehung des Leibes: eine problemgeschichtliche Unter-suchung der frühscholastischen Sentenzen-und Summenliteratur von Anselm von Laon bis Wilhelm von Auxerre* (Münster: Aschendorff, 1965), 86.
[19] Sigmund Freud, *Civilization and its Discontents*, trans. James Strachey (New York: Norton, 1989), 46–47 n1.

it senses, whereas smell, as Valerie Allen observes, gets into us; the

> companionable air attends us continually, sustains us in breath, and makes a community of one. Creaturely in itself, the air rearranges subject/object relations as a continuum, and causes our selfhood to expand and contract with the elements.[20]

By understanding their posture as optical and as non-haptic, by understanding their sensory engagement as unilateral, not interactive, humans promote what Judith Butler terms an "ontology of discrete identity"[21] and try to reject their precarious involvement in the "primary vulnerability," best exemplified—not incidentally for this chapter—by infants, a condition shared more or less willingly by all that is.[22] To make the inner and outer worlds "utterly distinct," to grant "the entire surface of the body . . . an impossible impermeability,"[23] the traditional conceptualization of the up-right human self allows humans to believe themselves to be pilgrims just passing through.

Mainstream medieval Christian resurrection doctrine is of a piece with this corporeal argument, because it too presents the human body as properly celestial

---

[20] Valerie Allen, *On Farting: Language and Laughter in the Middle Ages* (New York: Palgrave Macmillan, 2007), 37.

[21] Judith Butler, *Frames of War: When is Life Grievable?* (New York: Verso, 2009), 31.

[22] Judith Butler, *Precarious Life: The Powers of Mourning and Violence* (New York: Verso, 2004), 31–32; though Butler limits her insights to intrahuman relationships, her work lends itself easily to critical animal studies. See for example Kelly Oliver, *Animal Lessons: How They Teach Us to Be Human* (New York: Columbia University Press, 2009), 42–45.

[23] Judith Butler, *Gender Trouble: Feminism and the Subversion of Identity* (New York: Routledge, 1990), 170.

and unchanging amid a disdained nonhuman world. Resurrection doctrine argued that humans would receive their own body again, intact, in the Last Judgment.[24] One strain of Christian resurrection doctrine argued that humans had a core fleshly self, a "truth of human nature,"[25] that would remain the same regardless of how humans changed during their lives, regardless of what they ate and how they grew; another, simpler strain imagined that humans could wholly assimilate the animal flesh they ate to their human bodies. Meanwhile mainstream Christian resurrection doctrine, of whatever variety, denied plants and animals any place in the afterlife.[26] Once this world and change itself has passed away, there will be nothing left to accuse humans of what they had done. The doctrine allowed humans to imagine themselves as able to injure without being injured. To invoke Butler again: the differential allocation of vulnerability serves fantasies of discrete selfhood by allowing the "properly" invulnerable—in this case, the human subject facing a world of objects—to deny "its dependency [and] its exposure" to others by "exploit[ing] those very features in others, thereby making those features 'other to' itself."[27]

---

[24] For surveys of medieval Christian resurrection doctrine, see Caroline Walker Bynum, *The Resurrection of the Body in Western Christianity, 200-1336* (New York: Columbia University Press, 1995) and Richard M. Grant, "The Resurrection of the Body," *Journal of Religion* 28 (1948): 120–30, 188–209.

[25] Philip Lyndon Reynolds, *Food and the Body: Some Peculiar Questions in High Medieval Theology* (Leiden: Brill, 1999), 50–66.

[26] Francesco Santi, "Utrum Plantae et Bruta Animalia et Corpora Mineralia Remaneant post Finem Mundi: L'animale eterno," *Micrologus* 4 (1996): 231–64.

[27] Butler, *Precarious Life*, 41.

The human imagination thus seeks a body without what it means to be a body, without any of the vulnerability, parasitism, symbiosis, and indeed symmateriality of actual bodies. Conceptualizations of the human subject as lonely, centered, isolatable to an everlasting essence—as in *Everyman*, for example—cannot account for the richness of what thrives within us, in the human microbiome, the life through and with which and *for* which we are. Speaking of the "oxymoronic truism that the human is not exclusively human," Jane Bennett directs our attention to the six kinds of bacteria that process the raw fat exuded in the crook of our elbows.[28] They too are with us, and vice versa, in an interdependence that at once constitutes and dispossesses us. Donna Haraway observes that

> human genomes can be found in only about 10 percent of all the cells that occupy the mundane space I call my body [and that] the other 90 percent of the cells are filled with the genomes of bacteria, fungi, protists, and such, some of which play in a symphony necessary to my being alive at all, and some of which are hitching a ride and doing the rest of me, of us, no harm,[29]

a passage Isabelle Stengers praises for its engagement with

> the imbroglio, perplexity and messiness of a worldly world, a world where we, our ideas

---

[28] Jane Bennett, *Vibrant Matter: A Political Ecology of Things* (Durham: Duke University Press, 2010), 112–13.
[29] Donna Haraway, *When Species Meet* (Minneapolis: University of Minnesota Press, 2008), 1–2. See also Timothy Morton, *The Ecological Thought* (Cambridge: Harvard University Press, 2010), 34–36, 66–67.

and power relations, are not alone, were never alone, will never be alone.[30]

The ongoing shiftiness of being is what the assertion of human uprightness means to correct. But the Hessian boy prefers the muck.

Down on all fours, leaping like a wolf, yet, or better, *and* speaking, he refuses the logic of the dominant humanist traditions of the Middle Ages, in which someone gets to be the human subject and something has to be the animal object, there to be dominated, used, and observed by the one subject with a rational, studious posture. This tradition allies with the philosophers who, as Derrida remarked, "have never been *seen seen* by the animal." Suspending or refusing his human dominance, Derrida allows himself the uneasiness of being caught in his own cat's eyes; he does not conjure away his uncertainty; and he opposes those who take "no account of the fact that what they call 'animal' can *look* at them, and *address* them from down there."[31] The same belief in the unilateral availability of the unreflective animal object, the same commitment to a zero-sum game of subjects and objects, must underlay a belief as old as Plato's *Republic* and repeated throughout the Middle Ages, which held that a human would be rendered speechless if seen first by a wolf,[32] if, in other words, the human were made the object of a gaze. The boy, uncommitted to human mastery and, therefore, in no danger of losing it, has allowed himself to be seen. He has been seen seen by the scandalized adults, who see that the boy

---

[30] Isabelle Stengers, "Wondering about Materialism," in *The Speculative Turn: Continental Materialism and Realism*, ed. Levi Bryant, Nick Srnicek, and Graham Harman (Melbourne: re.press, 2011), 371 [368–80].
[31] Derrida, *Animal that Therefore*, 13. Emphasis in original.
[32] For example, see Albert the Great, *On Animals*, 2:1518.

has allowed wolves to address him without, presumably, losing his ability to address them in turn.

So far as the human system is concerned, this speaking, contentedly lupine boy should not be. By training the boy for a good, upright life, the adults rehabilitate themselves according to their own understanding at the same time as they rehabilitate the boy. *Circumiacientes* and *circumponentes* with the wolves, and then, with the humans, *circumligatis*, bound up, his wolf-family probably killed, the boy is now surrounded by people who want him to be happy; who just want him to be happy; who want him to be happy for them. Here I rely on Sara Ahmed's recent *Promise of Happiness*, which counters the notion of happiness as the presumptive highest good by charac-terizing several dominant social arrangements as "happiness script[s]," "straightening device[s]"[33] which render some lives impossible by compelling "would-be subject[s] to face the right way such that [they] can receive the right impressions,"[34] to disorient such subjects from—per classical models—the lower happinesses of the body and towards the higher happinesses of the mind.[35] For the Hesse child, it doesn't quite take. He would rather be back with the wolves. His discontent provides what Ahmed calls an "unhappiness archive," in which

> the sorrow of the stranger might give us a different angle on happiness not because it teaches us what it is like or must be like to be a stranger, but because it might estrange us from the very happiness of the familiar,[36]

---

[33] Sara Ahmed, *The Promise of Happiness* (Durham: Duke University Press, 2010), 91.
[34] Ahmed, *Promise of Happiness*, 54.
[35] Ahmed, *Promise of Happiness*, 12.
[36] Ahmed, *Promise of Happiness*, 17.

in this case, the self-satisfied happiness of being human, doing it right above a disorderly world.

The adults, reactionaries unreflectively dedicated to their community, show themselves to be far less capable of response than the wolves.[37] This is especially notable given wolves' infamously stubborn rapaciousness: one of Marie de France's fables uses a wolf to signify those who "ne peot lesser a nul fuer / sun surfet ne sa glutunerie" ["cannot abandon their gluttony for any price"];[38] another features one unable to learn the whole alphabet, because the only word he can form is "lamb."[39] Note too that one manuscript of the Hesse story has the child *raptus*, not *captus*, by wolves, which then *rapuerant* their prey: snatching this child is like snatching any meat, but for whatever reasons, something about this young meat strikes them differently. The wolves break with themselves by opening a new relation to humans. Under their care, the boy thrives. The wolves feed him the best food, and they shelter him from the cold by gathering leaves, by enveloping him with their bodies, by digging him a *foveam*. A *fovea*, the den, is a word also meaning "trap" or "pitfall," one of the methods for catching wolves. They have trapped the boy by making a home for it; by capturing the boy, they have given themselves over to being trapped or caught by a new way of life. As they care for him, the wolves find that winter moves them differently. They

---

[37] For a critique of the distinction between reaction and response, see Derrida, *Animal that Therefore I Am*, 119–40, and Jacques Derrida, *The Beast and the Sovereign, Volume I*, trans. Geoffrey Bennington (Chicago: University Of Chicago Press, 2009), 115–20.

[38] Marie de France, *Fables*, ed. and trans. Harriet Spiegel (Toronto: University of Toronto Press, 1994), Fable 50, ll. 24–25; my translation.

[39] Marie, *Fables*, Fable 82.

discover how the trees and their own bodies can form a kind of clothing or living, lupine home.

The Erfurt tale thus argues for the cultural basis of even animal nature; or that "culture" might better be called adaptation, if we allow "adaptation" to be impractical, excessive, never quite a perfect fit;[40] and that adaptation's shared work of struggle or fun—which might produce a human, a wolf, a tree, an idea—cannot neatly be registered along the axes of nature and nurture, object and subject, passive and active. The Hesse story should therefore not be thought of as a narrative of the return to nature, wherever or whatever that is, or a regressive narrative of the emergence of the beast within.[41] This is a story in which the wolf-boy happens, the wolves-boy happen. The boy has been captured and trained, captured and trained again; and, otherwise sleeping or withdrawn[42] qualities in boy, wolves, and trees have been activated or made apparent in this odd event. But the chronicle calls the

---

[40] For one treatment of this topic, see Morton, *Ecological Thought*, 30, 44–45.

[41] For the meanings of the word "nature" in the Middle Ages (which, unlike modern uses of the term, was not a place one could go out into), see Monica Brzezinski Potkay, "Natural Law in 'The Owl and the Nightingale,'" *The Chaucer Review* 28 (1994): 369–71 [368–83], Rebecca M. Douglass, "Ecocriticism and Middle English Literature," *Studies in Medievalism* 10 (1998): 144–47 [136–63], and Sarah Stanbury, "Ecochaucer: Green Ethics and Medieval Nature," *Chaucer Review* 34 (2004): 4–7 [1–16].

[42] The term is key to Graham Harman's object-oriented philosophy and, in part, means to replace the inadequate notion of "potential"; see, for example, Graham Harman, *Prince of Networks: Bruno Latour and Metaphysics* (Melbourne: re.press, 2009), 187. Adam Robbert, "Further Drafts of an OOE," *Knowledge Ecology: Nature, Media, Knowledge* [weblog], August 9, 2011 (http://knowledge-ecology.com/2011/08/09/further-drafts-of-an-ooe/), sketches an object-oriented ecology sympathetic to my project.

boy *deprehensus, captus, cogebatur,* because it lacks the imagination to find descriptive tools adequate to "horizontally arranged co-participants . . . vibrat[ing] with precious and vital potentialities."[43] Everything is always at once a subject and object, or even always countable as multiple objects generated by each of the distinct various modes in which other subjects—wolves, trees, winter, Chronicle—apprehend it. Given the boy's self-estrangement, we must also recognize that subjects are objects to themselves. For even without the insights of object-oriented ontologies, we know from psychoanalysis that the boy's experience and subjectivity are not wholly his to know or experience.

Further routes of engagement remain unexplored: the child's lupine boyishness as a sign of as yet unforeclosed hopes that proper adulthood seeks to erase or tame; his gender—I know of no medieval examples of feral girls—which may be yet another symptom of the presumptive universality of the male subject, but which may also exemplify one who refuses the pretenses of carnophallogocentrism.[44] In closing, however, I will attend only to the necessary verso of "precious . . . vital[ity]," namely, death and what sustains life, and the problem of eating well.

For the boy to be fed, something had to be killed. What does it mean to be a companion, or more precisely, *concarnian* in the woods with wolves; what does it mean to be their messmate, to be given the

---

[43] Eileen A. Joy, "Mattering, the Middle Voice, and Magnanimous Self-Donations: A Response to Jeffrey's 'Queering the In/Organic,'" *In the Middle* [weblog], September 5, 2010, http://www.inthemedievalmiddle.com/2010/09/mattering-middle-voice-and-magnanimous.html.

[44] For one use of this term, see Derrida, "Eating Well," 280.

meliorem partem?[45] In the Erfurt chronicle material, as in medieval textuality in general, wolves are notorious anthropophages.[46] The chronicle records an attack in 1271 in which wolves eschewed sheep and instead devoured 30 men.[47] *Melior* might, therefore, be read as describing not the portion size or the cut but the quality, so that the *meliorem partem* is better than the usual run of meat: not mutton, but human flesh, better than animal flesh because of its purported great savor and nutritiousness: Albert the Great observes that if a wolf has eaten a human, it will seek more out "because of the sweetness of their flesh" [propter carnis dulcedinem].[48] I recall a *Radiolab* story on Barbara Smuts' time among the baboons.[49] Abandoning the pretense of being only an observing subject among animal objects, Smuts learns to sit like a baboon and to sound like one. Though a vegetarian, she salivates when she witnesses the troop kill and dismember a young gazelle. Not witnessing, then, but sensorial communion. She feels this as an encounter with her

---

[45] Haraway, *When Species Meet*, 74: "the ecologies of significant others involves messmates at table, with indigestion and without the comfort of teleological purpose from above, below, in front, or behind. This is not some kind of naturalistic reductionism; this is about living responsively as mortal beings where dying and killing are not optional" (one of the many uses of "messmate" in this book).

[46] Aleksander Pluskowski, *Wolves and the Wilderness in the Middle Ages* (Woodbridge: Boydell, 2006).

[47] Holder-Egger, "Chronica S. Petri Erfordensis Moderna," 262.

[48] Albert the Great, *On Animals*, 2:1519; *De animalibus*, 2: 1410. For more on the flavor of human flesh, see Steel, *How to Make a Human*, 118–35.

[49] Jad Abumrad and Robert Krulwich, "The Shy Baboon" [radio broadcast], *Radiolab*, February 8, 2010, http://www.radiolab.org/blogs/radiolab-blog/2010/feb/08/the-shy-baboon/.

heritage, but her abandonment to another array of care, her gustatory betrayal of both her vegetarianism and the gazelle, might just be called a different framing, remaking certain parts of the world as grievable and others not.[50] This is not her past, then, but a slippage into another present, where baboons and their desires draw their own lines between subjects and objects, between what should be protected, what can be eaten, and what is outside notice. The boy, eating the *meliorem partem*, likewise may have slipped into being a species traitor.[51] We must wonder whether the boy fled or salivated as the hunters approached.

But to present anthropophagy as particularly shocking is to be a humanist. The Hesse story demands more of us. It demands that we let our *us* slip, come what may. The wolves might have given the child especially good cuts from sheep, according to the Erfurt chronicle, their proper food. Surely from the perspective of sheep, they would still have done a wrong. This point, inspired by critical animal theory's assault on the ethical uniqueness of the so-called rational subject, might be shifted towards still stranger questions of justice inspired by the nonhierarchical thinking of actor-network philosophy and its affiliated schools, which variously complicate divisions between life and death, subjects and objects, semipermanent subjects and shifting configurations, vulnerability and breakability, and so on. For these thinkers, the ethical call might come from anywhere, to anything, without limit.[52] I think of how Augustine jeers at those who want

---

[50] For grievable lives, see Butler, *Precarious Life*, 19–49, and *Frames of War*, 1–32.

[51] I borrow this locution from the motto of Noel Ignatiev's journal *Race Traitor*, "treason to whiteness is loyalty to humanity."

[52] See especially Émilie Hache and Bruno Latour, "Morality or Moralism?: An Exercise in Sensitization," trans. Patrick

to use the commandment "thou shalt not kill" to protect animals: "but if so," he asks,

> why not extend it also to the plants, and all that is rooted in and nourished by the earth? For though this class of creatures have no sensation, yet they also are said to live, and consequently they can die; and therefore, if violence be done them, can be killed . . . . Must we reckon it a breaking of this commandment . . . to pull a flower?[53]

Augustine is being sarcastic, but he might be taken at his word if we choose to think as a flower, which too must flourish. The Dutch physician Nicholaes Tulp (most well-known today from Rembrandt's 1632 *Anatomy Lesson*) describes an Irish boy, raised by sheep, who was "magis ferae, quam hominis speciem" ["more a beast than a type of human"], whose body and diet had become ovine, who "manducabat solum gramen, ac foenum, et quidem eo delectu, quo curiosissimae oves"[54] ["ate only grass or hay, with the same choice as the fussiest of sheep"]. The Irish sheep boy and his herd might also be condemned for what

---

Camiller, *Common Knowledge* 16.2 (2010): 311–30, who set no limits on where the call for justice might arrive; Jane Bennett is also useful here, though *Vibrant Matter* admits to identification "with members of my species, insofar as they are bodies most similar to mine" (104). See also the following exchange between Jean-Luc Nancy and Derrida in "Eating Well": "[Nancy]: When you decide not to limit a potential 'subjectivity' to man, why do you then limit yourself simply to the animal? [Derrida] Nothing should be excluded" (269).

[53] Augustine, *The City of God*, trans. Marcus Dods (New York: Modern Library, 1950), I.20, 26.

[54] Nicolaes Tulp, *Observationes medicae* (Amsterdam: Elzevir, 1652), 312–13; the book appeared first in 1641, but I cite this edition because of its ready availability online.

they do to flowers, even apart from the soil erosion caused by grazing, or the intrahuman economic inequities of early modern sheep farming, points that should be remembered even if they cannot be considered here.

I must therefore return to Haraway's designation of our co-constitutive environment as a "symphony." The term elides both the overflowing proliferation and the precarity of lives living together and off each other, whose competing orientations, framings, and interests may be with but not always for each other. A symphonic trope cannot account for what remains, for the irreducibility of wants and needs to a harmony. It is better to think not of a symphony but of a polity, if this polity can be thought of without the singular cephalic supremacy of the ancient metaphor of the body politic. There are uncountable polities, each with its own hierarchies and borders, each incapable in its own way of understanding its others. Object-oriented ontology does not do away with hierarchies, nor does it entirely do away with correlationism. Rather it concocts a nonanthropocentric, universalized correlationism whose infinite centers, to be sure, would be unrecognizable to Kant or perhaps even to Quentin Meillassoux, correlationism's greatest enemy. In this universalized correlationism, subjects are objects that are cared about. Each subject organizes its world, its polity, in its own way, unwilling and indeed unable to let everything into its borders and supremacy without sacrificing its own existence. This is therefore not a flat morality but one of infinite, incommensurable hierarchies.[55]

---

[55] I developed these ideas in a brief conversation with Graham Harman at the *Speculative Medievalisms 2* conference in New York City, September 16, 2011; see http://speculativemedievalisms.blogspot.com/2011/05/speculative-medievalisms-ii-laboratory.html.

With all this in mind, vertiginously shifting our attention and concern from one call to another, from one justice or injustice to another, with something or someone always slipping from our attention, always knowing—as Žižek demands—our attention to be anamorphic, we can speculatively think as trees, as the earth, as the forest law, as the pleasures of the court of Henry. They too have their thrivings; they have their interests in some polity; because each in its own way must eat, each needs its own limitrophic investigation. Each in its own way suffers the eating of others and thus has its own vulnerable *meliorem partem*. When we eat, as we must, we should at least eat as the Hesse story imagines the wolves do, unelevated, amid the eaters, not neglecting to remember that what we eat had its own best part that we have taken, perhaps irrevocably, and that we, not innocent, will be taken in turn.[56] All bodies can only pretend to be upright; all are down here, constitutively interconnected and subject to an end; all must be immanently somewhere; all belong to others in ways they can hardly know; all subjects; all objects. All can only pretend to have a good conscience.[57]

---

[56] This passage tries to meet the demands of Derrida, "Eating Well," 281–82.

[57] "Good conscience" echoes Derrida's many scornful uses of this phrase; for example, from "Eating Well": "Responsibility is excessive or it is not a responsibility. A limited, measured, calculable, rationally distributed responsibility is already the becoming-right of morality; it is at times also, in the best hypothesis, the dream of every good conscience, in the worst hypothesis, of the petty or grand inquisitors" (286).

ANIMALS AND THE MEDIEVAL CULTURE OF EMPIRE

Sharon Kinoshita

> [W]e must take into account the myriad ways in which animals, wild and domesticated, are entwined in human cultural history: animals, after all, are foes and friends, symbols and signs; they serve as talismans, as objets d'art, as markers of status, as commodities and presentations, as sources of entertainment; clothing, food, and medicine, and even as sources of wisdom and models of human behavior.
>
> Thomas T. Allsen, *The Royal Hunt in Eurasian History*

In the opening scene of the *Chanson de Roland*, the pagan king Marsile sends Charlemagne an offer of gifts, tribute, and loyalty if the Franks will lift their siege of Saragossa and go home. The suggestion originally comes from Blancandrin, Marsile's respected and most trusted advisor:

> Mandez Carlun, a l'orguillus, al fier,
> Fedeilz servises e mult granz amistez:
> Vos li durrez urs e leons e chens,
> Set cenz camelz e mil hosturs müers,
> D'or e d'argent quatre cenz muls cargez,
> Cinquante carre qu'en ferat carïer. (ll. 28–33)[1]

> [To the proud and haughty Charles, send your loyal (feudal) service and great friendship. [Say] you will give him bears, lions, and dogs, 700 camels and 1000 molted hawks, 400 mules loaded with gold and silver, 50 carts to haul it all away.]

For eleventh- or twelfth-century listeners, this scene (as I have suggested elsewhere) would likely have evoked the Iberian institution of *parias*, the tribute money that eleventh-century Muslim kings paid to their Christian counterparts in what one historian has called a medieval "protection racket." The early twelfth-century chronicle, the *Historia Silense*, records a remarkably similar scene in which the Muslim king of Toledo comes in person to offer the king of Castille-León "an immense amount of gold and silver coin and of precious textiles" if only he will pack up his tents and go home.[2] The one striking difference between that historical chronicle and the nearly contemporary *chanson de geste* is the catalogue of animals carefully detailed in our Old French "literary" representation.

---

[1] Citations of the *Chanson* are from *La Chanson de Roland*, 2nd edn., ed. and trans. Ian Short, Lettres Gothiques (Paris: Livre de Poche, 1990); translations are mine.

[2] Sharon Kinoshita, *Medieval Boundaries: Rethinking Difference in Old French Literature* (Philadelphia: University of Pennsylvania Press, 2006), 18–19. The chronicle is named after its (erroneous) attribution to the monastery of Santo Domingo de Silos.

This essay explores the resonances of that scene against the context of the role of animals in medieval society. Where the majority of Animal Studies approaches to the Middle Ages examines the ways in which medieval texts put the category of "animal" in conversation with the category of "the human"—a "zoontology," in Cary Wolfe's words, that poses "the question of the animal and of species difference in all its various dimensions"—this essay turns instead to a cultural zoohistory that looks at the way animals functioned in and mediated between different medieval cultures.[3] The permeable boundary I will be considering is not that between the human and the animal but between Latin Christendom and the Islamic world. Specifically, I am interested in animals—camels, elephants, falcons—as objects of exchange in a shared culture of empire, as manifested in historical examples and literary representations of a traffic that, even in the age of crusades, succeeded in cutting across political and confessional boundaries in the Mediterranean and throughout Central Asia.[4]

---

[3] Cary Wolfe, "Introduction," in *Zoontologies: The Question of the Animal*, ed. Cary Wolfe, xiii [ix–xxiii]. See, for example, Karl Steel's "How to Make a Human," *Exemplaria* 20.1 (2008): 3–27, which traces the genealogy of human-animal differentiation across "Christian thinkers as diverse as the foundational Augustine and the unorthodox ninth-century court scholar John Scotus Eriugena" (11), or Peggy McCracken's "Translation and Animals in Marie de France's *Lais*," *Australian Journal of French Studies* 46.3 (2009): 206–18, on the blurring of human-animal difference, as in the morphing protagonists of Marie de France's "Bisclavret" or "Yonec."

[4] Contrast the 2006 volume, *A Communion of Subjects: Animals in Religion, Science, and Ethics*, ed. Paul Waldau and Kimberley Patton (New York: Columbia University Press, 2006), in which the historical study of animals seems to call forth a kind of taxonomic imagination. Part II of the text,

The kind of procession imagined in the opening scene of the *Chanson de Roland* was not unique to medieval Iberia. In the late eleventh century, an eastern Mediterranean prince dispatching his daughter to be wed to a foreign ruler had her dowry conveyed by

> 130 camels, magnificently clothed with Byzantine brocades. Most of the loads consisted of gold and silver and three howdahs. The dowry was also borne on 74 mules, draped in various sorts of regal brocades, whose bells and harness were of gold and silver. On six of them were twelve silver chests, containing jewels and finery that were beyond price. Preceding the mules were 33 horses of excellent stock, whose stirrups were of gold encrusted with various gems. There was also a large cradle, much of it of gold.[5]

Some 120 years later, another king dispatching *his* daughter to marry another foreign ruler equipped a baggage train comprising

> soisante sommiers tous carkiés d'avoir et d'or et d'argent et de dras de soie et de rikes joiaus;

"Animals in Abrahamic Traditions," is subdivided into chapters on Judaism, Christianity, and Islam—a kind of Linnaean classification not of the animals themselves but of civilizations defined (as for Samuel Huntingdon) by religion. Part III is devoted to "Animals in Indian Traditions" (subdivided into Hinduism, Buddhism, and Jainism), and Part IV to "Animals in Chinese Traditions" (including Early Chinese Religion, Daoism, and Confucianism).

[5] *The Annals of the Saljuq Turks: Selections from al-Kamil fi'l-Ta'rikh of 'Izz al-Din Ibn al-Athir*, trans. D. S. Richards, Studies in the History of Iran and Turkey (London: RoutledgeCurzon, 2002), 232.

ne n'i avoit sommier qui ne fust couvers d'un vermel samit qui si estoit lons qu'il trainoit bien set piés ou uit a cascun par derriere, ne ja tant n'alaissent par boe ne par laides voies que j'a en fust nus des samis escorchiés, tout par cointise et par nobleche.[6]

[sixty pack animals loaded with riches: gold, silver, silk cloths, and rich jewels. Every single pack animal was covered with a piece of red samite, so long it trailed a good seven or eight feet behind. They never went through mud or bad roads, for none of the pieces of samite was damaged, all for daintiness and nobility.]

Clearly we are in the presence of a common cultural practice: a bride being conveyed to her future husband is accompanied by a convoy of pack animals laden with gifts or payments consisting of gold, silver, jewels and silks. In the first case, the convoy includes other animals ("33 horses of excellent stock") that themselves constitute part of the present. All the animals are swathed in magnificent silks, surely the equal of those they transport. Significantly, the two examples come from opposite sides of the Muslim-Christian "divide." In the first instance, the bride was the daughter of the Seljuk sultan Malikshah, sent to Baghdad to marry the 'Abbasid caliph.'[7] Here the magnificent brocades

---

[6] Robert de Clari, *La Conquête de Constantinople*, ed. Philippe Lauer, Classiques Français du Moyen Age 40 (Paris: Champion, 1924), §117.1. Around 1214 the Bulgarian king Boril gave his cousin and step-daughter, the daughter of his predecessor Kaloyan, in marriage to the new "Latin" emperor. Florin Curta, *Southeastern Europe in the Middle Ages, 500-1250* (Cambridge: Cambridge University Press, 2006), 384–86.

[7] The description comes from the Annals of the historian Ibn al-Athir. On Ibn al-Athir, see Francesco Gabrieli, *Arab Historians of the Crusades*, trans. E. J. Costello (Berkeley:

adorning the camels and mules may be read as part of the "culturally-determined 'textile-reflex' [that] whatever could be draped should be draped," exemplifying what art historian Lisa Golombek has dubbed "The Draped Universe of Islam."[8] In the second instance, however, the bride was the daughter of Boris, king of the Vlachs, dispatched to marry the "Latin" Emperor Henry of Hainault in the wake of the Fourth Crusaders' conquest of the Byzantine capital of Constantinople, in an incident recorded by Robert de Clari—the simple knight whose chronicle of the Fourth Crusade constitutes one of the earliest examples of Old French prose historiography.

That a Muslim sultan and an Orthodox king should equip their daughters' baggage trains in such similar fashion, described in practically identical terms by writers on opposite sides of the Crusades, marks this scene as a recognizable part of what I am calling the medieval culture of empire: a set of shared courtly forms and practices signifying imperial power. Originating in ancient Mesopotamia and transmitted through the Persian and Hellenistic empires to Rome and to the Islamic world, it constituted a kind of cultural package that—in contrast to the religiously-based identities, institutions, and practices on which historians tend so often focus—passed readily across not just political but confessional lines.[9] Caliphs and

---

University of California Press, 1984), pp. xxvii–xxviii. Since he died in 1232, the two accounts (as opposed to the incidents they record) are roughly contemporary.

[8] Lisa Golombek, "The Draped Universe of Islam," in *Content and Context of Visual Arts in the Islamic World: Papers from a Colloquium in Memory of Richard Ettinghausen, Institute of Fine Arts, New York University, 2-4 April 1980*, ed. Priscilla P. Soucek (University Park: Pennsylvania State University Press, 1988), 34 [25–38].

[9] In some ways, this culture of empire forms the complement to the Carolingian and post-Carolingian cultural complex

sultans, emperors and kings presided over magnificent palaces displaying the scope and power of their rule, calculated to awe subjects and foreign visitors alike. They posed as collectors of knowledge and patrons of learning, sponsoring the compilation, translation, and transmission of scientific, medical, and literary texts. They exchanged precious portable objects (today relegated to the category of "minor" or "decorative" arts) such as rock crystal vases, carved ivory caskets, luxurious silks, and other fine artifacts that—given as diplomatic gifts, offered as tribute, or bestowed as tokens of favor—circulated widely, constituting what the late art historian Oleg Grabar dubbed the "shared culture of objects." Decorated with the same stylized courtly motifs that adorned princely palaces, they created a kind of visual *lingua franca* linking the courts of the high medieval Mediterranean. Amidst the scenes of seated lords, musicians, dancers, and winepourers, at least two of the courtly motifs—hunters and mounted falconers—bespeak the common obsession with animals, as do the numerous mirror-image representations of stylized birds and beasts: "confronted" or "addorsed" lions, falcons, peacocks, or the widespread image of one animal dominating another, usually read as an expression of raw strength and power.[10]

The possession and exchange of rare and exotic animals were recognizable elements in the medieval culture of empire. In his magisterial 2006 study, his-

---

whose emergence Robert Bartlett describes in *The Making of Europe: Conquest, Colonization, and Cultural Change, 950-1350* (Princeton: Princeton University Press, 1993).

[10] Oleg Grabar, "The Shared Culture of Objects," in *Byzantine Court Culture from 829 to 1204*, ed. Henry Maguire (Washington, DC: Dumbarton Oaks, 1997), 115–29. These motifs were first articulated as a cycle under the Umayyads and likely diffused by the spread of portable objects like silks.

torian Thomas Allsen places the institution he calls the royal hunt at the heart of "the political and cultural life of many of the peoples of premodern Eurasia." Over a period of nearly four millennia, it radiated out in remarkably homogeneous form from a "core area" centered in Iran, North India, and Turkestan across much of Eurasia, so that "courts and cultures with little direct knowledge of one another nonetheless [came to share] a similar hunting style." With its "manifold linkages between nature, culture, and politics," the royal hunt, along with ancillary institutions such as the management of hunting parks and the exchange of animals, became a key component "in interstate relations, military preparations, domestic administration, communications networks, and in the search for political legitimacy" that reveals "the extensive historical connections among the peoples of the Old World."[11] Like the inanimate decorative art objects transported along what Eva R. Hoffman terms "pathways of portability," animals entered into the complex set of political and social relations materialized by the circulation of gifts.[12] "In exchanging unusual animals," Allsen speculates, "rulers quite consciously . . . helped to solidify each other's regimes through a kind of professional courtesy."[13]

> The sender demonstrated generosity and command over Nature, and the recipient's

---

[11] Thomas T. Allsen, *The Royal Hunt in Eurasian History*, Encounters with Asia (Philadelphia: University of Pennsylvania Press, 2006), 12.

[12] Eva R. Hoffman, "Pathways of Portability: Islamic and Christian Interchange from the Tenth to the Twelfth Century," *Art History* 24.1 (2001): 17–50. On the complexities of gift exchange, see Cecily J. Hilsdale, "Gift," *Studies in Iconography* 33 (2012): 171–82.

[13] Allsen, *The Royal Hunt*, 235.

status was elevated by a convincing display of distant connections.[14]

By the Middle Ages, such exchanges were facilitated by "well-established networks specializing in the transcontinental movement of animals" found throughout the Old World, linking the Islamic Mediterranean through West Asia all the way to China.[15] Egypt became a center of redistribution from which south- and central-African giraffes received as tribute or transported as part of the commercial traffic in exotic animals were "reexported or offered as royal presentations to caliphs and other Muslim rulers," by the thirteenth century reaching courts in Sicily and Central Asia.[16] Elephants originally from India or Southeast Asia were often "recycled" in princely gift exchanges that sometimes took them as far as Latin Europe.[17]

The most famous example is undoubtedly Abu'l Abbas, the elephant that the historical Charlemagne

---

[14] Allsen, *The Royal Hunt*, 234.

[15] Allsen, *The Royal Hunt*, 236. On the Latin West and the Muslim world's shared roots in classical antiquity, see, *inter alia*, Richard Bulliet, *The Case for Islamo-Christian Civilization* (New York: Columbia University Press, 2004), 1–45.

[16] Allsen, *The Royal Hunt*, 236.

[17] Allsen, *The Royal Hunt*, 253. Two sixteenth-century examples of re-gifted elephants are documented in Silvio A. Bedini, *The Pope's Elephant* (Nashville: J. S. Sanders, 1998), on the creature that the Medici pope Leo X received from Manuel I of Portugal in 1514, and *The Elephant's Journey*, trans. Margaret Jull Costa (Boston: Houghton Mifflin Harcourt, 2010), Nobel laureate José Saramago's posthumous novel on the elephant Manuel's son Joao III gave the Habsburg Archduke Maximilian in 1551. Both speak to the reterritorialization of power forged by the new Portuguese sea-link to the Indies as well as to the early modern persistence / transformation of a medieval phenomenon.

received, along with the other "large presents," from the 'Abbasid caliph Harun al-Rashid (referred to in the Royal Frankish Annals as "Harun Emir al Mumenin, the king of the Persians").[18] The fact that Charlemagne had apparently requested such an animal through the envoy Isaac the Jew, whom he had dispatched four years earlier, indicates that "the Frankish ruler had some inkling that elephants were considered proper animals of state by his peers to the east."[19] As Alessandro Barbero writes,

> the possession of an elephant or any other exotic animal had symbolic importance. It was the prerogative of the imperial figure to whom God had entrusted the government of a large portion of the world and whose name had been heard in infinitely distant lands. Both Charles and Harun were certainly well aware of all these connotations.[20]

As for the other unspecified "large presents," they may be gleaned from those Charlemagne received from the "king of Persia" in 807. These included a tent, canopy, and curtains "of unbelievable size and beauty;" precious silk robes, perfumes, ointments, and balsam; and an ingenious mechanical water clock featuring "twelve horsemen who at the end of each hour stepped out of twelve windows"—a magnificent display

---

[18] *Carolingian Chronicles: Royal Frankish Annals and Nithard's Histories*, trans. Bernhard Walter Scholz with Barbara Rogers (Ann Arbor: University of Michigan Press, 1970), 81–82.
[19] Allsen, *The Royal Hunt*, 253.
[20] Alessandro Barbero, *Charlemagne: Father of a Continent*, trans. Allan Cameron (Berkeley: University of California Press, 2004), 100.

indicating how thoroughly the ability to mobilize tributary splendor was on the side of the caliph.[21]

> There was every extravagance the East could provide . . . Charles could not compete with the splendor and ingenuity of such gifts, but he returned the compliment with *hounds, horses, mules, and precious fabrics*, which do not appear to have made a similar impression on Arab chroniclers.[22]

Already in this ninth-century chronicle, we see the kernel of the cultural practice the *Roland* poet will evoke three centuries later: an embassy between rulers of different religions, mediated by the transmission of rare and expensive objects. Closer to the time of the *Chanson de Roland*, Henry I of England (according to William of Malmesbury in his *Gesta Regum Anglorum*)

> took passionate delight in the marvels of other countries, with much affability . . . asking foreign kings to send him animals not found in England—lions, leopards, lynxes, camels—and he had a park called Woodstock in which he kept his pets of this description.[23]

---

[21] *Carolingian Chronicles*, 87.
[22] Barbero, *Charlemagne*, 100 (emphases added). On representations of Harun al-Rashid as a giver of gifts in the Arabic *adab* [refined courtly] tradition, see Jocelyn Sharlet, "Tokens of Resentment: Medieval Arabic Narratives About Gift Exchange and Social Conflict," *Journal of Arabic and Islamic Studies* 11.3 (2011): 83–92 [62–100].
[23] William of Malmesbury, *Gesta Regum Anglorum. The History of the English Kings*, 2 vols., ed. and trans. R. A. B. Mynors, R. M. Thomson, and M. Winterbottom (Oxford: Clarendon Press, 1998), 1:741. I thank Jeffrey Jerome Cohen for this reference.

In 1105, after his victory at Caen, Henry I "paraded a young lion, a lynx, camels, and an ostrich before a populace that followed the animals with exuberant pleasure and wonder. The message was of a ruler so powerful he could acquire and control even these fearsome, wild, and expensive creatures."[24] Willene Clark attributes this predilection for wild animals to the twelfth-century revival of Classicism:

> Among the most effective symbols of Roman might were the wild and exotic animals that the ancient emperor and statesmen imported for ceremonial processions, for the bloody but impressive games of the arena, and for their personal menageries.[25]

Though a self-conscious revival the practices of antiquity may have been involved, another model was closer to hand: that of the medieval culture of empire centered in the Islamic and Byzantine worlds. By cultivating forms and practices associated with the prestigious courts of places like Constantinople, Baghdad, or Cairo, Latin rulers could signify their participation in an ancient discourse of rulership recognizable across the Eurasian continent.

Henry I's compound of Woodstock provides a northern European echo of what Allsen identifies as an important component of the culture of empire: the cultivation of hunting parks—"secured, artificial environments . . . found in some form almost everywhere royal courts mounted royal hunts." Though dating as far back as Egypt in the third millennium BCE, it was in ancient Persia under Achaemenid rule that such parks

---

[24] Willene B. Clark, *A Medieval Book of Beasts: The Second-Family Bestiary: Commentary, Art, Text and Translation* (Woodbridge: Boydell, 2006), 17–18.
[25] Clark, *A Medieval Book of Beasts*, 17–18.

coalesced as an imperial institution. "[F]our or five times larger than any of its predecessors," the Achaemenid empire became

> the model for statecraft and kingly government in the core area. Everything associated with their state was consequently imbued with special properties; its very success . . . magnified the importance of all Achaemenid institutions and promoted them near and far as essential attributes of sovereignty and majesty, and as necessary ingredients for, and the ultimate measure of, political success.[26]

Achaemenid forms and practices were imitated and appropriated by rulers of client states (such as the Orontids of Armenia) and successor states (notably the Sasanian rulers of pre-Islamic Iran), moving from there into Islamic, especially 'Abbasid, culture, becoming wide-spread in the medieval culture of empire.[27] A suggestion of the symbolic capital invested in the royal hunting park may be glimpsed in *Relatio de Legatine*

---

[26] Allsen, *The Royal Hunt*, 36–37. For the formative role of ancient Persia in the elaboration of imperial visual culture, see Margaret Cool Root, *The King and Kingship in Achaemenid Art: Essays on the Creation of an Iconography of Empire* (Leiden: Brill, 1979).
[27] Allsen, *The Royal Hunt*, 37. The "selective appropriation and adaptation of hallmark Achaemenid Persian forms" have recently been identified among the first century CE Nabataeans, attesting to the "longevity of the Achaemenid legacy . . . in regions that were once strategic zones of its vast empire," in this case deployed in "conscious resistance to Roman cultural hegemony through the deployment of eastward-resonating visual paradigms": Björn Anderson, "Imperial Legacies, Local Identities: References to Achaemenid Persian Iconography on Crenelated Nabataean Tombs," *Ars Orientalis* 32 (2002): 163 [163–207].

Constantinopolitana—Bishop Liudprand of Cremona's first-person account of his embassy to the court of the Byzantine emperor Nicephoros Phocas on behalf of the German emperor Otto the Great in 968. During the course of his visit, Liudprand tells Otto,

> Nicephorus asked me whether you had preserves, that is, hunting grounds, or if, instead of preserves, you had wild donkeys or other animals. When I affirmed to him that you had preserves, and animals in the hunting grounds, with the exception of wild donkeys, he said: 'I will lead you to our preserve, whose enormity, as well as the wild, that is woodland, donkeys, you will marvel to see.'[28]

From the standpoint of the medieval culture of empire, we easily discern that Nicephorus's question represents not mere idle curiosity but a gambit in an aggressive game of cultural one-upmanship. (An eleventh-century Central Asian "mirror for princes" describes hunting parks as "a major attribute of majesty, like conquest, generosity, and the bestowal of justice."[29]) Led to a preserve that he finds "hilly, overgrown, [and] unpleasant," Liudprand continues, he was shown a herd of "wild" donkeys of the very same kind, he rather petulantly asserts, that are found *domesticated* in the markets of Cremona, "not bare-backed, but bearing

---

[28] *The Complete Works of Liudprand of Cremona*, trans. Paolo Squatriti, Medieval Texts in Translation (Washington, D.C.: Catholic University of America Press, 2007), 260.

[29] Yusuf Khass Hajib, *Wisdom of Royal Glory (Kutadgy Bilig): A Turko-Islamic Mirror for Princes*, trans. Robert Dankoff (Chicago: University of Chicago Press, 1983), 256; cited in Allsen, *The Royal Hunt*, 46.

loads."[30] His stubborn insistence on the domestication and hence utility of western (in contrast to Byzantine) donkeys turns a willfully blind eye to the widespread conventions of the medieval culture of empire.[31]

It is to the Italian-born emperor Frederick II, the *stupor mundi* whose exploits and antics dominated the first half of the thirteenth century, that western Europe's first great menageries are attributed.[32] Frederick's maternal grandfather was Roger II, the upstart Norman king of Sicily (r. 1130-54) who was the first Latin Christian ruler systematically to exploit the resources of the medieval culture of empire, cannily constructing a discourse of monarchical legitimacy out of elements (visual representations, titulature and coinage, administrative practices) drawn not from Capetian France or imperial Germany but from the Byzantine Empire and Fatimid Egypt. Roger's coronation cloak, a magnificent semi-circle of red silk woven (according to the Arabic inscription embroidered in gold thread around the lower hem) in the royal

---

[30] *Liudprand of Cremona*, 261. Today Liudprand's best-known work, the *Embassy* was little circulated in the Middle Ages. Its highly sarcastic tone, Paolo Squatriti argues, should be read as a calculated rhetorical strategy "better suited to literary analysis than to psychoanalysis." Given the admiration for Byzantine society and letters that Liudprand expresses elsewhere, "the unprecedented, persistent, and explicit anti-Byzantinism" he displays throughout the text is likely an attempt to justify to Otto "why he had failed to reach an accord with Nicephorus" (*Liudprand of Cremona*, 7, 32).

[31] The Byzantines collected exotic animals at least from the eleventh century, when Constantine IX received an elephant and a giraffe from the caliph of Fatimid Egypt. In the twelfth centuries, Byzantine emperors awed visiting crusaders with the display of wild lions and leopards. See Gustave Loisel, *Histoire des menageries de l'antiquité à nos jours*, vol. 2 (Paris: Octave Doin, 1912), 142–43.

[32] Loisel, *Histoire des menageries*, 145–47.

workshop in Palermo featuring mirror-image representations of a lion dominating a camel, ostentatiously proclaimed his participation in a visual discourse of power legible across the medieval Mediterranean and western Asia.[33] When Roger's grandson William II died in 1189, his successor (and Frederick's father), the German Emperor Henry VI, found a menagerie (including a giraffe and camels) that subsequently "excited great wonder from Rome northwards to Germany."[34] Reared in Sicily amidst the remnants of Roger's multicultural kingdom, Frederick II, like his grandfather, was entirely at home in the medieval culture of empire. The celebrated manuscript of *De arte venandi cum avibus* not only attests Frederick's lifelong passion for falconry but also fits a recognizable model of the sovereign as promoter of learning.[35] The diplomatic and cultural relations he maintained with Muslims in Egypt and the Levant that so scandalized the pope and the rest of Latin Europe also ensured him "a supply of weird and wonderful beasts" that stocked his zoological garden in Palermo and leopardarium, tended by Muslim slaves, at Lucera.[36] Among these was

---

[33] While the motif of one animal dominating another is widespread in the shared culture of objects, the particular choice of a lion and a camel has sometimes been read as a declaration of Roger's triumph over Islam. William Tronzo, *The Cultures of His Kingdom: Roger II and the Cappella Palatina in Palermo* (Princeton: Princeton University Press, 1997), 142–43.

[34] David Abulafia, *Frederick II: A Medieval Emperor* (Oxford: Oxford University Press, 1988), 54.

[35] See Sharon Kinoshita, "Translatio/n, Empire, and the Worlding of Medieval Literature: The Travels of *Kalila wa Dimna*," *Postcolonial Studies* 11.4 (2008): 371–85.

[36] Abulafia, *Frederick II*, 54; Loisel, *Histoire des menageries*, 146. Abulafia notes that "contrary to general assumption," Frederick's court expenditures were much smaller than those of his Norman predecessors or his Angevin successors; among

a giraffe from the sultan of Egypt, "the first to appear in mediaeval Europe."[37]

Historian David Abulafia reads Frederick's delight in rare animals "as evidence for the endless wonders of the natural world."[38] Clearly, however, such animals were also part of a calculated display of imperial power meant to awe the emperor's subjects and enemies alike, one of his "semi-Arab habits of leadership."[39] In 1231, Frederick visited Ravenna "with many animals unknown to Italy: elephants, dromedaries, camels, panthers, gerfalcons, lions, leopards, white falcons, and bearded owls," then crossed the Alps (using the camels for transport) "with monkeys and leopards, to the wonder of the untraveled Germans."[40] In 1237, an elephant received from the sultan of Egypt played a starring role in the triumphal procession at Cremona celebrating Frederick's victory over the Lombard

---

the exceptions were expenditures on hunting lodges and "fabulous gifts to Mediterranean rulers," such as the polar bear he sent the Egyptian sultan al-Kamil in 1232 in exchange for a "gorgeous planetarium, said to be worth 20,000 marks" (Abulafia, *Frederick II*, 266–67).

[37] Charles Homer Haskins, *The Renaissance of the Twelfth Century* (New York: Meridian Books, 1957), 328, quoting the Franciscan chronicler Salimbene. Contrast the claim that the giraffe that Lorenzo de Medici received (again from the sultan of Egypt) in 1487 was the first to be displayed in an Italian city since the time of Julius Caesar. See Christiane L. Joost-Gaugier, "Lorenzo the Magnificent and the Giraffe as a Symbol of Power," *Artibus et Historiae* 8.16 (1987): 94 [91–99]. Compare with Marina Belozerskaya, *The Medici Giraffe and Other Tales of Exotic Animals and Power* (New York: Little Brown and Company, 2006).

[38] Abulafia, *Frederick II*, 54.

[39] Mary Refling, "Frederick's Menagerie," paper presented at the Second Annual Robert Dombrowski Italian Conference, Storrs, Connecticut, September 17-18, 2005: 3; http://faculty.fordham.edu/refling/Frederick%92s%20Menagerie.pdf.

[40] Haskins, *Renaissance of the Twelfth Century*, 328.

League: "topped by a wooden tower bearing Frederick's pennant," it dragged the enemy's broken *carroccio* (an ox-drawn cart bearing the Italian cities' relics and civic banners, symbolizing divine protection) "to which various high-ranking captives were shackled."[41] And in 1238, when Frederick married the English king Henry III's sister Isabelle at Worms, he was accompanied (in a variation of the bridal cortege we saw earlier) by

> numerous quadrigas [two-wheeled victory chariots] laden with gold and silver, very fine linen, purple silk, gems, precious ceramics; camels, mules, and dromedaries led by Saracens; and, finally, monkeys and leopards tended by Ethiopians.[42]

In such carefully choreographed spectacles, exotic animals, material finery, and human captives or retainers all contributed to the strategic performance of Frederick's imperial power.

With all this in mind, let's circle back to the *Chanson de Roland*'s colorful inventory of creatures in the passage with which we opened:

> Mandez Carlun, a l'orguillus, al fier,
> Fedeilz servises e mult granz amistez:
> Vos li durrez urs e leons e chens,

---

[41] Abulafia, *Frederick II*, 303–4. The *carroccio* was an ox-drawn cart bearing saints' relics and sacred banners, solemnly drawn into battle by the Italian cities, a symbol of the divine protection they craved and a source of morale to the troops.

[42] Loisel, *Histoire des menageries*, 146 (my translation). Frederick's gift of three leopards is credited as being the origin of Henry III's Tower Menagerie. Later, Henry III received an elephant (famously documented by Matthew Paris) from another brother-in-law, French king Louis IX, who purportedly acquired it while on Crusade.

> Set cenz camelz e mil hosturs müers,
> D'or e d'argent quatre cenz muls cargez,
> Cinquante carre qu'en ferat carïer.
> (ll. 28–33)

> [To the proud and haughty Charles, send your loyal (feudal) service and great friendship. [Say] you will give him bears, lions, and dogs, 700 camels and 1000 molted hawks, 400 mules loaded with gold and silver, 50 carts to haul it all away.]

In contrast to the sultan of Rum or the king of the Vlachs, Marsile promises his conversion and feudal obeisance, guaranteed not by a daughter given in marriage but by sons proferred as hostages (ll. 40–42). Given the formulaic style of Old French epic, this passage is repeated virtually verbatim twice more; first, when Blancandrin delivers the proposal to the emperor Charlemagne:

> De sun aveir vos voelt asez duner,
> Urs e leuns e veltres enchaignez,
> Set cenz cameilz e mil hosturs muëz,
> D'or e d'argent .IIII. cenz muls trussez,
> Cinquante care que carïer en ferez.
> (ll. 127–31)

> [He wants to give you a good part of his wealth: bears, lions, and chained greyhounds, 700 camels and 1000 molted hawks, 400 mules loaded with gold and silver, 50 carts you will use to cart it away.]

And again when Charlemagne reports the offer to his vassals:

> De sun aveir me volet duner grant masse,

> Urs e leuns e veltres caeignables,
> Set cenz cameilz e mil hosturs muables,
> Quatre cenz muls cargez de l'or Arabe,
> Avoec iço plus de cinquante care.
> (ll. 182–86)

> [He wants to give me a great quantity of his wealth: bears, lions, and shackled greyhounds, 700 camels and 1000 molted hawks, 400 mules loaded with gold and silver, along with more than 50 carts.]

Except for the shift from "dogs" to "greyhounds," the list remains remarkably stable—its slight variations attributable largely to changes in assonance. That this represents the conscious reflection on the part of vernacular French literature of a recognizable cultural package is confirmed in Thomas of Kent's later twelfth-century Alexander romance, *Le Roman de toute chevalerie*. There, as Alexander prepares his mighty expedition to Persia, General Tholomé attempts to dissuade him by reminding him of the copious booty that the army has already amassed: "Your men," he says, "are loaded down with the wealth they have won" ["Vos ostz sunt mult chargé de ceo qu'il ont conquis," l. 5184]. And what is this wealth that Tholomé hopes will suffice to deflect Alexander's dreams of conquest? "Gold . . . and silver, purple and greyish-brown silk, *elephants, camels, and Arabian horses*" ["Or . . . e argent, pailles purprins e bis, / Olifanz e chameals e chevals arabis," ll. 5182–83]—adding to the precious metal coin and exotic animals of the *Chanson de Roland* the fine silks of both the *Historia Silense* and the dowries of the Seljuk and Vlach princess-brides described above.[43]

---

[43] On the role of silk in the medieval culture of empire, see Sharon Kinoshita, "Almería Silk and the French Feudal

Donkeys, as Richard Bulliet observes, are "much more interesting as symbolic animals than as beasts of burden." In this light, what can we make of the particular animals Marsile offers the Franks?[44] Clearly, the bears and lions given pride of place stand in for the even more exotic giraffes and elephants that historical rulers received from their Muslim counterparts. "The cultural history of lions is," notes Allsen, "quite complex." In contrast to other "powerful predators," the lion, transported throughout Eurasia, "had meanings and well-articulated cultural niches far beyond its home range," including China; its symbolic meanings were "diffused through varied cultural media—art, literature, and religion."[45]

Both dogs and molted hawks belong to the courtly culture of the hunt cultivated among ruling classes across Europe and Asia. Unlike great exotic animals like lions, elephants, and giraffes, they came from a variety of locations and thus made natural objects of exchange between sovereigns or lords of high rank. The particular prestige of birds from the far north spawned a "truly transcontinental market for raptors," especially the gyrfalcon from the subarctic taiga—a passion shared by thirteenth-century Mongol rulers and the western emperor Frederick II.[46] (When the khan of the Golden Horde sent Frederick a letter demanding that he surrender his empire in exchange for a position at the Mongol court, the emperor is reputed to have joked

---

Imaginary: Towards a 'Material' History of the Medieval Mediterranean," in *Medieval Fabrications: Dress, Textiles, Clothwork, and Other Cultural Imaginings*, ed. E. Jane Burns (New York: Palgrave Macmillan, 2004), 165–76.

[44] Richard W. Bulliet, *Hunters, Herders, and Hamburgers: The Past and Future of Human-Animal Relations* (New York: Columbia University Press, 2005), 144.

[45] Allsen, *The Royal Hunt*, pp. 235–36. On bears, see Robert E. Bieder, *Bear* (London: Reaktion Books, 2005).

[46] Allsen, *The Royal Hunt*, 243–44.

that "with his experience he was well qualified for the post of the khan's falconer."[47]) Greyhounds—specifically named in lines 128 and 183 of the *Chanson de Roland*—were the oldest, most widely diffused, and (along with the mastiff) most prized of hunting dogs. Attested in desert rock drawings in predynastic Egypt, they spread to the Mediterranean and southern Europe in Greco-Roman antiquity, becoming the "canine of choice" across the Islamic world and into medieval India and Georgia.[48] Significantly, hunting dogs were the one area in which Europeans had something unique to offer their Muslim counterparts. The Latin West developed

> an impressive array of indigenous sleuthhounds that tracked, flushed, and pursued by scent and sound. . . . no other region bred so many specialized hunters, each dedicated to a specific type of terrain or prey.

Such dogs were first sent east by the Carolingians as princely gifts; in the twelfth century, bird dogs were introduced via the Crusader states. In sum, Marsile's offer of *veltres* participates in a millenium-long tradition that resulted in "the dispersal of specialized

---

[47] On falcons and falconers in the medieval culture of empire, see Sharon Kinoshita, "'Noi siamo mercatanti cipriani': How To Do Things in the Medieval Mediterranean," in *The Age of Philippe de Mézières: Fourteenth-Century Piety and Politics between France, Venice, and Cyprus*, ed. Renate Blumenfeld-Kosinski and Kiril Petkov (Leiden: Brill, 2012), 47–49, 53–57 [41–60].

[48] Allsen, *The Royal Hunt*, 55–56. On the wide diffusion of the greyhound, known as *leporarius* as well as *veltres* in the Latin West, see Allsen, *The Royal Hunt*, 239.

breeds across Eurasia," resulting in "the accumulation of a great diversity of canine types at major courts."[49]

The 700 camels, on the other hand, stand out as a wrinkle in this otherwise seamless show of inter-confessional exchange. While the 400 mules mentioned in line 32 are clearly pack animals, the camels' position between the hunting dogs and the molted hawks seem to mark them as part of the gift. In the Middle Ages, camels were widespread across the Islamic world, but for utilitarian purposes—particularly as a mode of transport, an alternative to the carts and pack mules alluded to in the last two lines of our quotation.[50] In antiquity, desert cities such as Petra (capital of the Nabataeans) and Palmyra became transit centers for camel caravans crossing from the Arabian Peninsula or Persia to the Mediterranean.[51] Somewhere between the third and the seventh centuries, the one-humped camel (likely native to the southern Arabian Peninsula) became the standard pack animal for the transport of men and goods from Morocco to Afghanistan, even in areas where horse-drawn carts and chariots had

---

[49] Allsen, *The Royal Hunt*, 241. In his *Antapodosis* [*Retribution*], Liudprand of Cremona reports that King Hugh of Italy included in a gift sent to the Byzantine emperor Romanos "two dogs of a kind never seen before in that region" (*Liudprand of Cremona*, 119).

[50] The importance, or not, of Mecca in camel caravan routes in pre-Islamic Arabia is a fraught point in the historiography of Islam. For a summary, see Robert Irwin, *Camel* (London: Reaktion Books, 2010), 150–52. Under the 'Abbasid caliphate, she-camels (more efficient than mules, because requiring fewer relay stops) were used for the state postal network. Irwin, *Camel*, 152.

[51] Irwin, *Camel*, 145–46. The Nabataeans, as we saw above, self-consciously used and transmitted forms of the Achaemenid culture of empire.

flourished in antiquity.[52] In Central Asia, Richard Bulliet has speculated, the southward migrations of the Oghuz Turks, bringing them within the political and cultural orbit of the Muslim world, were prompted by climatic changes that affected their camels. Converting to Islam (and becoming known as Seljuk Turks from an eponymous ancestor), they throve politically and economically by developing a hybrid one-humped camel used for military campaigns and for supplying the caravan trade at Silk Road centers such as Bukhara and Samarqand.[53]

Notably, the one exception to the camel's predominance in the Muslim world was al-Andalus (conquered and settled by *non*-camel-raising North Africans), where native mules remained the pack animals of choice and the cart never entirely disappeared. Only briefly under the Almoravids (c. 1090-1170), Sanhaja Berber tribesmen from Mauritania, did camel breeding take hold.[54] (This dating coincides with the moment when Henry II of England received a gift of camels from the Muslim king of Valencia and has also been used in attempts to date the *Chanson de Roland*.[55]) In Latin Europe, there are sporadic references to camels (perhaps introduced by the Visigoths)

---

[52] Richard W. Bulliet, *The Camel and the Wheel* (New York: Columbia University Press, 1990), 28. Bulliet points out that Arabic had only one (rarely used) word for "cart" until the fourteenth century, when there was a sudden proliferation of loanwords from several languages. Depictions of ancient or mythical scenes including carts or chariots betray medieval artists' unfamiliarity with basic modes of harnessing.

[53] Richard W. Bulliet, *Cotton, Climate, and Camels in Early Islamic Iran: A Moment in World History* (New York: Columbia University Press, 2009), 96–126.

[54] Bulliet, *The Camel and the Wheel*, 229–30.

[55] Haskins, *The Renaissance of the Twelfth Century*, 328, and Michelle Szkilnik, "Roland et les chameaux: Sur la date de la *Chanson de Roland*," *Romania* 122.3-4 (2004): 522–31.

in the early Middle Ages (including an anecdote that the seventh-century Merovingian king Clotaire II had his queen paraded on a camel before having her executed).[56] Correspondingly, camels figure little in the Latin European cultural imaginary, in striking contrast to their prominence in Arabic and Islamic culture and society.[57] Two, Robert Irwin notes, play "walk-on roles" in the late twelfth-early thirteenth-century *Roman de Renart*, including one who

> came from Lombardy to bring my lord [the lion king] Noble tribute from Constantinople. He had been sent by the pope as his legate and friend, and he was very wise and a good jurist

pressed into service in the lawsuits of Isengrin the Wolf and Bruin the Bear.[58] As late as the fifteenth century, in his account of his visit to Egypt, the German pilgrim Felix Fabri gave a long description of camels he saw "in which detailed and accurate observation mingled with learned misinformation from literary sources."[59] As we are now in a position to see, the mingling of accurate observation and misinformation likewise characterizes the *Chanson de Roland*'s account of Marsile's offer of tribute. The camels that, historically, might have been used for the transportation of tribute are here miscast

---

[56] Irwin, *Camel*, 157–58.
[57] On the centrality of camels in medieval Arabo-Islamic cultures, see Irwin, *Camel*, 68–100. For visual representations of camels in Islamic art, see Bulliet, *Cotton, Climate, and Camels*, 123–26.
[58] Irwin, *Camel*, 107, citing *The Romance of Reynard the Fox*, trans. D. D. R. Owen (Oxford: Oxford University Press, 1994), 94–95. In the later medieval West, camels connoted everything from docility and patience to superfluity and sexual appetite; see Irwin, *Camel*, 110.
[59] Irwin, *Camel*, 155.

as part of the tribute itself. For all its apparently formulaic simplicity, the catalogue of animals in Marsile's offer of submission to Charlemagne reveals the commonalities, but also the differences, forming the backdrop for historical and literary-historical examples of interconfessional ex-change.

With their simultaneous reference to pack mules (*quatre cenz muls*) and carts (*Cinquante carre*), the final two lines of our quotation (ll. 32–33) move us back toward the camelless world of Latin Europe. Carts figure prominently in another twelfth-century epic, *Le Charroi de Nîmes*. Heading south from Paris to "the kingdom of Spain" ["Espaigne le regné," l. 450] to conquer the Saracen city of Nîmes, the landless hero Guillaume Fierebrace and his nephews devise the strategy of disguising themselves as merchants and sneaking their men and arms, Trojan-horse style, through the gates of the city in barrels mounted on ox-drawn carts. Their efforts make for some of the poem's many moments of comic relief:

> "Niés," dit li cuens, envers moi entendez.
> Fetes ces bués trestot cel val aler."
> Et dit Bertran: "Por neant en parlez.
> Ge ne sai tant ne poindre ne bouter
> Qe je les puisse de lor pas remüer."
> Ot le Guillelmes, s'en a un ris gité.
> Mes a Bertran est molt mal encontré,
> Qu'il ne fu mie del mestier doctriné,
> Ainz n'en sot mot, s'est en un fanc entré,
> Trusqu'as moieus i est le char entré;
> Voit le Bertran, a pou n'est forsené.
> (ll. 996–1006)[60]

["Nephew," said the count. "Listen to me. Get these oxen across this valley." Then Bertrand

---

[60] See also lines 1002–5, 1012–14.

said, "You're wasting your breath. I can't jab or whip them hard enough to get them to change course." Guillaume heard him and let out a laugh. But Bertrand had a hard time of it. Not being the least bit schooled in the discipline and not knowing the first thing about it, he got the cart into the mud up to its hubs. Seeing this, Bertrand almost went crazy.]

For the poem's audience, Bertrand's incompetence at his task undoubtedly evoked the huge social and economic gap separating the knight—however poor and landless—from the peasant from whom he has confiscated this cart. Named for the horses indispensable to their military function, *chevaliers* are by (cultural) definition helpless at driving oxen with their unwieldy carts.[61] Here again, if in a much different register, animals prove key indicators of social and cultural distinction in the vernacular world of the French feudal nobility.

CONCLUSION

In a brief episode in his autobiographical memoir, the *Libre dels feyts* (Book of Deeds, c. 1244), the Aragonese king, Jaume I "the Conqueror" recounts how, in the midst of his campaign against Muslim Valencia, a swallow built her nest atop his tent pole. Thereupon, he writes, "I ordered that the tent not be removed until she and her children had gone, since she had come under

---

[61] On some of the resonances of horses in the constitution of knighthood, see Jeffrey J. Cohen, "Chevalerie," in *Medieval Identity Machines* (Minneapolis: University of Minnesota Press, 2003), 35–77.

our protection [in our faith]."[62] Modern readers, as critic Samuel Armistead writes, invariably take this as a "delightful vignette" revealing "an attractive note of personal intimacy and kingly compassion" on the part of a ruler better known for his campaigns of conquest. However, an early thirteenth-century Arabic geographical dictionary slightly antedating the *Libre dels feyts* tells a remarkably similar tale about the seventh-century general 'Amr ibn al-'As. According to this source, during the original Muslim conquest of Egypt, a dove laid her eggs atop the general's tent pole, leading him to declare: "She is inviolable in our proximity [*jiwari-na*]. Let the tent remain standing until she hatches her chicks and makes them fly away." From an Islamic point of view, Amr's act signifies "the sacredness of the client," evoking "a whole system of values" rooted in ancient Arabian and earlier Semitic traditions. Without venturing into the question of intentionality and Jaume's (possible) manipulation of an important Arabo-Islamic social and cultural convention, Armistead underscores

> the richly intercultural ambience of medieval Iberia, in which narrative motifs, anecdotes, and episodes could easily have migrated . . . from one linguistic community to another,

insisting that

---

[62] Samuel G. Armistead, "An Anecdote of King Jaume I and its Arabic Congener," in *Cultures in Contact in Medieval Spain: Historical and Literary Essays Presented to L. P. Harvey*. Ed. David Hook and Barry Taylor (London: King's College London, 1990), 1 [1–8]. This section is adapted from my own previous citation of Armistead's reading in "Medieval Mediterranean Literature," *PMLA* 124.2 (2009): 603 [600–8].

> our perspectives on the development of medieval Hispanic literature . . . cannot be complete unless . . . the possibility of such exchanges is taken into account and . . . exhaustively explored.[63]

In the *Libre dels feyts*, as in Marie de France's lai "Yonec," a bird turns out to be a kind of shifter between civilizations—a node of intersection where Arab-Muslim convention imperceptibly breaks the surface of a royal Catalan memoir or the ruler of an occluded Celtic kingdom disrupts the border world of Anglo-Norman Wales.[64] In this essay, I have tried to demonstrate the way a half dozen lines at the outset of the *Chanson de Roland* likewise point us toward a shared culture that, hidden in plain sight, was capable of producing remarkable confluences across apparent religious and cultural divides. Providing a common language that facilitated contact and communication, exotic animals were at the heart of a long-standing political-cultural practice that stood alongside the philosophical and theological texts constituting the prehistory of "humanist" thinking.

---

[63] Armistead, "An Anecdote," 3.
[64] For this reading of "Yonec," see Kinoshita, *Medieval Boundaries*, 110–24.

THE FLORAL AND THE HUMAN

Peggy McCracken

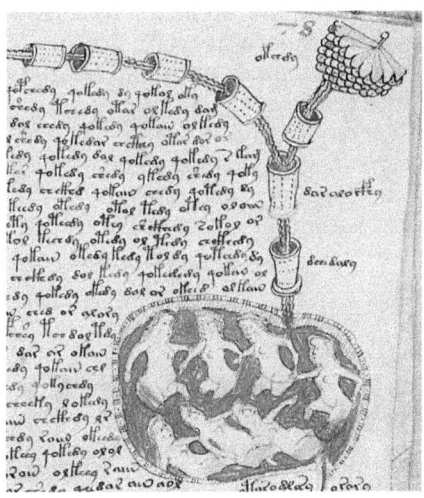

In twelfth-century versions of the *Roman d'Alexandre*, among the many curious beings Alexander the Great encounters during his exploration of India, we find a group of floral-human beings.[1] After many days in the

---

[1] I focus here on Alexander of Paris's romance, composed around 1180. The earliest French version of the *Roman d'Alexandre*, composed ca. 1110-25 by Alberic de Pisançon, survives only in a fragment. Lamprecht's *Alexanderlied* is a Middle High German adaptation of Alberic's poem, and contains a version of the flower maiden episode, which we assume Lamprecht found in Alberic's version. The episode was rewritten in the 1170s by Lambert le Tort de Châteaudun

desert, Alexander and his men come to a forest and they see there a maiden sitting at the base of every tree. The forest provides for the maidens—whatever they might wish for in the morning, they receive by evening. The flower maidens are somehow bonded to the sheltering wood. They will die if they leave the shadow of its trees. When winter comes, they disappear into the ground, and when the summer returns with warm weather, they are reborn as white flowers. The flowers hold the maidens' human form and the petals become dresses for the women.

When Alexander and his men arrive in the forest, the flower maidens welcome them eagerly. There is nothing these maidens love more than men, the text tells us, and Alexander's men have never seen more beautiful women.[2] Indeed, Alexander is "troubled"

---

and is found in the so-called Amalgam version of the *Roman d'Alexandre* in manuscripts A (Arsenal 3472, dated to before the mid-thirteenth century) and B (Venice, Museo Civico, VI, 665, dated to the first half of the fourteenth century). For editions and dates of the Amalgam versions, see *The Medieval French* Roman d'Alexandre, vol. 1, *Text of the Arsenal and Venice Versions*, ed, Milan S. La Du, Elliott Monographs, no. 36; gen ed. Edward C. Armstrong (Princeton: Princeton University Press, 1937), xi–xii, 346. It is generally assumed that Alexander of Paris develops the Amalgam version since he explicitly cites Lambert le Tort as his source. Alexander of Paris modifies the flower maiden episode in significant ways, as I will discuss below. The episode does not appear in Thomas of Kent's *Roman de toute chevalerie* (*The Anglo-Norman Alexander: Le roman de toute chevalerie*, ed. Brian Foster and Ian Short [London: Anglo-Norman Text Society, 1976-77]), the thirteenth-century French prose version (*Der Altfranzösishe Prosa-Alexanderroman*, ed. Alfons Hilka [Halle: Niemeyer, 1920]), or Jean Wauquelin's fifteenth-century *Les faicts et les conquestes d'Alexandre le Grand*, ed. Sandrine Hériché (Geneva: Droz, 2000).

[2] Mais plus aiment les homes que nule riens vivant,
Por ce q'en cuide avoir chascune son talant.

(*effreés*, l. 3367) by the sight of such beautiful creatures and he declares that he and his army will stay with them for four days. When his men enter the forest, the maidens receive them without hesitation. Each chooses a soldier, and encourages him to pursue his desires.[3]

The flower-human nature of the welcoming maidens is one mark of the strangeness that seems to trouble Alexander in this episode where boundaries between human and nonhuman, nature and culture, and conquest and hospitality are also troubled. Alexander and his men encounter a forest where the human and the vegetal merge, where nature includes the marvelous and the made, and where a conquering army is greeted with an unbounded hospitality that cannot pass the boundary of the forest.

THE CONQUEST OF NATURE

The *Roman d'Alexandre* recounts both Alexander's conquest of the known world and his exploration of unknown regions. He famously descends into the sea in a glass vessel in order to "know the truth about those

---

Cil de l'ost les conjoient si s'en vont mervellant,
Car de si beles femes ainc mais ne virent tant,
Ne ne fuissent trovees desi qu'en Oriant. (ll. 3358–62)
I cite from *The Medieval French* Roman d'Alexandre, vol. 2, *Version of Alexandre de Paris*, ed. Edward C. Armstrong et alia, Elliott Monographs, no. 37; gen. ed. Edward C. Armstrong (Princeton: Princeton University Press, 1937), as reproduced in *Le roman d'Alexandre*, trans. Laurence Harf-Lancner (Paris: Livre de Poche, 1994). All citations from Alexandre of Paris's *Roman d'Alexandre* are from this edition and all are from Branch III of the romance. All translations of the Alexander romance are mine.
[3] Les puceles n'i firent plus longe demoree,
Chascune prist le sien sans nule recelee.
Qui sa volenté vaut ne li fu pas veee,
Ains lor fu bien par eles sovent amonestee. (ll. 3459–62)

who live there," and he ascends into the heavens, pulled by griffins, to see the world from on high.[4] In his travels through India, he encounters many marvelous beings, both animal and human, and he depends on guides to explain what he finds. Just before he arrives at the forest of the flower maidens, Alexander has encountered two old men who offer to lead him to marvelous trees that will foretell the manner of his death. As Alexander and his men travel toward the arboreal oracle, they come to the forest where the flower maidens dwell. The lush forest promises a much-desired respite to Alexander and his men, who reach it after enduring the severe weather and trials of the desert, and the narrator dwells on the description of the welcoming green of the wood that extends along a river. We learn that trees of every kind are found there along with the most precious herbs and grasses.

Within the forest there is a garden filled with plants that can heal any man, no matter how sick or infirm—even the victim of the strongest poison will be restored to health, the narrator explains. The effect of the healing plants is different for women: these grasses and herbs restore lost virginity. Any damsel who had given herself over to the game of love and offered herself to her lover,

> if she spent a single night lying completely naked on the grasses, in the morning she would find herself a maid with her virginity restored simply from the sweet odor of the spices in the garden.[5]

---

[4] "De ciaus de la mer voil savoir la verité" (l. 397); "Je veul monter au ciel veoir le firmament . . . Sorveoir veul le siecle, si com li mons porprent" (ll. 4969–74).

[5] . . . Se une seule nuit i avoit reposé
Et son cors trestot nu sor les herbes posé,
Au main ne fust pucele s'eüst sa chasteé

The garden's restorative effects on women are described only in the Alexander of Paris romance; earlier versions limit the healing virtues of the garden to men. The gendering of the effects of the plants—they heal men and restore women's virginity—underscores the blurred boundary between nature and culture in this episode. The herbs and grasses appear to act both naturally and marvelously. No human intervention is necessary for their efficacy, yet their effects exceed "natural" healing processes, particularly for women. And for whose benefit do they act? The restoration of health is an obvious advantage for the man who is healed, but for whose benefit is the restoration of virginity? It seems that the virtues of the garden correspond to a valorization of intact female bodies located most commonly in patriarchal marriage politics, in the gift of a woman from one man to another, and not in the woman's gift of her own body to a lover. It seems that this apparently isolated forest in the middle of an Indian desert has been touched by the gendered cultural values of its Western audience.

Western courtly values also seem to have influenced the description of the flower maidens' clothing. When Alexander first sees the maidens, he comments at length on their beauty and on their clothes. He uses courtly conventions to describe the women's appearance and he details their clothing using a vocabulary that recalls the rich, often imported fabrics that clothe noble bodies in Western courts and courtly romances.

> Did you ever see such beautiful women in all your life? Their faces are brighter than meadow flowers, their eyes are smiling and livelier than a falcon's, and have you ever seen such perfect noses? Their mouths are well

---

De l'odour des espices et de la douceté. (ll. 3321–24)

made for kissing and you will never find such perfect ones in any place you travel! Their teeth are whiter than polished ivory or the summer lily. Their bodies are shapely, slender at the waist, with small breasts and round hips. Some are dressed in silk brocade, some wear richly dyed fabric and still others wear silk taffeta. They all have an abundance of silk. They lack nothing, they have everything they want except the company of men. There are many of them, let us stay with them since they want us so badly.[6]

Troubled by the extraordinary beauty of the women, Alexander does not question how they come to be dressed in extravagantly worked fabrics (nor does the text emphasize the eastern provenance of the silks).[7]

---

[6] Veïstes mais si beles en trestous vos aés?
Eles ont cler le vis plus que n'est flors de pres,
Les ieus vairs et rians plus que faucons müés.
Veïstes onc tels nes ne si amesurés?
Les bouches ont bien faites, ja mais teus ne verrés
A baisier n'a sentir, en cel païs n'irés,
Et ont les dens plus blanches qu'ivoires reparés
Ne que la flor de lis q'amaine li estés.
Bien sont faites de cors, grailles par les costés,
Mameles ont petites et les flans bien mollés.
Les unes sont vestues de bon pailes röés,
Les pluisors d'ostorins et li mains de cendés;
Toutes ont dras de soie tout a lor volentés.
Nule riens ne lor faut, ains ont de tout assés
Fors compaignie d'omes et si'n est grans plentés.
Or sejornons o eles, molt nos ont desirrés. (ll. 3372–87)

[7] For a discussion of the eastern fabrics that clothe courtly heroines in medieval French courtly romances, see E. Jane Burns, *Courtly Love Undressed: Reading Through Clothes in Medieval French Culture* (Philadelphia: University of Pennsylvania Press, 2002), esp. Chapter 6, "Saracen Silk: Dolls, Idols, and Courtly Ladies," 181–210. See also Sharon

Only when he prepares to leave the forest does he question how the women live there: "What kind of adventure has brought these women into the woods?" he asks, "Is it a law or a judgment? Where do they come from and where do they get their clothes?"[8] His two guides explain to him that the maidens are born as flowers, and that petals form their dresses.

> At the beginning of winter when it turns cold, they change their form and go into the earth. When summer returns with warm weather they re-emerge in the form of white flowers. Those who are born inside them have the form of a [human] body, and the outside of the flower is their clothing. Each dress is so well fitted to its wearer that there will never be need of scissors or sewing. . . . Whatever the maidens need, if they wish for it in the morning, they receive it by evening.[9]

Kinoshita, "Almería Silk and the French Feudal Imaginary: Toward a More 'Material' History of the Medieval Mediterranean," in *Medieval Fabrications: Dress, Textiles, Clothwork, and Other Cultural Imaginings*, ed. E. Jane Burns (New York: Palgrave, 2004), 165–76.

[8] Si lor a demandé: "Par com faite aventure
Sont en cel bos ces femes? Est ce lois ou droiture?
Dont vienent et que vestent?" (ll. 3523–25)

[9] A l'entrée d'yver encontre la froidure
Entrent toutes en terre et müent lor faiture,
Et qant estés revient et li biaus tans s'espure,
En guise de flors blanches vienent a lor droiture.
Celes qui dedens naissent s'ont des cors la figure
Et la flors de dehors si est lor vesteüre,
Et sont si bien taillies, chascune a sa mesure,
Que ja n'i avra force ne cisel ne costure,
Et chascuns vestemens tresq'a la terre dure.
Ainsi comme as puceles de cest bos vient a cure,
Ja ne vaudront au main icele creature
Q'eles n'aient au soir, ains que nuit soit oscure. (ll. 3531–42)

This is the only explanation Alexander receives for how the maidens live in the forest. The wise men who "know their nature" ["qui sorent lor nature," l. 3530] describe the seasonal re-birth of the maidens as part of a cycle of renewal in the forest, and the description of the clothes that are perfectly fitted without scissors or sewing emphasizes the marvelous bounty of the forest that provides for them—the maidens' dresses are not shaped by human skill. Yet this explanation of where the maidens get their clothes seems at odds with the earlier description of the embroidered and richly dyed silks the flower maidens wear: who worked these fabrics? The wise men's answer to Alexander's question ("Where do they come from and where do they get their clothes?") points to the conflation of nature and culture in this episode, a conflation further echoed in the merging of the floral and the human. And yet, any alignment of nature with the floral and of culture with the human is troubled by the representation of human-floral beings that wear richly worked clothing formed from flower petals.

As plants that grow in forests, flowers are part of the natural world, but of course flowers are also grown in gardens. Flowers are then part of culture, both because they are brought under cultivation and, as Jack Goody elaborates,

> because they are used throughout social life, for decoration, for medicine, in cooking and for their scents, but above all in establishing, maintaining, and even ending relationships, with the dead as with the living, with divinities as well as humans.[10]

---

[10] Jack Goody, *The Culture of Flowers* (Cambridge: Cambridge University Press, 1993), 2.

Flowers also have a history. Goody notes that after the fall of Rome, both the knowledge and practice of flower culture in Europe declined. Botanical learning was lost, and Christian condemnations of luxury, along with the promotion of spiritual understandings of nature, meant that flowers were less prominent in decoration and in ritual practices. Only during the twelfth century did flowers regain importance in cultural practices and representations in Europe. This was in part due to a growing trade in scents and luxury items, particularly trade eastward with China, India, and the Spice Islands. The opening up of learning and increased contact with the Islamic world were other factors leading to what Goody calls "the return of the rose" in twelfth-century Europe. We see manifestations of the renewed importance of flowers in twelfth- and thirteenth-century literature in an attention to the practical and symbolic use of flowers.[11] In Marie de France's *Eliduc*, a weasel cures its partner with a red flower, and a flower symbolizes a beloved lady in both *Romances of the Rose*.

A new importance for flowers in the twelfth century may contribute to the elaboration of Alexander's encounter with the flower maidens in romances from that period, but flowers are not symbols in Alexander's encounter with the floral-human women. Flowers share being literally and materially with the maidens. Nor does the romance describe the practical use of flowers. In fact, it insists that the healing virtues of the garden come from its herbs and grasses, not from its flowers. To be sure, flower petals form the maidens' clothing, but in a process of growth whose difference from craft or making is emphasized by the narrator in his description of the dresses that are perfectly fitted to the maidens without scissors or sewing. The romance

---

[11] See Goody's Chapter 5, "The Return of the Rose in Medieval Western Europe," in *The Culture of Flowers*, 120–65.

seems deliberately to refuse the use value of flowers both in the explanation of the healing properties of the garden and in the description of the maidens' clothing. Indeed, the naturalness of the garden itself is defined by the absence of human intervention in the forest and the garden it encloses. We learn that "Trees of various kinds were planted there, never had any of them been cut, and no man had ever dared to strike a blow to them."[12] This is a virgin forest, it has not been used by men. Similarly, the garden enclosed in the forest contains the herbs and grasses that heal men and restore women's virginity as well as fruit trees "that came there by nature, they were never planted."[13] The "natural" properties of the forest seem to be defined according to an opposition between what is made and not made. This distinction is particularly evident when the description of the flower maidens is compared to the description of the two automata that guard the bridge leading into the forest and that were created through magical arts. "The one who made these young men was too full of pride," says Alexander as they come crashing down as the result of his guides' countermagic ("Cil qui fist ces enfans fu molt outrecuidiés," l. 3445).[14] By contrast to the "made" statues, the flower-maidens take their form in a process of renewal. They emerge each spring in the flowering of the forest that has never been cut by men.

---

[12] Arbres i ot plantés de diverse maniere,
Ainc n'en fu uns trenchiés ne devant ne derriere,
Ja n'iert hom si hardis qui un seul caup i fiere. (ll. 3288–90)
[13] "I vinrent par nature, ainc n'i furent planté" (l. 3303).
[14] For an exploration of literary representations of automata in relation to twelfth-century knowledge of machines, see E.R. Truitt, "'Trei poëte, sages dotors, qui mout sorent di nigromance': Knowledge and Automata in Twelfth-Century French Literature," *Configurations* 12 (2004): 167–93.

In the paradoxical representation of a forest that provides for the maidens but is not used by them, the *Roman d'Alexandre* imagines a nature untouched by human intervention, but responsive to human needs, desires, and values. Indeed, the forest offers an apparently unbounded plenitude that is, however, limited by its boundary, since the flower maidens may not leave its shadow. They may take lovers ("Chascune prist le sien," l. 3460), but they may not be taken away, as Alexander learns when he wishes to capture the most beautiful among them and take her with him: "If one could get her away from this place and hold her in his own country, she would be made a richly crowned queen."[15] Alexander describes a process of incorporating the maiden's beauty into a value system that would reward her and whoever would take her from the forest into his land. But this maiden cannot be taken away. When Alexander's men attempt to seize her, she faints four times and pleads with Alexander not to take her out of the forest: "Noble and honorable king, do not kill me. If I am taken out of the forest by one foot, if I leave even one of the shadows, I will die immediately, that is my destiny."[16] The bond that holds the flower maidens in their forest disrupts Alexander's practice of collecting people, animals, and things as he travels. It

---

[15] Qui ceste feme avroit de cest convers getee
Tant que il la tenist en la soie contree
Bien en devroit on faire roïne coronee. (ll. 3493–95)
On Alexander's inability to take the maiden, see Emmanuèle Baumgartner, "La formation du mythe d'Alexandre au XIIe siècle: le Roman d'Alexandre et l'exotisme," *Conter de Troie et d'Alexandre: Pour Emmanuèle Baumgartner*, ed. Laurence Harf-Lancner, Laurence Mathey-Maille, and Michèle Szkilnik (Paris: Presses Sorbonne Nouvelle, 2006), 137–58, esp. 155.
[16] Gentieus rois, ne m'oci, franche chose honoree,
Car se g'iere plain pié de la forest getee,
Qu'eüsse une des ombres seulement trespassee,
Sempres seroie morte, tels est ma destinee. (ll. 3501–4)

also locates the flower maidens' hospitality within the boundary of the forest they cannot leave and identifies the forest as a dangerously desirable place of pleasure. At the end of their sojourn, Alexander's attempt to take the beautiful flower maiden away with him reminds his men of the women's beauty and the pleasures they offered, and they want to turn back into the forest and instead of following Alexander away from it. Only the king's threats prevent their return. The forest is dangerous to Alexander and his men precisely because of its hospitality.[17]

The *Roman d'Alexandre* includes another episode in which hospitality proves dangerous.[18] Before Alexander and his men reach the forest where the flower maidens live, they encounter women who "live in the water like fish." These women are clothed only by their long shining hair and they are marvelously beautiful.[19] They are like sirens, since they invite the ad-

---

[17] In Lamprecht's *Alexanderlied*, the men spend three months and twelve days in the forest and they leave only when the flower maidens die with the arrival of winter (ll. 5332–44). Thanks to James A. Schultz for help with Middle High German. For a comparison of the German and French versions, see Danielle Buschinger, "Les filles-fleurs dans l'Alexandre de Paris, l'Alexandre de Strasbourg, et le Parsifal de Richard Wagner," in *Romans d'antiquité et littérature du nord: Mélanges offerts à Aimé Petit*, ed. Sarah Baudelle-Michels et alia (Paris: Champion, 2007), 88–98.

[18] For a discussion of the two episodes, see Catherine Gaullier-Bougassas, *Les romans d'Alexandre: Aux frontières de l'épique et du romanesque* (Paris: Champion, 1998), 160–61, and Philippe Ménard, "Femmes séduisantes et femme malfaisantes; les filles-fleurs et la forêt et les créatures des eaux dans le Roman d'Alexandre," *Bien dire et bien aprandre* 7 (1989): 5–17.

[19] En l'eaue conversoient a guise de poisson
Et sont trestoutes nues si lor pert a bandon
Qanque nature a fait enfresi c'au talon;
Li chevel lor luisoient com pene de paon,

vances of Alexander's men only to draw them to their deaths, but unlike other medieval representations of sirens as hybrid women-fish or women-birds, these water creatures have women's bodies from head to toe. Full of desire, Alexander's men rush to join the women. They lie with them and when they are too tired to do anything more and want to leave, the women hold them tight, draw them into the water, and drown them.[20]

This encounter is both like and unlike the encounter with the flower maidens. Like the maidens in the forest, the water women seem to live on the boundary between the human and nonhuman. They live in the water, like fish, but they are not fish or even partly fish. Unlike the flower maidens who will die if they pass the boundary of the forest's shadow, the water women can leave the water, and they come onto shore to meet Alexander's men. Like the flower maidens they welcome the men with sexual availability, but theirs is a lethal hospitality.

Both sets of creatures threaten to derail Alexander's march through India. The flower maidens' welcome tempts Alexander's men to abandon their king to remain in a pleasure garden, and even though the water women's embrace draws their lovers to death in their realm of water, Alexander's men would still go to join them were it not for the king's prohibition. The two encounters promise similarly distracting and even

---

Ce sont lor vesteüres, n'ont autre covrison. (ll. 2904–8)

The water maidens are in most versions of the Alexander story and they appear in a very condensed form in the Greek romance that is the source of the French versions. See *The Greek Alexander Romance*, trans. Richard Stoneman (New York: Penguin, 1991), 124.

[20] Qant il ierent si las que faire nel pooient,
Volentiers s'en tornassent, mais eles les tenoient;
Celes levoient sus, en l'eaue les traioient,
Tant les tienent sor eles qu'eles les estrangnoient. (ll. 2918–21)

dangerous interludes for Alexander's men, but the sexual availability of their human or semi-human lovers seems to have different values in each episode. Whereas the water creatures that Alexander encounters are only once called "water maidens" (puceles de l'eau) and they are repeatedly called "women" (femes),[21] the text continues to refer to the flower beings as maidens (puceles). The flower maidens give themselves, they take lovers, but they remain *puceles*, even after spending four days having sex with Alexander's men. At the end of the army's sojourn with them, the text tells us, the "maidens" accompany Alexander and his men to the edge of the forest's shadow ("Les puceles les guïent tant com li ombres tent," l. 3546). It may be that "puceles" is used here to connote youth or to suggest the unspoiled beauty that draws Alexander's men back to the flower maidens. However, the narrator's use of "puceles" seems noteworthy when read alongside the description of the virginity-restoring herbs and grasses that opens the episode. Both the garden and the descriptions of the flower maidens suggest that women's virginity is valued in this episode; they also suggest that it is never definitively lost.

It is perhaps their ever-renewed virginity that explains the relationship of the flower maidens to the trees that have never been cut. Although the text does not use the term "virgin" to describe the forest, it does emphasize that its trees have never been touched by men. If the use-value of the trees is relocated to the ever-virgin bodies of the flower maidens who welcome Alexander's sex-starved men, the floral-human beings seem to escape the possession that such a shift might imply. The culturally defined value of a maiden and her maidenhead is subverted in the isolated garden where perpetual virgins willingly give themselves to men.

---

[21] In the episode we find "puceles" at l. 2934 and "femes" at ll. 2900, 2923, and 2927.

Moreover, if virginity is a cultural value defined at least in part by succession concerns, the ever-renewed virginity of the flower maidens points to the valorization of renewal over reproduction. The maidens are reborn each spring as flowers, but they themselves do not give birth. In fact, the cycle of flowering in which the maidens live is one that defies human death and birth. One of the things that troubles Alexander is the absence of tombs in the forest: "Where have they found such enduring youth? I see no tombs or sepulchers here."[22] Alexander's question is perhaps motivated by his earlier failed quest for the fountain of youth, or perhaps he is already thinking of the prophecy of his own death toward which he will journey, but the question is also provoked by Alexander's troubled reaction to the beautiful and mysterious floral-human beings who cannot be taken from the forest. In fact, Alexander himself introduces death into the flower maidens' forest, since to take them away is to kill them. The flower maidens cannot be taken. They cannot be subjected to Alexander's will and they cannot become his subjects.

GIVING AND TAKING

Alexander encounters various forms of hospitality in his travels through the East—he comes upon people who offer to guide him, he meets some women who make love with him and his men, and he encounters others, like the Amazons, who make peace with him. In all his encounters, the hospitality of the flower maidens remains unique. The welcome is also rather unique in the context of medieval narratives. Hospitality has codified forms and conventions in medieval romances, as Matilda Tomaryn Bruckner has shown, none of

---

[22] Ou ont eles trové jovent qui tant lor dure,
Qant je n'i ai trové tombe ne sepulture? (ll. 3528–29)

which correspond very closely to the flower maidens' welcome. The maidens' sexual desire for their guests is not unique (in Chrétien's *Chevalier de la charrette* we find the example of a lady who offers Lancelot lodging in exchange for his promise to sleep with her), but the apparent unconditionality of their hospitality is rare.[23] In fact, the flower maidens' welcome of Alexander's men anticipates some of the terms in which hospitality is elaborated in Jacques Derrida's exploration of the concept.[24] When read alongside the *Roman d'Alexandre*, Derrida's description of hospitality offers a vocabulary that underscores the relationship between the flower maidens' hospitality and the encounters that lead to conquest and tribute elsewhere in the *Roman d'Alexandre*. In turn, the romance may enter into a conversation with Derrida about the gendered values that define hospitality in his and other accounts.

Here is Derrida's description of the arrival of the *étranger*, the foreigner, the stranger, or the "strange stranger":[25]

> ... the stranger, here the awaited guest, is not only someone to whom you say "come," but "enter," enter without waiting, make a pause in our home without waiting, hurry up and come in, "come inside," "come within me,"

---

[23] Matilda Tomaryn Bruckner, *Narrative Convention in Twelfth-Century French Romance: The Convention of Hospitality, 1160-1200* (Lexington: French Forum, 1980).

[24] *De l'hospitalité: Anne Dufourmantelle invite Jacques Derrida à répondre* (Paris: Calmann-Lévy, 1997), translated as *On Hospitality: Anne Dufourmatelle Invites Jacques Derrida to Respond*, trans. Rachel Bowlby (Stanford: Stanford University Press, 2000). See also Jacques Derrida, "Hostipitality," in *Acts of Religion*, ed. and trans. Gil Anidjar (New York: Routledge, 2002).

[25] "Strange stranger" is Timothy Morton's translation in "Queer Ecology," *PMLA* 125.2 (2010): 277 [273–82].

> not only toward me, but within me: occupy me, take place in me, which means, by the same token, also take my place ... it's *as if* the master, *qua* master, were prisoner of his place and his power.... So it is indeed the master, the one who invites, the inviting host, who becomes the hostage, and who really always has been. And the guest, the invited hostage, becomes the one who invites the one who invites, the master of the host. The guest becomes the host's host. The guest becomes the host of the host.[26]

Derrida plays here with the double meaning of the French word "hôte," which means both guest and host, and he suggests that the resemblance is more than homophonic or semantic. The two terms, the two positions, are in relation to each other: one slips into the other, one comes within the other, one is taken hostage by the other.

The narrative of Alexander's encounter with the flower maidens offers a strange anticipatory echo of this passage. The men come into the forest and they come into the flower maidens who eagerly welcome Alexander and his army. Moreover, the flower maidens offer not just themselves, but also the plenitude of the forest to Alexander and his men:

> They have great pleasure all night long until day comes with the light of morning. When they wanted to eat, they found a meal prepared for forty thousand men. They asked for water and it was brought to them.... Every food in the world was brought to them, and each one found it seasoned to his taste. After the meal, they went to amuse them-

---

[26] Derrida, *On Hospitality*, 123–25.

selves in the meadow. Whoever wanted fruit of any kind, or precious spices could have as much as he wished without constraint.[27]

The hospitality of the flower maidens includes the hospitality of their forest. They invite Alexander and his men into the forest, they invite them within themselves, and they become the hostages of Alexander, or at least that is what Alexander's decision to take a flower maiden away with him suggests. But Alexander's attempt to take a hostage also suggests that his men have been taken hostage by the flower-maidens: the men see the beauty of the maiden Alexander would take away and they turn back to the forest and its pleasures. Alexander's attempted hostage-taking further reveals that the flower maidens are already hostages. They cannot leave the forest that provides so well for them and that offers them such hospitality—these hosts are hostages not just of their guest but of their own host, the forest. They are already taken.

We might also describe the flower maidens as taken, or taken up, by the Alexander romance itself. They are found only in twelfth-century versions of Alexander's story, and the interpolation of the flower maiden episode into the narrative may offer the occasion (or the provocation) to think about the transmission history of the Alexander romance itself in

---

[27] Trestoute icele nuit ont grant joie menee
Tant que biaus fu li jors, clere la matinee.
Qant li vaurent mengier, la viande ont trovee,
A quarante mil homes la truevent conreee;
Il demanderent l'eaue si lor fu aprestee.
. . .
Sous ciel n'en a devise la ne soit a portee,
Chascuns a son talent la treuve asavoree.
Aprés mengier se vont deporter en la pree;
Qui vaut fruit de maniere ne chiere herbe loëe
Assés en pot avoir sans chose dev[e]ee. (ll. 3466–79)

terms of Derrida's definition of hospitality. So, for example, translations, rewritings, and repetitions might be described as visitations that take possession, that take hostages, that is, that take prior texts hostage through rewriting. They might also be described as visitors in a textual terrain that recreate themselves as hostages to a prior text. What is a medieval text if not a coming into place, a taking place that depends on an encounter with a strange stranger? Hospitality seems a particularly appropriate concept for describing the transmission of the Alexander story, which had a vast circulation dating from the death of Alexander and extending into the late Middle Ages. Its astounding ubiquity included translations into virtually every language of culture from India to Iceland.[28] Daniel Selden has called this pattern of circulation a "text network," that is,

> an autopoietic body of related compositions whose origins largely escape us, and whose evolution, in the second and third centuries BCE, remained far from complete.[29]

Selden identifies the Alexander romance, with its world-wide circulation for over more than a millennium, as an exemplary text network.[30]

We can never know with certainty why such texts were so popular. Selden suggests that the development of text networks is linked to the fact that they thematize their own dissemination: "cross-cultural transmission is less an arbitrary matter dependent on taste than

---

[28] Daniel Selden, "Text Networks," *Ancient Narrative* 8 (2010): 12–13 [1–23].
[29] Selden, "Text Networks," 7.
[30] Other examples Selden points to are the Life of Ahiqar, the Fables of Bidpai, and the Balavariani ("Text Networks," 12).

structurally encoded in the work."[31] Another way to say this: text networks invite translation and rewriting; this is why Selden describes them as autopoietic. To describe texts as self-reproducing is to shift focus away from the author, translator, or compiler as the agent of dissemination and to consider the text as having an agency of its own. That agency would be located in the text's invitation, through thematic representation, to its own reproduction through translation and rewriting. In the Alexander romance, for example, Selden identifies a structural encoding of dissemination in Alexander's serial conquest of every nation in the world, one after the other.[32] Alexander's political and territorial conquests figure the text's own serial conquest of languages and cultures.

Alexander is a conqueror and a collector. He captures and collects people, as in his attempt to take the flower maiden out of the forest, but he also collects objects, and most of all, he collects gifts. In fact, Alexander demands gifts as tribute from the peoples he conquers.[33] In its representations of tributary exchange, the *Roman d'Alexandre* may recall its own origins, just as it thematizes its own dissemination in representtations of conquest. Text networks originate in tributary empires, according to Selden; they are the most characteristic form of fiction produced by such polities.[34] But hospitality would seem to counter tribute with a different model of taking in the *Roman d'Alexandre*. Both tribute and hospitality involve gifts,

---

[31] Selden, "Text Networks," 13.
[32] Selden, "Text Networks," 14.
[33] On tribute in the Alexander story, see Paul Goukowsky, "Les sources de l'histoire d'Alexandre," in Edouard Will, ed., *Le monde grec et l'orient*, 2 vols. (Paris: Presses Universitaires de France, 1972-75), 2:314–19, 322–23; and Laurence Harf-Lancner, *Le Roman d'Alexandre*, 13–14.
[34] Selden, "Text Networks," 14.

but whereas in the first, giving and taking constitute an exchange that recognizes sovereignty, in the second, pleasure substitutes for obligation and pleasure can be taken, but not taken away. If, as Selden suggests, Alexander's serial conquests represent a structural encoding of the romance's dissemination, the flower maiden episode would seem to challenge the model of conquest with welcome, and to limit Alexander's habit of taking away by his inability to take a flower maiden past the boundaries of the forest. The forest's boundary contains the pleasure found there and limits Alexander's desire to take (in contrast to all the other boundaries that Alexander passes with ease). The episode represents not conquest and taking away, but welcome and taking within. In other words, the *Roman d'Alexandre* imagines an alternative form of encounter with the would-be conqueror and collector of tribute, and in this it may participate with other twelfth-century French texts in a broader conversation about tributary relationships. For example, Sharon Kinoshita has argued that *The Song of Roland* reimagines an Iberian relationship of cross-cultural accommodation, secured by the payment of tribute, as a conflict motivated by an intransigent crusading fervor.[35] The Alexander stories do not overtly imagine conflict in terms of crusade values. However, a shift analogous to the one identified by Kinoshita operates in Alexander's encounter with the flower maidens. In a fleeting and temporary way, the episode imagines an encounter that upends relations of taking, taking away, and being taken. The episode moves away from the perspective and values of a tributary exchange structure to imagine a marvelous

---

[35] Sharon Kinoshita, "'Pagans Are Wrong and Christians Are Right': From Parias to Crusade in the Chanson de Roland," *Medieval Boundaries: Rethinking Difference in Old French Literature* (Philadelphia: University Pennsylvania Press, 2006), 15–45.

hospitality represented as the plenitude of a forest full of sexually available virgins who in giving themselves are taken and who in being taken, also take Alexander and his men ("Chascune prist le sien," l. 3460).

This mutual taking seems important, as does the maidens' desire for Alexander and his men. These women take lovers and they give themselves. They seek their own pleasure even as they offer pleasure ("plus aiment les homes que nule riens vivant," l. 3358). The pleasure offered and the pleasure received are not described as an exchange, however. The flower maidens welcome their guests with gifts of themselves and they give themselves for their own pleasure, but they are not offered by a host. The forest that provides the flower maidens also provides for Alexander and his army, but the text's insistence on the women's welcome and their taking of the men locates sexual hospitality not in the forest's bounty but in the flower maidens' desire. The episode thus rewrites stories in which the host's gift of a woman for a guest's pleasure or protection is taken as an exemplary act of hospitality—from the Biblical account of Lot and his daughters to Pierre Klossowski's 1953 novel, *Roberte ce soir*—and it poses a challenge to critics, like Derrida, who take these stories as foundational accounts of hospitality.[36] By rewriting the

---

[36] Genesis 19:1-9; see also Judges 19:23-30; Pierre Klossowski, *Roberte ce soir* (Paris: Minuit, 1953). Derrida discusses both texts at length in *On Hospitality*. For feminist critiques of the gendering of hospitality in Derrida's account, see Maureen Sander-Staudt, "Su Casa es Mi Casa? Hospitality, Feminist Care Ethics, and Reciprocity," and Helen Daley Schroepfer, "Hospitality: Agency, Ethics, and Gender," both in *Feminism and Hospitality: Gender in the Host/Guest Relationship*, ed. Maurice Hamington (Lanham: Lexington Books, 2010), 19–38, 39–52, respectively; and Nancy J. Holland, "'With Arms Wide Open': Hospitality and the Most Intimate Stranger," *Philosophy Today*, SPEP Supplement, 45 (2001): 133–37. For a critique of readings that take Judges 19 as a "study in

host's gift of a woman's body as an invitation issued by desiring women, the flower maidens episode subverts the exchange of women between men that establishes social relations between men and grounds social institutions.[37] The ever-renewed virginity of the flower maidens further removes them from hierarchies defined by exclusive possession—their virginity cannot be taken away. Finally, the episode defines hospitality not as a gift to be taken, but a pleasure to be enjoyed. It describes not exchange but invitation, not reward but welcome. And in this, hospitality troubles the definition of generosity, or *largesse,* one of the founding virtues of kingship in the *Roman d'Alexandre.*

The Alexander story is a story about empire, about the conquest of an empire and, in its medieval versions, about kingship.[38] From the lessons that Alexander receives from Aristotle to the lessons that he himself gives to Darius on the duties of a king, to the gift of his lands to his vassals at his death, the Alexander story

---

hospitality," see Mieke Bal, *Death and Dissymmetry: The Politics of Coherence in the Book of Judges* (Chicago: University of Chicago Press, 1988), 80–93. On Klossowski, see also René Schérer, *Zeus hospitalier: Eloge de l'hospitalité* (Paris: Armand Colin, 1993). I thank Maxime Foerster for introducing me to Schérer. For an essay that identifies the "fraternalistic" nature of Levinas's notion of hospitality, see David J. Gauthier, "Levinas and the Politics of Hospitality," *History of Political Thought* 28 (2007): 158–80.

[37] The foundational study is Gayle S. Rubin's "The Traffic in Women: Notes on the 'Political Economy of Sex," *Toward an Anthropology of Women,* ed. Rayna R. Reitner (New York: Monthly Review Press, 1975). See also Rubin's own commentary on the essay in *Deviations: A Gayle Rubin Reader* (Durham: Duke University Press, forthcoming).

[38] Alexander also becomes an exemplary ruler for authors of mirrors for princes. See Catherine Gaullier-Bougassas, "Alexander and Aristotle in French Alexander Romances," in *The Medieval French Alexander,* eds. Donald Maddox and Sara Sturm-Maddox (Albany: SUNY Press, 2002), 57 [57–73].

promotes the virtues of the judicious and generous ruler who establishes and maintains relationships through sovereign generosity or *largesse*.[39] The value of generosity is particularly emphasized in Alexander of Paris's romance, but always in terms of return and reciprocity.[40] Alexander's gifts reward past service and ensure future loyalty; Alexander gives in order to take.

The hospitality of the flower maidens troubles the hierarchies established and maintained through the acts of sovereign generosity and reciprocal tribute so firmly promoted by Alexander's teacher, Aristotle. In this it may participate in what Emmanuèle Baumgartner has identified as

> the questioning that lies at the heart of Alexander of Paris's version . . . of whether a durable power base [can] be founded on unlimited exercise of prowess and generosity [and] the systematic dispensation of wealth—the 'conseil' or rule of government that Aristotle steadfastly proffers to his "pupil."[41]

The virtues of kingship are addressed in other parts of the romance more than in the Marvels of the East section, where Alexander is represented more as an explorer than a conqueror, but even as he moves through the uncharted lands of India, Alexander uses

---

[39] Stephen D. White, "Giving Fiefs and Honor: Largesse, Avarice, and the Problem of 'Feudalism' in Alexander's Testament," in Maddox and Sturm-Maddox, *The Medieval French Alexander*, 127–41.

[40] William W. Kibler, "'A paine a on bon arbre de malvaise raïs': Counsel for Kings in the Roman d'Alexandre," in Maddox and Sturm-Maddox, *The Medieval French Alexander*, 112 [111–125].

[41] Emmanuèle Baumgartner, "The Raid on Gaza in Alexandre de Paris's Romance," in Maddox and Sturm-Maddox, *The Medieval French Alexander*, 34 [29–38].

either generosity or force to find his way. He rewards his guides with gifts, slaughters his enemies, and threatens the guides who lead him astray. In the flower maidens' forest, Alexander encounters a place that he cannot win through force, since it does not resist him; he cannot rule through generosity, since he can give the women nothing that they do not already have; and he cannot demand tribute, since the maidens deny him nothing except the possibility of taking them beyond the shadow of the forest.

The flower maidens trouble Alexander from the beginning of the encounter:

> When he sees the maidens, he is troubled by them, and he is so taken by their beauty that he swears by his head crowned in gold that he will not leave this place before four days have passed.[42]

Alexander's oath on his own crowned head may implicitly suggest that sovereignty is at risk in his determination to stay with the flower maidens. If so, it is surely because, as in most of his encounters in the desert, the natural wonders of India are dangerous—precisely because they are marvelous. Like the bountiful forest where the flower maidens live, full of naturally occurring plants but somehow able to provide delicious meals and embroidered silks for the women, the animals, plants, and people that Alexander encounters in his travels are both natural and marvelous, both in the sense that they provoke marvel because they have never been seen before, but also because they act marvelously—trees prophesy Alex-

---

[42] Quant il vit les puceles, molt en est effreés
Et de la biauté d'eles est issi trespensés
Q'il en jure son chief, qui d'or est corounés,
Que ne s'en movra mais si iert quars jors passés. (ll. 3367–70)

ander's death, women are born as flowers, a forest provides finely fitted dresses.

In the flower maidens episode the narrator focuses explicitly on the idea of nature, the garden full of naturally occurring plants, the forest untouched by men, the herbs and grasses that heal without human intervention, the "nature" of the maidens who are reborn as flowers. And yet, the forest is also characterized by apparently human work. Alexander finds the beautiful maiden he would take with him under a vermillion carob tree whose leaves have been decorated, literally "worked," with golden birds ("Et iert a oisiaus d'or menüement ouvree," l. 3484), but the text does not specify who did this work. Perhaps then it is no wonder that Alexander cannot understand the maidens' inability to leave the shadow of the trees as a natural being-with the forest. They must have been exiled there through some law or punishment, he thinks. "What kind of adventure has brought these women into the woods?" he asks, "Is it a law or a judgment? Where do they come from and where do they get their clothes?"[43] The forest, the garden it encloses, and the flower-women who inhabit it, represent a nature both touched and untouched by human work, by human craft, by trade, by tribute. The unconditional hospitality of the flower-maidens resists the model of conquest and tribute, it imagines a space of shared being and of sharing, of welcoming, of inviting in, of being taken, and of taking. In this it reflects, too, the invitation of the text network—to share and to take, but not to take away, to join, to come again, to repeat.

---

[43] See footnote 8 above.

EXEMPLARY ROCKS

Kellie Robertson

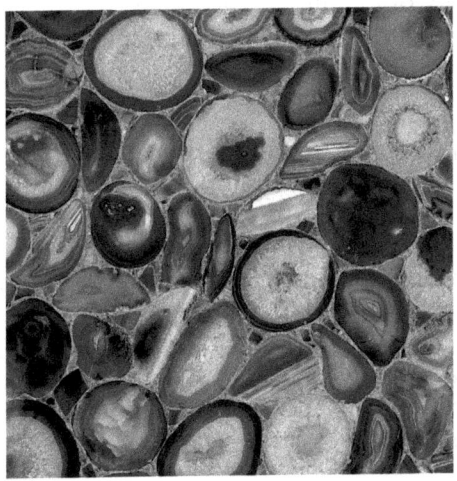

> The stone is worldless [*weltlos*], the animal is poor in world [*weltarm*], man is world-forming [*weltbildend*].
>
> Heidegger, *The Fundamental Concepts of Metaphysics: World, Solitude, Finitude*

Rocks are usually synonymous with insentience: to say that so-and-so has "a heart of stone" or is "dumber than a box of rocks" is to give insult by degrading the dynamic into the inert. In such comparisons, the rock contaminates the human to the extent that the latter is drained of all sensation and vitality. Such popular wisdom is codified into metaphysical precept in Heidegger's attempt to define "world" by parsing it according to levels of perceived sentience and a capacity for active engagement with the environment. Heidegger's theses have been much discussed by critics interested in "the animal" and "the human:" both Derrida and Agamben lament how these rigid categories obscure the common ground of animality and humanity especially with respect to language. Despite this desire to resist the singularity of the human, it is only recently that critics such as Graham Harman, Jane Bennett, and (within Medieval Studies) Jeffrey J. Cohen have challenged the third leg of Heidegger's ontological stool: the poverty of the inanimate world.[1]

This essay examines the types of world-making to which medieval stones were thought to contribute as well as how this creative capacity gradually dimmed over the course of the early modern period. Far from being "worldless," medieval stones were irrepressibly vital: inner "virtues" bestowed on them quasi-animate

---

[1] Heidegger's theses are articulated in his 1929-30 seminar, which appeared in translation as *The Fundamental Concepts of Metaphysics: World, Finitude, Solitude*, trans. William McNeill and Nicholas Walker (Bloomington: Indiana University Press, 2001), 176. The theses concerning the human and the animal are discussed by Jacques Derrida in *Of Spirit: Heidegger and the Question*, trans. Geoffrey Bennington and Rachel Bowlby (Chicago: University of Chicago Press, 1991), 48–49, and in *The Animal That Therefore I Am*, ed. Marie Louise Mallet and trans. David Wills (New York: Fordham University Press, 2008), 145; and by Giorgio Agamben, *The Open: Man and Animal*, trans. Kevin Attell (Stanford: Stanford University Press, 2003), 49–62. On the philosophical status of inanimate objects, see Graham Harman, *Tool-Being: Heidegger and the Metaphysics of Objects* (Chicago: Open Court, 2002) and Jane Bennett, *Vibrant Matter: A Political Ecology of Things* (Durham: Duke University Press, 2009). On the status of medieval stones, see Jeffrey J. Cohen, "Stories of Stone," *postmedieval: a journal of medieval cultural studies* 1/2 (2010): 56–63; doi:10.1057/pmed. 2009.1.

powers of motion and action, while "mineral souls" linked them to the plants, animals, and humans further along the *scala naturae*, or ladder of nature. Lapidaries and encyclopedias documented the endlessly entertaining charisma of ostensibly insensible stones: coral, for instance, was thought to make fields fertile and to drive away evil spirits, while magnetite could be used to test the fidelity of wives, since it would "repulse" an unfaithful woman. A staple of such lapidary accounts were the piroboli, the so-called "fire stones" [*lapides igniferi*] that spontaneously burst into flame when brought together. This apparently lifelike behavior was explained as the natural attraction between a "male" and a "female" stone, a sexual dimorphism that was often allegorized as an exemplum against carnal lust. Bestiaries and versions of the *Physiologus*, a popular treatise of moralized natural history, find in this natural phenomenon a cautionary lesson for clerics and monastics, who were advised to eschew the company of women lest they burn for the sin of lechery. These anthropomorphizing accounts of fire-producing stones suggest a natural world motivated by recognizably human desires and behaviors. The habit of moralizing rocks in this way seems to reduce the inanimate object to a screen on which the human is projected in grainy but recognizable form.[2] Yet these accounts cannot be

---

[2] For the stories concerning piroboli, see the bestiary preserved in Aberdeen University Library MS 24, which is helpfully found on-line: "The Aberdeen Bestiary," http://www.abdn.ac.uk/bestiary/index.hti. A virtually identical account is found in Oxford, Bodleian Library, Ashmole MS 1511; see F. Unterkirche, *Bestiarium: Die texte der Handschrift Ms. Ashmole 1511 der Bodliean Library, Oxford in lateinischer und deutschen Sprache* (Graz, 1986). The *Physiologus* is extant in many Latin versions; see, under the rubric "De lapidus quos vocant terobolem," Francis J. Carmody, *Physiologus Latinus versio Y* (Berkeley: University of California Press, 1941), 95–134; and *Bestiario Latino, versio BIs*, ed. Emilio Piccolo

written off as an ideological false-consciousness that sees rocks as merely humans in petric drag. Instead, they would have raised complex moral questions for an audience who understood stones to have, not inner lives per se, but a recognizable potential agency. This context would lead a medieval reader to ask: what kind of cleric or citizen gets precipitated out of these rocks? What kind of rock from these clerics and monastics? While the natural world was seen as a signifier for hidden spiritual truths, this allegorized world is one of mutual, rather than unidirectional, influence; in this world, even the ostensibly insentient parts of the Great Chain of Being (as it came to be known after A. O. Lovejoy) carry lessons legible to the careful reader. Moreover, if a penchant for auto-combustion would seem to raise the stone up a few notches on this chain, the cautionary exemplum suggests that "natural" sexual desire brings the human down a few steps to the quasi-animal or even mechanical, rendering it less than fully human. Such episodes become an object lesson in the potentially incendiary nature of abstract human systems that seek to assign meaning to natural phenomena with certainty, only to have them destabilize the very terms whose meaning they were intended to reinforce.

Such lapidary episodes may seem inscrutable or even tendentious to a modern reader conditioned to see a stone's value in purely instrumental terms: what is

---

(Napoli: Dedalus, 2000), 12. There is much recent work on lapidary and bestiary descriptions; see, for instance, "Learning from Nature: Lessons in Virtue and Vice in the Physiologus and Bestiaries," in *Virtue & Vice: The Personifications in the Index of Christian Art*, ed. Colum Hourihane (Princeton: Princeton University Press, 2000), 29–41; and Dorothy Yamamoto, *The Boundaries of the Human in Medieval English Literature* (Oxford: Oxford University Press, 2000).

a gem worth? what type of rock is suitable for building what kind of structure? From this perspective, lapidaries seem to document a fetishistic relation of human to inhuman object, an object deprived of its own voice and continually ventriloquized in the service of shoring up human custom. However, the medieval habit of moralizing rocks also documents the pre-modern continuum that ran from the human to the nonhuman, a spectrum both flexible and subtly shaded. While rocks were regularly (and sometimes facilely) moralized objects, the allegorical undertaking as a whole allowed the rock entrée to the charmed circle of world-making.

Rocks became, over the course of the later medieval period, a recognizable place to test where the material world ended and the immaterial began, an experiment undertaken by both poets and natural philosophers. This shared undertaking points us toward knowledge-making practices common to both late medieval fiction-writing and physical inquiry, practices that, unlike their post-Enlightenment counterparts, did not of necessity cordon off the human from the natural nor see the human as the centripetal point around which the non-sentient converged. Such a *mentalité* does not see the rock-human assemblage as a nostalgic, narcissistic closeness to nature but rather suggests that a particular historical understanding can be recuperated by modern feminist ecological thinking, an inquiry conditioned by the "locational possibilities" (in the words of critic Lorraine Code) that allow us to follow the epistemic positions supported by medieval rocks.[3] This view of nature had profound implications for how the contrasting domain of "art" was viewed: in an Aristotelian world, nature was privileged as self-directed, superior to a human artifice that merely copied its original. The first half of this essay charts a

---

[3] Lorraine Code, *Ecological Thinking: The Politics of Epistemic Location* (Oxford: Oxford University Press, 2006).

course between the exemplary rocks of natural philosophy and the hard places of late medieval poetry in order to explore how the rock became a topos from which to adjudicate not just physical but metaphysical questions. The second half of the essay looks at how the relation of art to nature, human to rock, changed during the early modern period by focusing on a single case study: an agate that has come to be known as the "Chaucer Pebble." The fortunes of this stone as it moved from Egypt to the British Museum sheds light on the history of how rocks became "mere objects," doomed only and always to reflect the human, never to shape it. The stone's well-documented career suggests the ways in which "Nature" was redefined in Britain and the consequences of this redefinition for literary aesthetics as well as the sciences.

SEEKING THE STONE: MEDIEVAL ROCKS AS PHYSICAL AND METAPHYSICAL OBJECTS

The qualities attributed to the piroboli and other rocks expressed a medieval worldview that granted an inanimate object—such as a stone—limited powers of self-motion. The most conspicuous "activity" of medieval rocks was perhaps the healing power attributed to them in lapidaries. Precious stones were thought to be capable of correcting an imbalance in bodily humors; a hot and dry stone such as garnet was thought to alleviate sorrow and despair, since it would counteract an overabundance of cold and wet humors that led to melancholy. What appears as supernatural to a modern reader was characteristic of an Aristotelian physical world in which all material objects, from rocks to sticks to human bodies, are an elemental gallimaufry endowed with substantial forms that directs both *potentia* and actual motions. Albertus Magnus observes that stones (even of the same type) can differ greatly in their powers. This difference results from the interaction of matter and form in an individual rock, which could, in certain circumstances, even be subject to death:

> the specific form of individual stones is mortal, just as men are; and if [stones] are kept for a long time, away from the place where they are produced, they are destroyed.
>
> [lapidum species ad individua quodammodo esse mortalia, sicut et homines, et extra loca generationis suae diu contenti corrumpuntur, et non nisi aequivoce retinent nomen speciei.][4]

The moralizing on rocks found in lapidaries, bestiaries, encyclopedias, and scientific literature is more than mere fetishism, in part because the premodern realm of objecthood was not *a priori* a passive one. Rocks were regularly used as examples in scholastic philosophy for analyzing the limit conditions of cognition. How, for instance, does a material rock generate the immaterial idea of a rock in the viewer's mind? When Aquinas looked at a rock, he imagined himself possessing an inner representation of the rock in his mind—called a "species" or an "intentional object"—which was in turn cognized by his intellect. The species (or "inner rock") was thought to be generated by the rock, thus linking the rock to the viewer through a quasi-material medium. Aquinas's meditation followed the Aristo-telian "intromission" model of perception, one that assumed an exterior object imprints itself on the percipient's

---

[4]*De mineralibus*, II.i.4. The Latin text of *De mineralibus* is taken from *Alberti Magni opera omnia,* ed. Auguste Borgnet and E. Borgnet, 38 vols. (Paris: L. Vives, 1890-99), vol. 29. The English translation is taken from Dorothy Wyckoff, *Book of Minerals* (Oxford: Clarendon Press, 1967), 66.

sense faculty.[5] Unlike later medieval and modern theories of cognition, the Aristotelian version did not assume the utter passivity of the object. These cognitive assumptions followed from an Aristotelian physical world where the elements (and those objects composed of them) were endowed with an inherent nature that directed the object's movements. Rocks did not fall to the ground from a height on account of gravity, but rather because their "natural place" was earth and their natural habit to return to it. Aristotle defined nature as opposed to art by saying that a natural object possesses an inner principle of motion and rest, while an object created by art (say a bed or a cloak) would lack such motion and possess only those motions inherent in its constituent parts.[6] This understanding of matter as having *potential*—the potential to move or act in certain ways—is not to be confused with panpsychism or animism—the belief that mind inheres in the stuff of the material universe—though Aristotle's sixteenth-century detractors would later level this charge against him.

The Aristotelian world view was reinforced by the idea of the *scala naturae* that linked together all forms of being. In the *History of Animals*, Aristotle describes a chain of material entities arrayed on a sliding scale of

---

[5] The competing theory, known as "extramission," argued that the mind emitted rays that went out to apprehend the largely passive object; this theory was championed by Peter Olivi and William Ockham. For a concise summary of debates over cognition, see Robert Pasnau, *Theories of Cognition in the Later Middle Ages* (Cambridge: Cambridge University Press, 1997).

[6] For a discussion of Aristotle's definition of nature as motion, see Mary Louise Gill and James G. Lennox, *Self-Motion: From Aristotle to Newton* (Princeton: Princeton University Press, 1994).

sentience, from rocks to plants to animals to humans.[7] Medieval encyclopedias such as Bartholomeus Anglicus's *De proprietatibus rerum* borrowed this hierarchic structure as a formal textual principle, beginning with a description of God and his angels and working its way through man and his parts to the physical world and its creatures including animals, plants and rocks. While the rock occupies the lowest rung on this ladder, it is nonetheless part of the reciprocal linkages that bound all things together in this ontological chain. Yes, the rock may be inanimate, but it is part of a teleological cosmos connected with the divine in its essence. On this view, the human soul is not something "extra" or "apart" from the rest of the material world, since it is imagined to be composed of multiple parts—vegetable, animal, and rational—that reflect the contributions of the lower levels of sentience. Some alchemical texts even posit a "mineral soul" responsible for the apparent liveliness of magnets and amber.[8] Such an

---

[7] See the *Historia Animalia* 588^{b}1: "Nature proceeds little by little from things lifeless to animal life in such a way that it is impossible to determine the exact line of demarcation, nor on which side thereof an intermediate form should lie. Thus, next after lifeless things in the upward scale comes the plant, and of plants one will differ from another as to its amount of apparent vitality; and, in a word, the whole genus of plants, whilst it is devoid of life as compared with an animal, is endowed with life as compared with other corporeal entities. . . . And so throughout the entire animal scale there is a graduated differentiation in amount of vitality and in capacity for motion": Jonathan Barnes, ed., *Complete Works of Aristotle: The Revised Oxford Translation*, 2 vols. (Princeton: Princeton University Press, 1984), 1:922.

[8] John Trevisa, *On the Properties of Things: John Trevisa's Translation of Bartholomaeus Anglicus De Proprietatibus Rerum: A Critical Edition*, ed. M. C. Seymour, 3 vols. (Oxford: Clarendon Press, 1975-89), 1:96. Dominik Perler describes the partitive soul as the dominant way of thinking about the soul until the early modern period; see the introduction to

understanding of the interconnectedness of all material bodies suggests that the allegorical reading of stones found in lapidaries were not mere analogies; rather, in a physical world where the rock and the human differ more by degree than by kind, where the divide between the material and the immaterial was not yet so indelible, the reciprocity of moral lessons was underwritten by an ontological connection manifest in the *scala naturae*.

Beyond lapidaries and encyclopedic descriptions, moralized stones became an avenue for poets to raise questions about how the lower orders of the *scala naturae* related to the higher ones. Robert Henryson's Middle Scots translation of the fable of "The Cock and the Jasp" uses a jasper (a type of chalcedony or quartz) as a place from which to speak about the complex (and even fraught) relation of worldly knowledge to spiritual understanding. Taken from the popular Latin fable collection known as the *Romulus*, this story recounts how a cock, scratching in a dunghill for worms, happens across the valuable stone. In an aureate monologue, the cock praises its beauty and its suitability for "ane lord or king" (l. 81); as for himself, however, he would have preferred to have come upon "draf or corne, small wormis or snaillis" (l. 94) with which to assuage his hunger.[9] The cock leaves the stone where he found it, and the story ends as he goes off in further search of food. This tale is followed by a

---

Dominik Perler, ed., *Transformations of the Soul: Aristotelian Psychology, 1250–1650*, special offprint of *Vivarium* 46.3 (2008) (Leiden: Brill, 2009), 1–9.

[9] All citations from Henryson refer to Denton Fox, ed., *The Poems of Robert Henryson* (Oxford: Oxford University Press, 1981), cited by line number. Henryson's Latin source can be found in Aaron E. Wright, ed., *The Fables of Walter of England*, Toronto Medieval Latin Texts 25 (Toronto: Pontifical Institute of Medieval Studies, 1997), 23–26.

substantial "moralitas" expounding the jasper as a symbol of prudence, the "science" or knowledge that can "with na eirdlie thing be bocht" (l. 151). The narrator's moral (much amplified from its Latin source where it occupies a scant two lines) elaborates on the lapidary characteristics associated with the stone and asserts that such knowledge is less valued now than it used to be ("Bot now allace this jasp is tynt and hid," l. 155). He ends by enjoining the reader to "Ga seik the jasp" (l. 161) wherever it may be found.

Henryson's injunction to "go seek the jasper" assumes a strict division between earthly and spiritual things: material substance and earthly riches are to be eschewed in the search for the immaterial goods of prudence and truth. This lesson is reinforced by comparison with a more familiar biblical scene of animal-mineral misrecognition: the narrator adds that the cock is like "ane sow"—a pig—that doesn't recognize the pearls in its trough (ll. 145-47). As Edward Wheatley has perceptively observed, Henryson's collection demonstrates how spiritual wisdom can be fashioned out of the schoolroom curriculum and its commentary tradition, a tradition that offers multiple (sometimes competing) types of allegory—natural, social, biblical—as hermeneutical tools for uncovering moral lessons.[10] Both Wheatley and Henryson's modern editor note the seeming incompatibility of the significant amount of space the fable dedicates to detailing the stone's earthly powers when measured against its moral, a reminder to readers that the most precious things are "mair excellent than ony eirthly thing" (Henryson, l. 130). This is less of a paradox in a

---

[10] Edward Wheatley, *Mastering Aesop* (Gainesville: University Press of Florida, 2000), 157. For the details of Henryson's borrowings from lapidaries, see Ian Bishop, "Lapidary Formulas as Topics of Invention: From Thomas of Hales to Henryson," *Review of English Studies*, n.s. 37 (1986): 469–77.

fable that repeatedly brings us back to "earthly things" to a much greater degree than any of its extant analogues in either Latin or the vernacular. In Henryson's version, the cock's mistake echoes that of the human actor whom the narrator blames for the loss of the jewel in the first place. The narrator imagines a slatternly house servant accidentally sweeping the precious stone out of doors:

> As damisellis wantoun and insolent
> That fane wald play and on the streit be sene,
> To swoping of the hous thay tak na tent
> Quhat be thairin, swa that the flure be clene;
> Iowellis ar tint, as oftymis hes bene sene,
> Vpon the flure, and swopit furth anone.
> Peraduenture, sa wes the samin stone.
> (ll. 71–77)

The narrator's casual misogyny, an addition to his source, reinforces the tale's moral that the search for prudence necessitates a vigilant awareness of one's physical surroundings at all times. Like the cock preoccupied with his search for food, the female servant has her mind on "play" rather than the spiritual lessons that might come from a conscientious performance of her day-to-day duties. In order to find the hidden treasure in the trash, the material world must be an object of constant and close scrutiny. In order to find knowledge, the wise man must first observe his own surroundings in order to glean knowledge from it. This is what both the cock and the servant girl fail to do. The paradox at the heart of Henryson's first fable is that, in order to extract an immaterial good, one must spend a lot of time staring at the dunghill.

This insight has consequences for how Henryson understands the right relation of art to nature in the tricky project of moralizing both the world present to our senses and the fictional world of the fable. The prologue to Henryson's fables announces that his audience should not disdain the lowly beast fable, since "mony men in operatioun / Ar like to beistis in conditioun" (ll. 48–49). Readers were to be vaccinated against a fall into bestial behaviors by way of animal exempla. This *contrapasso* suggests a straightforwardly mimetic relation between the human and non-human worlds, one in which animals teach and humans learn. Yet this reflective relation between the aesthetics of the fable and the moral lessons of the natural world breaks down in the very first fable, "The Cock and the Jasp," which presents a world in which neither animals nor humans are capable of learning, much less teaching. In a world where humans and animals fail to exercise their higher faculties, it is left to the mute stone to give voice to the transcendent virtue of prudence.

In Henryson's version of this fable, the animal world is not intelligibly didactic; instead, learning is accomplished only through a circuit that connects animal, mineral, and human. Henryson's exemplary choices can be clarified by contrasting it with an earlier vernacular version, John Lydgate's *Isopes Fabules*. In Lydgate's version, it is the cock rather than the rock who plays the leading role. While Henryson's version foregrounds the lapidary material, Lydgate's version highlights the noble qualities of the cock with a blazon of this impressive animal borrowed from the bestiary tradition. Furthermore, the cock's industrious scratching in the dunghill for food serves as a positive example for the human world, filled as it is with "losengowres," the deceitful, ablebodied poor who prefer to beg rather than gain a living through honest work.[11] Nature, in the

---

[11] All references to Lydgate's version of "The Cock and the Jasp" are taken from *The Minor Poems of John Lydgate, Vol. 2: The Secular Poems*, ed. H. N. MacCracken, EETS o.s. 192 (1934; repr. London: Oxford University Press, 1961). The fable is found on pp. 568–74.

shape of the busy cock, teaches the human world "to auoyde sloupe by dylygent trauayle, / By honest labour hys lyuelood to procure" (ll. 115–16). In Lydgate's version, the cock is affirmed rather than vilified: he symbolizes the lowly man who is diligent in his duties, accepts his position in the natural order of things, and does not desire inappropriate wealth or complain about his poverty. For Lydgate, the animal world models right behaviors, much as it does in bestiaries.[12] The jasper is reduced to the role of prop in this exemplary world, a thing whose value resides in a nexus of exchange overseen, not by wise lords, but by thrifty jewellers ("Late þese merchantis, þat go so ferr & ryde, / Trete of þy valew, wheþer hit be late or sone," ll. 164–65). The stone is part of a material nexus of trade and commerce that leaves little room for the spiritual values it later acquires in Henryson. Mimesis in Lydgate's fable is a one-way street running from the animal to the human. Nature does not teach wisdom but rather the social value of industriousness in the face of idleness and sloth. Whereas Henryson's narrator disdains the cock's instrumental view of the stone, Lydgate's narrator affirms it as a class-appropriate model of mercantile behavior. Lydgate's exemplary world is one in which the non-human is ventriloquized for the benefit of the human social order, while Henryson's exemplum foregrounds the ethical question of how the human engages the non-human world. Henryson's jasper exemplifies a metaphysical rather than a social truth; it teaches that the search for prudence is not confined to the social world that humans inhabit in isolation, rather it forces us to ask what is ethical in the wider context of a shared natural ecosystem. For Henryson, the natural meaning of the stone cannot be

---

[12] For a discussion of how the animal world functions mimetically in relation to the human, see Yamamoto, *The Boundaries of the Human*.

decoupled from its moral and allegorical meanings. The relations among animal, human, and rock form a complex moral circuit that shows meaning-making to be produced by the interchange among different levels of the *scala naturae*, across different categories of sentience.

Such instances of what might be termed "inorganic exemplarity" appear frequently in medieval poetry outside of the beast fable. For some medieval writers, the human-rock assemblage provoked the asking of difficult ethical questions about the relative value of human as opposed to divine knowledge. When Dorigen in the *Franklin's Tale*, for instance, looks over the sea cliff at the "grisly feendly rokkes blake" (l. 868) below her, she sees not only an imminent threat to the safe return of her beloved husband, but also the "hundred thousand bodyes of mankynde" (l. 877) that such dangerous outcroppings have slain in the past.[13] Her Boethian meditation on these perils casts the rock in the role of the "antihuman," a representative of a hostile inanimate world that is not merely indifferent to, but actively antagonistic towards, the realm of the human. Yet the rocks come to symbolize just how potentially porous the line between the human and the natural world really is, an instability that, for Dorigen at least, renders God's providential vision questionable. Critics have usually condemned Dorigen's "naive" questioning of the rocks and, through them, her implicit questioning of divine omnipotence; however, the questions raised by Dorigen's rocky meditation resemble those posed by Aquinas and other scholastics insofar as they imagine the limits of cognition and attempt to refine the blurry line between material and

---

[13] All citations from Chaucer are taken from Larry D. Benson, gen. ed., *The Riverside Chaucer*, 3rd edn. (New York: Houghton Mifflin, 1987).

mental entities.[14] In a medieval world where rocks were not merely passive objects of the human gaze, but active participants in shaping the mental reality of percipients, rocks have the capacity to organize the humans who look at them, based on what they see, rather than being simply subject to human desire. When Dorigen looks at the jagged rocks, she sees an imminent threat to her husband but also to her own sense of humanity; when her would-be lover Aurelius looks at the rocks, he sees the possibility of his own amorous success; and when the magician with whom Aurelius contracts to dispatch the rocks looks at them, he sees his £1000 fee. Since the species of the rock—its mental representation—appears to each character in a very different light, the rocks cannot be said to be a merely passive reflector of competing human desires. Perhaps the question posed by the Franklin at the tale's end—"Which was the mooste fre, as thynketh yow?" (l. 914)—is less about individual generosity of spirit (as critics commonly read it) and more about the extent to which humans collectively can be said to exercise free will at all in a world whose physical constraints not only limit human choices but actively shape what choices are available in the first place. If the *Franklin's Tale* can be said to have a moral, it would be that sometimes inanimate objects organize human communities (rather than the other way around) and that abstract notions of "trouthe" are meaningless unless grounded in the matter of the natural world.

---

[14] See Warren Ginsberg, "'Gli scogli neri e il niente che c'è': Dorigen's Black Rocks and Chaucer's Translation of Italy," in Robert M. Stein and Sandra Pierson Prior, eds., *Reading Medieval Culture: Essays in Honor of Robert W. Hanning* (Notre Dame: University of Notre Dame Press, 2005), 387–408; and John B. Friedman, "Dorigen's 'Grisly Rokkes Blake' Again," *Chaucer Review* 31 (1996): 133–44.

A similar materialization of the medieval concept of "trouthe" emerges from an encounter between stone and knight at the climactic moment of *Sir Gawain and the Green Knight*. As Gawain stoically prepares to endure the third and final stroke of the Green Knight's axe, he stands "as still as a stone," a conspicuous simile complicating any easy division between the competing claims of court and wilderness that the poem so insistently thematizes throughout. As Gawain prepares to receive this blow, he is transformed into an insensible fixture of the wasteland:

> But [he] stode stylle as the ston, other a stubbe suther
> That ratheled is in roché grounde with rotez a hundredth. (ll. 2293–94)[15]

The courtly knight has been transformed into either a rock or a stump rooted in rocky soil. Unlike modern comparisons between humans and rocks, imputed inertness is a positive rather than negative attribute. The usual chivalric circuit comprised of knight and horse (as outlined by Jeffrey J. Cohen) is here supplanted by a circuit comprised of insensible natural objects and the human.[16] At this instant, Gawain as rock-human hybrid is effectively turned into a creature not unlike the Green Knight himself, half courtly, half wild. What Gawain lacks, however, is the ability to see

---

[15] References to *Sir Gawain and the Green Knight* refer to Malcolm Andrew and Ronald Waldron, eds., *The Poems of the Pearl Manuscript*, 5th edn. (Exeter: University of Exeter Press, 2007).

[16] See Jeffrey J. Cohen, "The Inhuman Circuit," in *Thinking the Limits of the Body*, eds. Jeffrey Jerome Cohen and Gail Weiss (Albany: SUNY University Press, 2003), 1–10, and "Chevalerie," in Jeffrey Jerome Cohen, *Medieval Identity Machines* (Minneapolis: University of Minnesota Press, 2003), 35–77.

his ontological kinship with the Green Knight, a
blindness that echoes his inability to "see" the green
girdle he wears for protection as more than just an
inanimate object. Like the rocks of the *Franklin's Tale*,
the gold-encrusted girdle (referred to as a "juel")
organizes the human in ways that only become evident
when the inanimate is recognized as constitutive of
rather than ancillary to the ethical world of the court.
That Gawain never recognizes this shared moral circuit
suggests that his flaw is more than just a failure of
spiritual fortitude. While it is true that this passage
highlights the mutuality of human and non-human—
"that man is always already in nature, and nature,
forever in him," as one recent critic puts it[17]—it is
Gawain's failure to recognize this mutuality and to
acknowledge it that stands behind his misunder-
standing of the nature of the covenant that he makes
first with the Green Knight and later with Bercilak. The
moment Gawain stands petrified, both literally and
metaphorically, before the Green Knight's glancing
blow suggests not just that the court-wilderness
dichotomy is a false one but also that the poem's moral
quandary frames the problem of self-knowledge as one
of everyday cognition. The fact that Gawain's transformation into a rock marks his apotheosis as a knight
stands as a critique of both the activity valued by
chivalry and an alternate model to the Christian ideal of
passive suffering embodied in Christ.

While poetry used exemplary rocks to question the
relative values of human and divine modes of knowledge, natural philosophy was likewise interested in
how "nature" was framed in relation to "art." The rock-
human assemblages of Henryson, Chaucer, and the
Gawain-poet offer literary instances of the exemplarity

---

[17] William F. Woods, "Nature and the Inner Man in *Sir Gawain and the Green Knight*," *Chaucer Review* 36.3 (2002): 209 [209–27].

of rocks; lapidary accounts of so-called "figured stones" [*lapides figurati*] offered both poet and natural philosopher a case study in the right relation of art to nature. Perplexed by rocks with markings resembling landscapes, plants, animals, and even crucifixions, Albertus Magnus and other writers attributed them to a hidden (or "occult") "virtue" in the earth's depths that allowed for their spontaneous generation.[18] The category of *lapides figurati* included both rocks that portrayed recognizable images (usually as a result of color variations from iron oxides or manganese) as well as embedded fossils or fossil impressions. Albertus was especially interested in rocks that contained human images; his description of how they were fabricated relies on Aristotle's *Physics*: under certain unusual celestial conditions, the generative force impresses the human form "upon a seed of an entirely different kind and in opposition to the formative power inherent in that seed" ["in semine valde difformi contra vim formativam illi semini insitam imprimit formam humanam"].[19] Through a process that impresses human "form" on stony matter, rocks acquire human faces. The medieval fascination with these stones is explained in part by the fact that their existence and the mysterious details of their generation affirmed divine power by celebrating its capacity to confound human powers of reason. Moreover, these naturally occurring images, imprinted as if by design, troubled the medieval distinction between those things created by human art and those created by nature. Medieval writers often voiced the prevailing opinion that these stones were evidence that Nature's craftsmanship would always outshine anything produced by artifice. John Lydgate describes such stones in *Reson and*

---

[18] *De mineralibus*, II.iii.1, discusses naturally occurring images and seals [*sigillum*] on stones.
[19] *De mineralibus*, II.iii.2.

Sensuallyte, a love allegory in which the claims of the material world (in the person of Venus as the representative of natural philosophy) are contrasted unfavorably with those of the spiritual realm (in the person of Diana as the dreamer's would-be theological guide). Envisaging love as a game of chess, the poem describes the fair lady's retinue at length, right down to the shields carried by her pawns, which are fabricated out of figured stones:

> Ymages thervpon depeynt
> With freshe colours no thing feynt;
> Somme in the mater depe grave,
> And many stonys that they have,
> Which of figures ofte varie,
> Be called in the lapidarie,
> Stonys in ysrael yfounde,
> Somme square and somme rounde,
> Enprinted of ther owne kynde,
> For craft was ther set behinde,
> For I trowe that no man
> Swiche seelys grave kan.
> For nature, who taketh kepe,
> Passeth soothly werkemanshepe;
> For crafte ys subget vnto kynde,
> And mannys wyt kan nat fynde,
> By resemblaunce of no figure,
> To be egal vnto Nature. (ll. 6119–36)[20]

This passage reinforces the idea that human art, whether the engraver carving seals or the poet describing the material world, can never surpass the original found in Nature. In affirming that "craft is

---

[20] Citations from this text are taken from *Reson and Sensuallyte*, ed. Ernst Sieper, EETS e.s. 84 (London: K. Paul, Trench, Trübner, and Co., 1901). This text is a loose translation of *Les Échecs amoreux*.

subject unto kind," it also suggests that the human world of love and the material world are likewise governed by a natural order that guarantees certain outcomes in both realms. For Lydgate, the figured stone was more true that the engraver's art; Nature, as original, witnessed the divine plan more eloquently than any social creation could. Thus medieval natural philosophy determined not just what was believed about the formation of rocks in the earth's core but also how the natural world was represented in the poetry that sought to reproduce it.

In both learned and popular medieval texts, there appears to be no such thing as an uninterpreted (or uninterpretable) rock. The model of nature that emerges from these petric encounters suggests that the medieval relation between the natural world and the human was not one of unidirectional mimesis for all writers. Learning did not always occur simply by looking at nature. Instead, exemplarity was the product of an ecosystem rather than a simple reflection of "things out there." As a single but important node in this representational web, the mineral suggests something about the human relationship to the world that a human being cannot, unprompted, comprehend by itself. In this way, stones are both marvelous and monstrous. Stones allow for a projection into the space of the other, a conscious leap made through the medium of an ostensibly unconscious instrument. Returning to Heidegger's vocabulary, world-making was just as much a product of inanimate rocks as of animate creatures in this period.

So how did the medieval view of rocks as having natural motion, which in turn made them suitable vehicles for philosophical reflection on the limits and possibilities of the material world, lead to Heidegger's conclusion that rocks lack all metaphysical interest? The final part of this essay explores the Enlightenment career of a particular figured stone whose appearance in museum catalogues and popular writings attest how ideas about the relative values of art and nature had shifted by the eighteenth century. The career of this rock—half-pebble, half-poet—reveals the ways in which scientific and cultural beliefs remain intertwined even as the line that ostensibly separates the human from the natural, the animate from the inanimate, the subject from the object, was redrawn more indelibly and policed more vigorously.

The Chaucer Pebble and the Fate of the Exemplary Rock

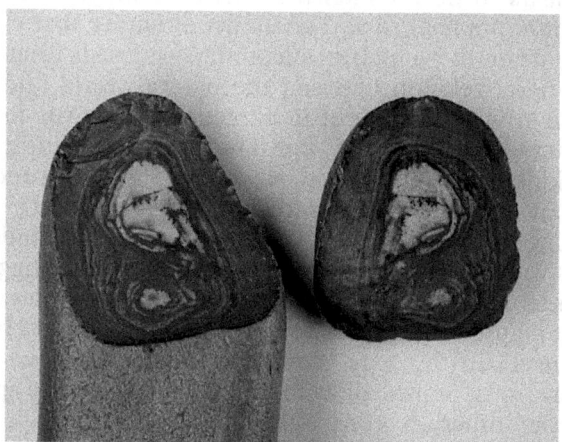

Figure 1. British Museum 58506, Egyptian jasper. Used by permission, copyright Natural History Museum, London.

A 1778 catalogue highlighting "objects of interest" in the newly established British Museum contains a description of the following item [Figure 1]:

> A Rough Egyptian Pebble . . . on which is a striking Likeness of the Head of *Chaucer*, father of the English Poets, and is entirely by

the Pencil of Nature, without any assistance of Art.... And now we will give a slight Description of another kind of Diamond, meaning Chaucer: ... [quotes from Leland on Chaucer's biography]. As to his genius as a Poet, Dryden speaking of Homer and Virgil, positively asserts, that our Author exceeds the latter, and stands in Competition with the former. In respect of Painting the Portrait, or Character of this great Genius; one may see his very Temper on this Egyptian Pebble, which is a Composition of the Gay, the Modest, and the Grave.[21]

A much later mention in *Strand Magazine* purports to relate the circumstances under which this curious stone was found:

This stone was picked up outside Cairo by a native donkey driver, whose ass had become violently obstreperous. It seems the native threw the stone with all his force at poor Neddy, with the result that part of it broke away, revealing on both sections *a portrait of Chaucer!*"[22]

Such figured stones would remain a common attraction for fashionable nineteenth-century London society:

---

[21] Jan van Rymsdyk, *Museum Britannicum*, 71–72. This reference is noted in Caroline Spurgeon, *500 Years of Chaucer Criticism and Allusion*, 3 vols. (Cambridge: Cambridge University Press, 1925), 3:95.

[22] William G. FitzGerald, "The Romance of the Museums," *Strand Magazine* 11 (1896): 62–71. Of this story, the writer admits, "I learn that this piece of jasper was brought to the British Museum before registers were made, and therefore the story does not figure in any of the official publications" (70).

after admiring Chaucer in stone at the mineral gallery in the Natural History Museum, a visitor could view a likeness of Voltaire, also in agate, at Strawberry Hill. The Chaucer Pebble found its way into popular guidebooks as well as scientific mineralogy treatises. It even makes a "cameo" appearance in a serialized novel about a lovelorn jeweller involved in an intrigue over a diamond necklace.[23] Today, the Chaucer Pebble resides in the "Enlightenment" gallery of the British Museum among other eighteenth-century curiosities, such as taxidermied dodos, bronze medals, and a colossal marble foot. There are many things that can be said about this curious pebble and its afterlife. Its existence could license a postcolonial critique of the early British entry into Egypt where even the stones were made to affirm the superiority of British colonial power. Or the pebble could direct our attention to the ideological orientation of the fledgling geological sciences and museum curation during the eighteenth century. This essay will conclude by exploring the differences between what medieval poets and natural philosophers saw when they looked at rocks and what their eighteenth-century counterparts saw. Rocks continued to play a role in the materialist two-step that is the

---

[23] It appears epiphenomenally in British print throughout the eighteenth and nineteenth centuries, particularly in serials such as *London Magazine* and *Gentleman's Magazine*. It is mentioned as an example of the "playful operations of nature" by Isaac D'Israeli, *Curiosities of Literature*, 2 vols. (1793), 2:66, and as an example of Egyptian jasper by George William Traill, *An Elementary Treatise on Quartz and Opal* (Edinburgh: Machlachlan & Stewart, 1870), 26–27; and it also appears in James Payn's novel, *A Confidential Agent*, first serialized in the literary magazine *Belgravia* from January to December 1880, later printed in 3 volumes (London: Chatto and Windus, 1880). It is still being mentioned as a notable tourist stop as late as 1918 in the first Blue Guide, *London and its Environs*.

nature-art dyad, though in a very different key, and the reception of the Chaucer Pebble as a "figured stone" sheds light on how changing literary aesthetics and the fledgling science of mineralogy continued to influence one another in surprisingly direct ways.

In *An Inquiry Into Meaning and Truth*, the twentieth-century logician and philosopher Bertrand Russell wrote that, "the observer, when he seems to himself to be observing a stone, is really, if physics is to be believed, observing the effects of the stone upon himself."[24] Just as for his scholastic predecessors, looking at rocks for Russell was a topos for thinking about the limits of human knowledge. How do we know whether the exterior world comes in to meet us or whether we go out to meet it? For Russell, the scientific axiom that rejected our "common sense" experience of the rock—it is passive; humans are active—destabilized both modern epistemology and modern science, since these two disciplines had both assumed a tacit infallibility with regard to their respective objects of knowledge. And yet Russell's assessment of the consequences of rock-gazing is only possible in a philosophical world already premised on the assumption that there is a definitive break between the rock and the human, between a "real" world that is external to the human viewer and an internal world whose reality is separate from the rock. Such a view would have been difficult to comprehend for a late medieval scholastic (such as Aquinas) whose medical, scientific, and literary understandings of the natural world would have assumed a shared reality created out of the continuous interchange between humans and rocks. The inherent division assumed by Russell's critique of modern science is one whose origins can be found in early modern Britain, when both poets and natural

---

[24] Bertrand Russell, *An Inquiry Into Meaning and Truth* (1950; rprt. New York: Routledge, 1995), 15.

philosophers began to reimagine the prevailing medieval understanding of how humans were related to rocks, and, by proxy, how art was related to nature. As historians Steven Shapin and Pamela Smith have argued, the art-nature dichotomy dissolved in the *ateliers* and laboratories of the sixteenth and seventeenth centuries, as artisan-made machines and the workings of nature were thought to operate according to structurally similar principles, differing only in degree.[25] Whereas the medieval Book of Nature trope was the original from which humans diligently read and copied the divine plan, early modern Nature was now imagined as a clock or an automaton, the human invention providing the blueprint for understanding the secret behind nature's regularity. A nascent humanist literary criticism came to similar conclusions: Sir Philip Sidney famously argued that human art does not slavishly imitate nature; it instead completes (and in some cases, improves) it.[26] If medieval poets and natural philosophers had imagined human craft to be a deficient version of Nature's more perfect original, their early modern counterparts began to view the human and the natural as complementary.

This new understanding of the art-nature relation found ardent expression in John Dryden's writing on the Father of English Poetry; he observes that, "Chaucer follow'd Nature every where; but was never so bold to

---

[25] See Pamela Smith, *The Body of the Artisan: Art and Experience in the Scientific Revolution* (Chicago: University of Chicago Press, 2004), and Stevin Shapin, *The Scientific Revolution* (Chicago: University of Chicago Press, 1996).

[26] On Sidney's interest in mimesis and nature, see S.K. Henninger, *Sidney and Spenser: The Poet as Maker* (University Park: Pennsylvania State University Press, 1989). For the overlap between scientific and literary discourse in the early modern period more generally, see the essays collected in Peter Dear, ed., *The Literary Structure of Scientific Argument* (Philadelphia: University of Pennsylvania Press, 1991).

go beyond her."[27] By the eighteenth century, literary criticism had turned Chaucer into nature's amanuensis, with the Chaucer Pebble as a readily identifiable witness to this newly articulated mimesis between art and nature.[28] The description of Chaucer as "another kind of Diamond" by the geological compiler and illustrator responsible for the British Museum catalogue, Jan van Rymsdyk, echoes Dryden's somewhat condescending assessment of Chaucer's art:

> Chaucer, I confess is a rough Diamond, and must first be polish'd, e'er he shines. I deny not likewise, that, living in our early Days of Poetry, he writes not always of a piece.

Like the perhaps apocryphal donkey driver, Dryden finds a rough outline of poetic form emerging from Nature, just in need of a little buffing. Both Dryden and Rymsdyk assumed an implicit analogy between the forms of nature and the forms of art. Dryden's well-known "polishing" of Chaucer notwithstanding, it would stretch the limits of interpretation to suggest that the effect of Chaucer's poetry (even less its intention) was the sort of realistic description that these later writers attributed to him.

If for Dryden and other eighteenth-century writers, Chaucer's poetry exemplified the effortless capacity of art to imitate nature, the Chaucer Pebble became yet

---

[27] John Dryden, *Fables, Ancient and Modern* (London: Jacob Tonson, 1700). Both this quotation and the one below are taken from the unpaginated preface.

[28] The eighteenth-century reception of Chaucer emphasized his realism and framed him as an "illusionist"; on this tendency, see Derek Brewer, *Geoffrey Chaucer: The Critical Heritage* (London: Routledge and Kegan Paul, 1978), 1:14–15. Alexander Pope similarly remarks on Chaucer's "natural way" (quoted in Brewer, *Geoffrey Chaucer*, 1:173).

another pretext for a discussion of nature's marvelous capacity to imitate art for some eighteenth-century scientists. Whereas earlier natural philosophers were prone to see petrified saints and monsters, eighteenth-century naturalists now saw English poets and animal remains. In addition to the Chaucer Pebble, the extensive mineral collection of the famous antiquarian Hans Sloane also included stones whose markings were thought to resemble a papal crown, figures of trees and landscapes, and a duck rising out of the water. The display of unusually shaped stones in museum collections emphasized this recently acquired taste for verisimilitude over wonder: "a stone resembling a dryed pear" is juxtaposed with a real dried pear (nos. 376-77) and "a stone resembling a cake of Chocolate" with a slice of chocolate cake (nos. 403-4). This collection, including over ten thousand minerals, would become the core of the British Museum.[29] Like the medieval scholastics, eighteenth-century natural philosophers were perplexed by *lapides figurati* and debates about their origins remained intense. Athanasius Kircher's monumental study of all things underground, *Mundus subterraneus* (1665), largely follows the medieval view that these stones were created by a *Natura pictrix* whose "lapidifying moisture" [*spiritu lapidifico*] occasionally misfired and imprinted organic images on inorganic matter.[30] Kircher is particularly

---

[29] On Sloane's mineral collection, see Jessie M. Sweet, "Sir Hans Sloane: Life and Mineral Collection. Part II: Mineral Collection," *Natural History Magazine* 35.5 (July 1935): 97–116; and John Thackray, "Mineral and Fossil Collections," Chapter 7 in *Sir Hans Sloane: Collector, Scientist, Antiquary, Founding Father of the British Museum*, ed. Arthur MacGregor (London: British Museum Press, 1994), 123–35.

[30] *Mundus Subterraneus*, VIII.1.10. Kircher's work is available in facsimile: *Mundus Subterraneus*, ed. Gian Battista Vai (Bologna: Arnaldo Forni Editore, 2004). On the debate over these stones, see "Figur'd Stones and Plastick Virtue,"

interested in the human images "drawn" by nature on stones and he included many plates depicting not just crucifixions, virgins, and saints but individual hearts, heads, eyes, ears and feet. While the idea that fossils and animal-like petrifacts had once been living creatures, transformed over time through geological processes, was gaining currency in the early eighteenth century, figured stones such as the Chaucer Pebble remained perplexing, with most naturalists—while believing that scientific laws and "decorum" governed nature—attributing their spontaneous generation to the same "plastic force" that Albertus Magnus had proposed centuries earlier. As a *lusus naturae* or "joke of nature," the figured stone challenged the eighteenth-century scientific community because it seemed to perform no function in itself, to play no role in the natural order of things; it seemed, in Lorraine Daston and Katharine Park's words, "at once a triumph of ingenuity and a dismissal of utility."[31] This dismissal of utility was often framed as rejection of the specifically Aristotelian view of teleology in the natural world, the view that had underwritten the medieval belief in the quasi-active powers of medieval stones, those perceptible side effects arising from a stone's striving toward its appropriate natural place. This medieval view had been strenuously questioned in the sixteenth century, and, by the middle of the eighteenth, Leibniz, formerly a fan of Kircher's work, would ridicule those who

---

Chapter 6 in John A. Moore, *Science as a Way of Knowing: The Foundations of Biology* (Cambridge: Harvard University Press, 1999), 102-28; Paula Findlen, "Jokes of Nature and Jokes of Knowledge: The Playfulness of Scientific Discourse in Early Modern Europe," *Renaissance Quarterly* 43 (1990): 292–331; and Gary D. Rosenberg, ed., *The Revolution in Geology from the Renaissance to the Enlightenment* in *Geological Society of America Memoirs* 203 (2009).

[31] Lorraine Daston and Katharine Park, *Wonders and the Order of Nature* (New York: Zone Books, 1998), 287.

believed in figured stones, noting that "the more one looked, the less one saw."[32]

Leibniz's skepticism aside, this scientific fascination with the artlessness of nature gets transposed into the "naturalness of art" in the literary criticism practiced by Dryden and his fellow antiquarians. Dryden repeatedly commends Chaucer's ability to "follow Nature," particularly in his realistic recounting of the Canterbury pilgrims. For Dryden, poetic work is a disappearing act; the writer's goal was to become a transparent lens through which a reader may view nature, defined as both human nature and the natural world. This equation of nature and art discounts conspicuous poetic labor as a failure; according to Neoclassical aesthetics, poetic labor should ideally be just as "occult" as the virtues behind magnets or *lapides figurati*. Such a reading of Chaucer must, of necessity, suppress the many moments where Chaucer discusses his own poetic work *qua* work and even foregrounds its failure. It is here that the controversy over the origins of figured stones (like the Chaucer Pebble) overlapped most conspicuously with eighteenth-century discussions of literary aesthetics. If the Chaucer Pebble is scientifically valuable to the extent that there is no apparent human labor in it, then so too the *Canterbury Tales* are valuable as literature to the extent that the poet's hand remains hidden. This is a model of authorship that elides labor through authorial absence just as the geological "explanation" of the fossil record elided natural work still preferring (despite mounting

---

[32] Leibniz in *Protogaia* (1749), quoted in Lorraine Daston, "Nature Paints," in Bruno Latour, ed., *Iconoclash: Beyond the Image Wars in Science, Religion, and Art* (Cambridge: MIT Press, 2002), 138 [136–38]. On Leibniz's views on figured stones and fossils more generally, see Cohen Rodarmor, *The Fate of the Mammoth: Fossils, Myth, and History* (Chicago: University of Chicago Press, 2002), 53–54.

evidence to the contrary) to see figured stones as fully formed plastic creatures (rather than the outcome of eons of natural change). Just as the Chaucer Pebble was thought to have been formed without the intervention of art, so too Chaucer, in Dryden's terms, was a fourteenth-century diamond in need only of having its "luster" polished by an eighteenth-century translator.

If, as Dryden had asserted "Chaucer follow'd Nature every where," by the eighteenth century, Nature was politely returning the favor in the form of the Chaucer Pebble. In order to understand poetry as "following" and, hence, completing nature, writers such as Dryden had to suppress a view of the natural world as having a potentially active engagement with the human world. No longer a dialectical relation, the non-human now functions mimetically in relation to the human. The rock, no longer a necessary node in an exemplary ecosystem, becomes a reflection or merely a further extension of the human. Moreover, nature no longer occupies a privileged and authorizing position in relation to human artifice; instead, poets were lauded for their agonistic ability to strive with nature and, occasionally, to surpass her in their own "naturalness." Rocks, even ones resembling humans, were no longer in a position to complicate the moral assumptions of the human world, since the inanimate had effectively been walled off from the animate. Figured stones merely confirmed that nature copied the human rather than the other way around. By the eighteenth century, the Chaucer Pebble bore witness to a world where rocks had lost their exemplary value and were reduced to echoing human values, a world where even Egyptian pebbles uncomplainingly reflected the Father of English poetry.

MINERAL VIRTUE

Valerie Allen

"I became a wanderer, making long journeys to mining districts, so that I could learn by observation the nature of metals," writes Albertus Magnus in his treatise *De Mineralibus*.[1] Perhaps it was then that he asked so

---

With thanks to participants of the George Washington Medieval and Early Modern Studies Institute conference on "Animal, Vegetable, Mineral," in particular Jeffrey Cohen for feedback; also to Ruth Evans for feedback.

[1] *De Mineralibus*, Book 3, Tractatus 1, Chapter 1, hereafter abbreviated (*DM* 3.1.1). The authoritative translation is by Dorothy Wyckoff, *Albertus Magnus: Book of Minerals* (Oxford: Clarendon Press, 1967), 153, hereafter cited as "Wyckoff," by page number. The Latin comes from volume 5:59 of Albert's complete works, *Opera omnia*, ed. A. Borgnet (Paris, 1890-1899), hereafter cited as "Borgnet," by page number.

"assiduously in different parts of the world" after a complete text of the *Lapidary of Aristotle*, a work he only knew through excerpts.[2] Albert's hardships testify to his commitment to the rigors of natural science (*physica*), the evidentiary standards of which are higher than for astrology or magic, draw as he still does from those lesser authorities.[3] But Albert has his limits, being quick to demarcate between science and divinatory practices of geomancy, necromancy, and so on—all "nonsensomancy" [*garamantia*], as he likes to call it.[4]

The irony is that however much earth scientists today salute Albert's observational scruples (translator Dorothy Wyckoff was a geologist), the alchemical learn-

---

Borgnet's edition is online at http://arts.uwaterloo.ca/~albertus/index.html. A more reliable Latin edition is underway, although *Mineralia* (part 2 of volume 6) has not yet appeared: see http://www.albertus-magnus-institut.de. For Albert's sources, see Wyckoff, xxxiv. For a general summary of Albert's treatise, using Borgnet and Wyckoff, see J. M. Riddle and J. A. Mulholland, "Albert on Stones and Minerals," in *Albertus Magnus and the Sciences: Commemorative Essays 1980*, ed. James A. Weisheipel (Toronto: Pontifical Institute of Mediaeval Studies, 1980), 203–34. For a general overview of geological knowledge in Albert's time, see Isabelle Draelants, "La science encyclopédique des pierres au 13e siècle: l'apogée d'une veine minéralogique," in *Aux origines de la géologie de l'Antiquité au Moyen Âge*, eds. Claude Thomasset, Joëlle Ducos, and Jean-Pierre Chambon (Paris: Champion, 2010), 91–139.

[2] The work appears to have been a fifth- or sixth-century Syriac or Persian lapidary; see Wyckoff, 263 (Appendix A, §14).

[3] *DM* 2.1.3; Wyckoff, 63; Borgnet, 5:27.

[4] Cited in Bernard M. Ashley, "St. Albert and the Nature of Natural Science," in Weisheipl, *Albertus Magnus and the Sciences*, 89 [73–102]. Ashley notes how Albert's natural science yields general knowledge that does not derive from the first principles of metaphysics but that itself is confirmed by observed experience and that validates the epistemic independence of sense data: "Natural science precedes metaphysics in the order of knowing" (97).

ing, the metaphysical invocation of mineral powers, even the observed properties of stones and metals amount only to pseudoscience. Four years before Wyckoff's scholarly and critical translation, Karl Popper published a lecture on a question that had been bothering him for most of the century: "Is there a criterion for the scientific character or status of a theory?" His answer, in brief, was that confirmations are two a penny and that theories should be praised insofar as they make bold, surprising predictions that run a high risk of being falsified.[5] Demarcation has continued to evolve its terms and criteria since then, for Popper's characterization of scientific rigor is neither complete nor unproblematic, but investment in testing for falsification (and by consequence, for a qualified confirmation) continues to influence scientific practice, with all that experiment entails: construction of hypotheses, bridging hypotheses, planning, implementation, monitoring, modification, repetition, control for variables, explanation, building of models, and extrapolation from outcome to untested situation.[6] The claim to the special epistemic status of science relies on demarcation, which perforce must label *De Mineralibus*, along with most of Albert's other writings, pseudo-scientific. Can Popper's question be reformulated in a way that enables a consideration of

---

[5] Karl R. Popper, *Conjectures and Refutations: The Growth of Scientific Knowledge* (1963; repr. New York: Harper Torchbooks, 1965), 33–39. The division between science and pseudoscience is not the same as that between empiricism and metaphysics.

[6] For consideration of scientific practice as a performative "dance of agency" between human and machine, see Andrew Pickering, "The Mangle of Practice: Agency and Emergence in the Sociology of Science," *American Journal of Sociology* 99.3 (1993): 559–89, and his subsequent book, *The Mangle of Practice: Time, Agency, and Science* (Chicago: University of Chicago Press, 1995).

medieval science (that is, of "pseudoscience") without the need either to denounce or rehabilitate it? That is the general question driving this exploration of Albert's treatise on minerals.

What is a mineral? In geological terms, three features are noted. First, minerals have a uniform chemical structure. A mineral is homoeomerous, its chemical structure a signature that equally marks any part of it. Common stones picked up from the ground are more likely to be rock, which conglomerates different minerals in proportions that vary from one sample to another. Second, minerals are elemental, comprising either a single element (like gold, sulphur, or diamond, which is pure carbon) or a compound of elements (e.g. silicone dioxide, which combines oxygen and silicone atoms to form quartz). Indeed, the most common minerals are such combinations of silicon and oxygen (silicates), and include some of the most familiar precious and semiprecious stones: tiger's eye, amethyst, agate, garnet, topaz, beryl, emerald, aquamarine, serpentine, chalcedony, carnelian, jasper, onyx, opal, lapis lazuli, and others. Third, a mineral is inorganic, quite lifeless, a definition that excludes pearl, coral, amber, and fossil fuels like coal because all are formed from once-living matter.

How does Albert answer the "what is a mineral" question? For him also, a mineral is composed of the elements. By "elements," earth scientists refer to the hundred and more substances that do not break down into other substances by ordinary chemical or mechanical means, but with these "natural kinds," Albert's elements share but a name, for his number only four—earth, water, air, fire—which transmute through the interaction of their sensible qualities. Although one element may predominate, it never exists in complete purity but is always compromised by the presence of the other elements.[7] If the elements can traffic thus, so can (metallic) minerals under certain conditions—that is the assumption on which alchemy works. Albert's mineral thus has a distinct substantial form, but with the theoretical capability of attaining a different form—at least in the case of metals, which are the most complex and fusible of the minerals. It is like all other mineral forms and not like them, each relating to the other by potentiality. Although elemental constitution is a necessary condition of a mineral, it is not sufficient, for all things—minerals, plants, animals—are composed from the four elements. The question of what makes a mineral a mineral remains open.

Figure 1. Rock Crystal, polished.

---

[7] How a compound could possess its own substantial form yet somehow retain the substantial forms of its component elements was a problem, partially solved by the claim that elements could unite and compound by means of their sensible qualities (heat/coldness, dryness/moisture): see Edward Grant, ed., *A Source Book in Medieval Sciences* (Cambridge: Harvard University Press, 1974), 603–14, for discussions by Aquinas and Albert of Saxony.

In stones, earth predominates, although a transparent stone such as rock crystal (*crystallus*) possesses a "wateriness approaching airiness" ["aqueitas declinans in æreitatem"], which is hardened and compacted by the "attacking" [*apprehendens*] earthy material [Figure 1].[8] The noun "mineral," which descends from post-classical Latin (*mineralis* adj., *minerale* n.), is cognate with the noun "mine," itself a post-classical Latin word [*mina*], referring to the underground excavation of treasures stored in the earth's bowels.[9] So it follows that a mineral, which comes from the earth, should predominantly contain earth. The same association is in Greek. *Ta orukta*, literally "things dug up," translates into Latin as *fossilis* from the past participle of *fodere*, "to dig." That is what a stone is: something dug up, a "fossil" in the early sense of the word.[10] Similarly, the word "metal" derives from the Greek for "mine" or "quarry" [*to metallon*], which synecdochally refers to the metal that comes from the mine.

The earthiness of a mineral makes it heavy. Albert's pre-Newtonian cosmos, where earthiness and heaviness elide, is founded on natural place and motion, a doctrine that, summarized briefly, runs as

---

[8] *DM* 1.2.2; Wyckoff, 39; Borgnet, 5:15. By being so compressed (*comprimere*) and compacted (*compingere*), the stone is very hard (*durissimus*), and can be highly polished (*polire*): *DM* 1.2.4; Wyckoff, 47; Borgnet, 5:19. The word *crystallus* means "ice." Theophrastus claims that water predominates in metals while earth predominates in stones: *De Lapidibus*, §1, ed. and trans. D. E. Eichholz (Oxford: Clarendon Press, 1965), 56–57 (see also 4). Yet Aristotle says that some (unnamed) stones have water predominant: *Meteorologica*, 389a8–9, ed. and trans. H. D. P. Lee (Cambridge: Harvard University Press, 1962), 364–65. Avicenna also claims aquosity in many stones: Grant, *Source Book*, 616.

[9] *OED*, s.v. *mineral* (n.), 2b and etymological notes.

[10] Aristotle, *Meteorologica*, 378a18–22 (286–87). *OED*, s.v. *fossil* (n.), 2a.

follows: were the four elements of earth, water, air, and fire not already mixed up within sublunary bodies they would settle naturally into four strata of density, like a pousse-café cocktail with earth on the bottom, followed by water, then by air, and fire on the top. Heavy things drop not because of gravitational pull but because the prepondering element of earth in them "desires" to return to base, and thus makes objects move in downward direction. Natural place preempts Newtonian gravity as a universal vector, rendering all motion "analogous with the canter of horses keen to return to their stables," remarks Karl Popper derisively.[11] Let drop a stone from the hand and it moves downward to meet its earthy friends. Objects move "naturally" according to their elemental disposition, and if not, then their motion is "violent." A stone being lifted or thrown upward was the classic example of violent motion. In this pre-Newtonian cosmos, levity—far from being mere lack of gravity—is a centrifugal urge, a natural tendency to flee earth's center and move to the terrestrial circumference as the place where it is happiest, most itself. Space is not continuous, not homogeneous, not neutral. It has a limit, internal variation, and distinct properties. Medieval space is place, meaning that it is defined in terms of its resident contents rather than being an empty container antecedent and indifferent to its inhabitants. A stone has a sense of place, yet its earthward love is not simple, for the sensible qualities belonging to the other elements compromise its purity, rendering it a microcosm of concord-in-discord. Once more, however, the same can be said of any old rock: that it is composed of the elements; that its earthiness or congealed wateriness

---

[11] Karl R. Popper, *The Open Society and its Enemies, Volume II. The High Tide of Prophecy: Hegel, Marx, and the Aftermath*, 5th rev. edn. (Princeton: Princeton University Press, 1966), 6.

drives it downward; that it is a little miracle of balance between conflicting elemental tendencies.

What makes a mineral is mineral virtue, which is the power the stone or metal receives, in the immediate from earthy exhalations, ultimately from the heavens, because "all the powers of things below come from above."[12] The efficacy of any individual mineral might be weakened by disorderliness in its matter (*confusio* or *inordinatio materiæ*) and/or by celestial powers acting in opposition at the critical moment of its generation. Kept for too long away from their place of origin (*extra loca generationis suæ diu contenti*), stones (*lapides*) deteriorate and no longer fit their names properly, for they have lost their power although retained their outward petrified form, rather like a body looks at death, so similar to former appearance but without life.[13]

Mineral virtue raises the question of whether Albert's minerals are organic or inorganic. For geology, the answer is the latter; for Albert, it is both and neither. On the one hand, he is clear about the difference between mineral and animate substance: minerals neither feed nor reproduce, nor do they have souls. He explicitly rejects arguments in favor of stones possessing souls, which commit the error of Pythagorean vitalism, holding "all things to be full of gods" [*omnia plena diis*].[14] On the other hand, minerals behave like the living kingdom. Those stones that have no souls do have substantial forms, bestowed by the power of heaven and by their distinctive elemental

---

[12] "Omnium inferiorum virtutes a superioribus descendere": *DM* 2.1.3; Wyckoff, 63; Borgnet, 5:27.
[13] *DM* 2.1.4; Wyckoff, 65–67; Borgnet, 5:28–29.
[14] *DM* 2.1.1; Wyckoff, 57; Borgnet, 5:24.

admixture.[15] In its operation as an efficient cause, the mineralizing *virtus* has no special name and can only be understood, Albert explains, *per similia*:

> Sicut in semine animalis . . . vis formativa animalis, quæ format et efficit animal . . . sic est etiam in materia aptata lapidibus virtus formans et efficiens lapides et producens ad formam lapidis hujus vel illius.
>
> [Just as in an animal's seed . . . there comes . . . a force capable of forming an animal, which forms and produces an animal . . . so in material suitable for stones there is a power that forms and produces stones, and develops the form of this stone or that.][16]

Where human seed is the efficient cause of a baby, some *virtus* that behaves like but is not actually an animal seed brings a gemstone into existence. Animal seed it may not be, yet Albert cannot stop himself from using reproductive terms to explain mineralization. Egregiously having it both ways, he uses the reproductive analogy while insisting on its inapplicability. The divisions between the kingdoms are porous, without clear division between the end of a mineral and the beginning of a living creature:

> Et si hoc dicatur, quod unus solus lapis concipit alium, tamen non intelligitur quod de parte sui seminis generator . . . nisi forte sit medium inter lapidem et plantam, sicut

---

[15] "Lapides igitur animas non habent, sed alias formas substantiales virtutibus cœlestibus et propriæ elementorum commixtioni datas": *DM* 1.1.6; Wyckoff, 25; Borgnet, 5:9.

[16] *DM* 1.1.5; Wyckoff, 22; Borgnet, 5:7.

multa media inter plantam et animal inveniuntur, sicut spongia.

[And if it is said that one stone conceives another, yet it is not to be thought of as being produced by its own seed . . . unless perhaps there is something intermediate between stone and plant, just as there are many things intermediate between plant and animal, such as the sponge.][17]

The reproductive analogy derives from alchemy and is elaborated more fully in Albert's discussion of metals rather than of stones. (Like geologists, Albert classifies both metals and stones as minerals.) He begins his consideration of individual metals with sulphur (*sulphur*) and quicksilver (*argentum vivum*) that "are, as it were, universal in metals, like their Father and Mother."[18] Quicksilver or mercury is the female matter in metals and sulphur functions like the father with his male semen (*masculus semen*), which has the power of impressing its form upon things rather than receiving impressions. Polymorphic sulphur has the theoretical capability of turning into any metal.[19]

---

[17] *DM* 3.1.6; Wyckoff, 171; Borgnet, 5:67. On stone's in/organic status and its locomotive powers, see Jeffrey Jerome Cohen, "Stories of Stone," *postmedieval: a journal of medieval cultural studies* 1.1-2 (2010): 60–61 [56–63].

[18] ". . . quasi universalia metallorum sunt sicut pater et mater": *DM* 4 (single tractatus), chap. 1; Wyckoff, 204; Borgnet, 5:83. Classified today as a non-metal (not being a conductor of an electrical current), sulphur is a metal in alchemy.

[19] *DM* 4 (single tractatus), chap. 1; Wyckoff, 205; Borgnet, 5:84. Albert here follows Hermes Trismegistus, mythical author of a group of alchemical writings. See David Porreca, "Albertus Magnus and Hermes Trismegistus: An Update," *Medieval Studies* 72 (2010): 245–81 (especially 274–78).

Quicksilver or mercury, to complete the analogy, provides the matter, "as the menstrual fluid is to the embryo: out of it, by the force of the Sulphur . . . all metals are produced."[20]

Seeing metals frequently occurring in rocks, Albert takes stones to be a matrix or "womb," a material cause of metal, "as if the substance of stones were, so to speak, a place peculiarly suitable for the production of metals."[21] As Hermes says, "the Mother of metal is Earth, that carries it in her belly."[22] Metals form in the fissures of rocks through the natural sublimation (*sublimatio naturalis*) of moisture (*humidum*) and earth (*terreum*).[23] The force of rising fumes opens and spreads through the pores of the surrounding stone, concentrating, purifying, and eventually hardening into metal. The rising vapor (subtle, refined, and highly capable of interpenetration) forces passageways, the size of which determine whether the metals form as veins or disperse throughout the rock [Figure 2]. Rocks are thus in the most passive sense a receptacle that provides the ideal lithic conditions under which metals gestate, and in this sense they provide the models mimicked by alchemists with their hermetically sealed vessels of glass. In a more active sense, and earlier in the process of genesis, rocks act as a mould, bestowing outer shape upon fusible metal. More actively and earlier again, rocks provide the material cause of metal by means of their exhalation of subtle vapors. In the

---

[20] ". . . sicut menstruum est embryonis: ex quo virtute sulphuris . . . omne metallum generatur": *DM* 4 (single tractatus), chap. 2; Wyckoff, 207; Borgnet, 5:85.

[21] ". . . tanquam lapidum substantia sit quasi locus proprius metallicæ generationis": *DM* 3.1.1; Wyckoff, 153; Borgnet, 5:59.

[22] "Genitrix metalli est terra quæ portat ipsum in ventre suo": *DM* 3.2.1; Wyckoff, 186; Borgnet, 5:75.

[23] *DM* 3.1.10; Wyckoff, 182; Borgnet, 5:72. See whole chapter for the following explanation.

same way, the woman, in the Aristotelian model of reproduction, provides both the matter of the foetus and its natural place for gestation. As to whether a mineral is organic or inorganic, then, it is not alive and does not reproduce, yet reproduction remains the only way of understanding it.

Figure 2. Copper Ore, Trimountain Mine, Houghton County, Michigan, Baltic Lode.

This ghostly quality of a mineral unites the worlds of hagiography and lapidary, saint and stone. Take the pearl, which although not a geological mineral because it contains organic matter is so classified in medieval lapidaries, and possesses special powers.[24] "Margaret" means "pearl" (Latin *margarita*), and so, when it comes to lives of Saint Margaret, the possibilities for word play are rich. Nicholas Bozon, a friar writing in England sometime around the end of the thirteenth/beginning of the fourteenth century, speaks of "Margarete, sa chere gemme," who is small, white,

---

[24] *DM* 2.2.11; Wyckoff, 105–6; Borgnet, 5:41.

Et vertuouse en treble manere
Cum treis vertuz ad la pere:

[And virtuous in a threefold way just as the stone has three virtues:]

De asez plus fu Margarete
Virtuouse ke margarite.[25]

[Margaret was far more virtuous than the margarite.]

Making a "virtue" of double entendre, Bozon turns the stone/saint pun into rhyme, and further puns on *virtuouse*, playing between minerality and morality. Without change of register, it is possible to shuffle between the powers of holiness and of a gemstone.

Albert posits a mineral virtue the nature and operation of which can only be explained by reference to what it is not, namely, animal generation. That is, he proceeds by analogy, an argumentative method of sometimes doubtful logic that he uses without embarrassment in this confidently scientific treatise. His "scientific method" is Aristotelian—the terms in this context are interchangeable—and this means that he thinks theoretically about his subject (*speculatio*) before constraining himself to individuating descriptions, descending from the general (*a communibus*) to the particular (*usque ad elementa particularia*).[26] This is

---

[25] Nicholas Bozon, *Three Saints' Lives by Nicholas Bozon*, ed. and trans. Sister M. Amelia (Klenke) (New York: Franciscan Institute, 1947), l.45 (31), and ll. 13–14, 19–20 (29), respectively.

[26] *DM* 4 (single tractatus), chap. 1; Wyckoff, 204; Borgnet, 5:83. For Albert's disentanglement of Platonic from Aristotelian conceptions of form, thereby allowing him to strengthen the case for natural science's ability to demonstrate necessary

why he opens his treatise by describing minerals in terms of the four causes.

The material cause is the elements, which by their varying determinate forms give rise to the subgroups of minerals—stones, metals, and intermediates; the efficient cause is the mineralizing power or virtue that operates by means of the exhalations or fumes given off by the elemental substances;[27] the formal cause is the celestial power of the heavens; and the final cause—not one Albert much addresses—is presumably exhausted by its function of exercising its mineral virtues or powers, for in physical things formal and final cause are the same thing.[28] Mineral virtue then derives from the heavens but uses as its instruments the fumes of the elements as they are acted upon by heat and cold. With roots running deep into Arabic and hermetic traditions of knowledge, mineral virtue, qua concept, does not fit squarely into Aristotle's four causes, for it seems to slither between explanations of the physical process of petrification and a stone's specific therapeutic properties.[29] The equivocation arises in part from the distinction made between stones in possession of active powers and those same stones having lost their special powers, as lifeless lumps dug out of the earth,

---

causes, see Michael W. Tkacz, "Albertus Magnus and the Recovery of Aristotelian Form," *The Review of Metaphysics* 64 (2011): 735–62.

[27] Albert acquired the concept of mineral virtue from Avicenna. For the four causes, see Wyckoff's introduction, xxxi–xxxii; also *DM* 1.1.5; Wyckoff, 21–23; Borgnet, 5:7–8.

[28] *DM* 1.1.6; Wyckoff, 24–26; Borgnet, 5:8–9.

[29] For the hermetic context of Albert's treatment of *virtus*, see Isabelle Draelants, "La *virtus universalis*: un concept d'origine hermétique? Les sources d'une notion de philosophie naturelle apparentée à la forme spécifique," in *Hermetism from Late Antiquity to Humanism*, eds. Paolo Lucentini, Ilaria Parri, and Vittoria Perrone Compagni, Instrumenta Patristica et Mediaevalia 40 (Turnhout: Brepols, 2003), 157–88.

still somehow enjoying the name of *lapides*. Regarding these "mysteries of the mineralizing power," the best one can do is approximate:

> For Albert, God was not in each rock, but he had put certain powers into them through secondary causes, including the celestial bodies. Those powers, whatever they are, can be discovered only by observation of their effects.[30]

Albert's method relies upon the "empty verbiage" of the four causes and intuited essences, as Popper meanly says of Aristotlean logic.[31] Causation was never quite the same after Hume and his billiard balls, when he points out how it is never possible to see one *causing* the other to move.[32] Events and phenomena are only correlated, causation only an inference rather than any insight into the order of things. Most difficult of all to justify is the *causa finalis*, which claims a present condition to have been brought about by a future condition, as if effects can precede their causes in time.

Even if mineral virtue, mysteriously present in stony exhalations by celestial influence, were as observable as a billiard ball it could still never be caught in the act of causing the mineral nature of stones. As a power it is identifiable only in its actuancy, as cause, in its effect. Ground to a powder, mixed with honey, and

---

[30] Riddle and Mulholland, "Albert on Stones and Minerals," 215, 214.
[31] Popper, *The Open Society, Volume II*, 9–12.
[32] David Hume, *An Inquiry Concerning Human Understanding*, ed. Charles W. Hendel (Indianapolis: Liberal Arts Press, 1955), §7.2, 85. For a "weird" communication between objects, see Graham Harman, "On Vicarious Causation," *Collapse*, Vol. II: Speculative Realism (London: Urbanomic, 2007), 187–221.

administered to a woman, *crystallus* (rock crystal) will make her lactate. Placed under the tongue, it will decrease thirst.[33] The *virtus* of crystal causes the decrease in thirst when placed under the tongue, and by means of the decrease in thirst when crystal is placed under the tongue one posits its mineral powers, and on it goes. The tautology evokes Molière's famous caricature of scholastic learning, when Argan, candidate for a degree, asked the cause and reason for why opium sends one to sleep, replies that it is because of its dormitive virtue, the nature of which is to dull the senses. The examining board is delighted:

> *First Doctor*: Domandabo causum et rationem, quare
> Opium facit dormire.
> *Argan*: . . . Quia est in eo
> *Virtus dormitiva*,
> Cujus est natura
> Sensus assoupire.
> *Chorus*: Bene, bene, bene, bene respondere.[34]

By the same circular inference, natural place is posited. It is the nature of an earthy stone to descend because it is heavy, and it is heavy because it is the nature of earth to descend. As theories, natural place and mineral virtue rudely commit metaphysics in the negative sense. Philosophy of science, for much of the twentieth century, has been absorbed in developing a logical vocabulary that avoids such metaphysical circularity while achieving something more explanatorily ambitious than mere summary of what happens, which is

---

[33] *DM* 2.2.3; Wyckoff, 83; Borgnet, 5:34.
[34] Molière, *Le Malade imaginaire*, Third Interlude, *Œuvres complètes: Vol. 2*, ed. Robert Jouanny (Paris: Garnier Frères, 1962), 848.

all that Humean empiricism will allow itself to do. Contemporary post-positivist science pays the same respect to explanatory or theoretical language as it does to observational language, yet mineral virtue remains beyond the pale, resistant to quantification and therefore unable to offer any predictive or retrodictive outcomes—in contrast to gravity, for example, which is equally unobservable but still measurable in its effects.

If Albert's observational method is at risk for his look-and-see approach to causes, his logical method of argument *per similia* is equally vulnerable. Molière's ridicule of scholastic causation is at least fiction, but the analogy made in all seriousness by Franciscus Sitius (Francesco Sizzi) in objection to Galileo's claim about Jupiter's four moons has been unkindly treated by the scientific community. Sizzi argues that there are and can only be seven planets. From the seven lamps on the candlestick in the Jewish tabernacle (*tabernaculum*), he points to the microsocmic dwelling (*domicilio*) of the human head, with its seven windows (*fenestræ*) of eyes, nostrils, ears, and mouth, thence to the macrocosmic sky (*cœlum*) and its seven planets for lamps (Hebrew Bible writers routinely describing the heavens as a tented dwelling). A multitude of nature's heptads (e.g. metals, days of the week) follow as effects (*effectus*) which "it would be long and most tedious to specify [*enumerare*]" but which lead the reader, he hopes, to infer the necessity of the seven-planet theory.[35]

Analogy is a complex topic, running the gamut from Sizzi's outlandish adjacencies to the most justly measured ratios (*a:b :: c:d*), as when Aristotle uses the term to claim justice as a kind of proportion.[36] By

---

[35] Francisco Sitius, *Dianoia Astronomica, Optica, Physica* (Venice, 1611), 15–16.
[36] *Nicomachean Ethics*, from 1131a29-30 to 1131b24, ed. and trans. H. Rackham, rev. edn. (Cambridge: Harvard University Press, 1934), 268–73.

expressing the ratio as fraction, $a/b = c/d$, and if three of the terms are known, the fourth term can be computed: thus, $a = bc/d$. True, the knowledge generated is analytic only, teasing out what is already latent in the original terms, and not supplying any new information. But it makes connections within experience that are meaningful and practical, enabling fifteenth-century mariner Michael of Rhodes to ask, "If a load of pepper which weighs 400 pounds is worth 49 ½ ducats, how many ducats will I have for 315 pounds? And to solve this by the rule of three, we will say: . . ."—and thereby to make equivalence between a world of incommensurables.[37] This quantitative proportionality is not the sense in which Albert uses analogy, which has been described as being more like Aristotle's category of relation (*pros hen*).[38] Albert's appeal to human reproduction to describe the genesis of stones seems closer to the function of a scientific model, which in modern science idealizes phenomena in order to visualize and explain them. Just as there can come a point when a scientific model so aptly illustrates its phenomena that it steps out of the realm of metaphor to *describe* rather than fictionalize those phenomena, so the reproductive model stops analogizing and starts describing: thus Albert refers to the female peranites, which conceives

---

[37] *The Book of Michael of Rhodes: A Fifteenth-Century Maritime Manuscript*, 3 volumes, eds. and trans. Pamela O. Long, David McGee, and Alan M. Stahl (Cambridge: MIT Press, 2009), 2:11. For the rule of three and early modern economics, see Richard W. Hadden, *On the Shoulders of Merchants: Exchange and the Mathematical Conception of Nature in Early Modern Europe* (Albany: State University of New York Press, 1994), 92.

[38] Victor Salas, "Albertus Magnus and Thomas Aquinas on the Analogy between God and Creatures," *Medieval Studies* 72 (2010): 290–91 [283–312].

and gives birth (*concipere et parere*) to a baby peranites.[39]

Analogy, broadly defined, seems fundamental to all reasoning from experience insofar as thought itself is impossible without inferring from perceived resemblances.[40] From the earliest speculative thought in Greek philosophy, two basic and interconnected logical models prevail: explaining phenomena by reference to their opposites (polarity), and by reference to similitude with something else (analogy).[41] Analogy enables counting. The very word "calculation" is a reminder of analogies between thoughts and stones. Some of the earliest concrete counting systems function by means of a one-to-one correspondence between things counted and pebbles (*calculi*). The accumulated pebbles give a sense of quantity without words or cardination. In Latin and Greek, "stone" and "number" are the same word (*calculus, pséphos*); while in Arabic, "stone" and "a tally" share the same root.[42] When a thought so resposes within a stone, it becomes nearly meaningless to posit intellection without pebbles. At that point of convergence between mental life and external *realia*, how to find the words to characterize their relationship: correlation between thinking subjects and external objects that otherwise have nothing to do with each other? cold instrumentality by which mind uses matter to think, much as one might use a paper towel to dry the hands and then toss it? panpsychism in all things,

---

[39] *DM* 2.2.14; Wyckoff, 112; Borgnet, 5:43.
[40] G.E.R. Lloyd, *Polarity and Analogy: Two Types of Argumentation in Early Greek Thought* (Indianapolis: Hackett Publishing, 1992; originally published Cambridge: Cambridge University Press, 1966), 172–73.
[41] Lloyd, *Polarity and Analogy*, 7–8.
[42] Georges Ifrah, *The Universal History of Numbers: From Prehistory to the Invention of the Computer*, trans. David Bellos et al. (New York: John Wiley, 2000), 96.

animate and inanimate? clunky cognitive machinery that somehow manages to get mind to understand matter? or what? Is it any more desperate for Sizzi to argue, by a kind of early fractal logic, that patterns writ large replicate patterns writ small, and that when sense data belie hard earned beliefs, that one should trust in the smooth equivalences supplied by analogy? Indeed, insofar as animals appear to be capable of calculating abstract quantity on the reasoning that *a* is to *b* as *c* is to *d*, analogy seems really to operate outside the human mind.[43] Only when nature is demystified into the bearer of purely positive data does Sizzi's argument by analogy diminish into amphibology.

So committed to metaphysics is Albert's causal method of analysis and argument by analogy that he waxes uncomfortable with the system he adopts in the lapidary section of his treatise, where he discusses stones and their special properties individually. Gingerly, he resigns himself to listing them in order of spelling:

> And for the most convenient order [*ordo*] in Latin, let us proceed alphabetically [*secundum ordinem alphabeti*] with the names of the stones and their powers, as the medical men are accustomed to do in describing medical simples.[44]

The arm's length distance at which the grouping system is held comes across in the phrasing of the rubrics: "Chapter 4: Names Beginning with the Fourth Letter, which is D."[45] Although alphabetic grouping began to

---

[43] Stanislas Dehaene, *The Number Sense: How the Mind Creates Mathematics*, rev. edn. (New York: Oxford University Press, 2011), 12–15.
[44] *DM* 2.2.1; Wyckoff, 69; Borgnet, 5:30.
[45] *DM* 2.2.4; Wyckoff, 85; Borgnet, 5:34.

dominate as a classificatory method among thirteenth-century encyclopedias Albert finds it insufficient to the task of philosophical analysis. Wyckoff notes the tenuousness of his system: alphabeticization does not extend to the second and subsequent letters of the names, and no attention is paid to orthographic variation.[46] In *De Animalibus*, when obliged to list animals alphabetically, he notes the unsuitability of the method to philosophy (*hic modus non proprius philosophiæ*).[47] Listing stones by letter subordinates natural forms to the arbitrary conventions of language (even if it is Latin) and bends the physical world into random orthographic shapes. Where division by Aristotle's four causes carves nature at her joints, alphabetic classification like an unskilled butcher hacks physical taxa into unrecognizable lumps.[48]

One of the most compelling and famous descriptions of taxonomic strangeness comes in Foucault's preface to his *Order of Things*, where he talks about Borges's alleged Chinese encyclopedia that groups animals according to categories such as whether they are embalmed, or frenzied, or drawn with a fine paintbrush, or at a distance look like flies.[49] Foucault's inquiry is into the discursive field or epistemic network that makes such category divisions meaningful. Its rule—the order of things—is subterranean and

---

[46] Wyckoff, 68.

[47] *De Animalibus* 22.1.1; Borgnet, 12:365. The alphabetical list of animals is given in the second tractatus, while his disclaimer comes in the first.

[48] Plato, *Phaedrus*, 265E, ed. and trans. Harold North Fowler (1914; repr. Cambridge: Harvard University Press, 2005), 534–35.

[49] Michel Foucault, *The Order of Things: An Archaeology of the Human Sciences*, (New York: Random House, 1970), xv. The reference is to Borges's essay, "The Analytical Language of John Wilkins."

has no existence except in the grid created by a glance, an examination, a language; and it is only in the blank spaces of this grid that order manifests itself in depth as though already there, waiting in silence for the moment of its expression."[50]

Buried too deep for enunciation in ordinary language, these epistemic rules cannot break surface into daily chatter, to be taken or left as caprice prompts, so instead they are intuited only in the interstices between utterances that themselves only appear true by those same epistemic rules. No ropes and pulleys of the mind will rectify this indirection, for as the great "masters of suspicion" (Marx, Nietzsche, Freud) have it, reality arrives already in structural contradiction with itself, and expression of its inner logic will only ever manifest itself as double.[51]

Without an underlying affinity to hold the phenomena together, Sizzi's alignment of cephalic orifices and Ptolomaic planets seems as counterintuitive as the adjacency between embalmed and frenzied animals. But such defamiliarization applies to any discursive field, including that of modern science. Discernible only in its instantiations, the Foucauldian episteme looks not unlike dormitive virtue: the rule is implied in the utterance, which is made meaningful by the rule, which is implied in the utterance. . . . Sometimes circularity is the shape of truth; all deductive arguments bite their own tails.

Epistemic assumptions juxtapose and correlate taxa into syntactic arrangements to make sense of adjacencies encountered in the world out there. When Albert looked at metal in the matrix of rock he "saw"

---

[50] Foucault, *Order of Things*, xx.
[51] Paul Ricoeur, *Freud and Philosophy: An Essay on Interpretation* (New Haven: Yale University Press, 1970), 32.

with eyes that could pierce through to essences the rock as material cause of the metal rather than as later scientists came to see it, namely, a mix of metal and ore, each having its own chemical identity.[52] When rock functions as both container and material cause, it "posits" metal, serving as origin and archive, the place of commencement and governance, its relationship to metal both jussive and sequential, to borrow a distinction made explicit by Derrida.[53] The topological and nomological converge in the natural place of rock as matrix, which mothers metal even as it orders it into being. While there could be many geological reasons why metals occur where they do, their adjacency to rock for Albert means origination and a gradual evolution from one state to another. His process of reasoning, so it seems now, is faulty twice over: first in the assumption that metal's adjacency to rock implies a temporal relation, that it occurred after rock; second, that it occurred because of the rock—a geological version of *post hoc ergo propter hoc*. Metaphysical Albert's reasoning may be, but by describing rock as an environment that summons its resident metals into being and sustains them in that mode, he demonstrates a deeply ecological sensibility, a sense of connection between things.

It is this principle of the connection that places Albert's treatise within a "history of resemblance,"[54] as Foucault calls it. Earlier, it was noted how the elements transmute into each other. It is the extent to which they are mixed well that determines the quality of a mineral—in particular, its density. Albert makes no

---

[52] Riddle and Mulholland, "Albert on Stones and Minerals," 221.
[53] Jacques Derrida, *Archive Fever: A Freudian Impression*, trans. Eric Prenowitz (Chicago: University of Chicago Press, 1998), 1–2.
[54] Foucault, *Order of Things*, xxiv.

systematic distinction between weight and density, which he calls compactness (*compactio*). Although the concept of specific gravity (or relative density) was known in Arab science, Albert follows Aristotle's theory of natural place, which explains density in terms of elemental constituency rather than mass relative to unit volume.[55] Compactness is created by the even mixing of earth and water, causing total interpenetration:

> But compactness is caused especially by moisture that penetrates everywhere throughout the material of the stone, causing every part of it to flow into every other part. And so the stone becomes compact.[56]

Metals represent a more complex mixing of the elements than what occurs in stones, for "we say that a stone is not a combination, but a simple mixture, solidified into its own form by a mineralizing power."[57] By mixture, Albert means a profound uniting of elements, approximate to chemical bonding.[58] This is why Albert proceeds to metals after stones, because stones are an "easier mixture" [*facilior commixtio*], closer to the original elemental mixture of earth and water.[59] The waters in metals are highly rarefied,

---

[55] Wyckoff, 49 (editorial comments).

[56] "Compactio autem præcipue facta partium est ab humido undique penetrante lapidis materiam: propter quod quamlibet partem ejus fluere facit ad quamlibet partem: et ideo compactus factus est lapis": *DM* 1.2.6; Wyckoff, 50; Borgnet, 5:20.

[57] "Dicimus lapidem esse mixtum non complexionatum virtute mineralium ad formam coagulatum": *DM* 1.1.6; Wyckoff, 26; Borgnet, 5:9.

[58] Riddle and Mulholland, "Albert on Stones and Minerals," 208.

[59] *DM* 3.1.1; Wyckoff, 155; Borgnet, 5:60.

thoroughly acted upon by the other elements, for "their parts are connected like [the links of] a chain and cannot easily be torn apart."[60] In metals, "an unctuous, subtle moisture" [*humidum unctuosum subtile*] is

> incorporated and thoroughly mixed with subtle Earth, so that large amounts of the two are combined, not merely with, but actually in, each other.[61]

The fusion of ingredients here exceeds counterpoint, suggesting complexity of internal composition. In this principle of *non tantum cum sed etiam in*, we encounter an engagement with difference-insimilitude that anticipates Emmanuel Levinas's radical alterity of the face-to-face encounter, which is a relation of the between-two, sans any third term, an "affront," to borrow from heraldic vocabulary. In contrast, Heidegger's *Miteinandersein* is found by Levinas to be a collectivity of self and other alongside and in relation to a common third term, an heraldic "accost" that ultimately stops short of full difference.[62]

Even though metals are more rarefied minerals than stones, not all metals are mixed as well as they might be or as internally coherent as stones are. Tin is brittle according to Albert, for it has a very "stuttering constitution" [*balbutientem habet valde composi-*

---

[60] "... harum partes connectuntur sicut catenæ, et una earum de facili evelli non potest": *DM* 3.1.2; Wyckoff, 156; Borgnet, 5:61.

[61] "... est incorporatum terrestri subtili fortiter commixto, ita quod plurimum utriusque non tantum cum plurimo utriusque, sed etiam in plurimo utriusque": *DM* 3.1.2; Wyckoff, 159; Borgnet, 5:62.

[62] Emmaunel Levinas, *Time and the Other*, trans. Richard A. Cohen (Pittsburgh: Duquesne University Press, 1987), 40–41, 93.

tionem].[63] For this reason it "does not mix well with anything else and is not capable of becoming continuously joined to anything near by," and it makes other metals mixed with it to stutter also.[64] When tin stutters, its parts discohere. Lack of interpenetration means inability to attain the similitude within difference that facilitates mixing:

> It is called a "stuttering" mixture because the mixing attains the proper proportion in some parts and not in others; but of real union, so to speak, there is very little. [It is] just like a man who stutters, being able to say some words and not others.[65]

If tin stutters, gold, as it were, sings. Gold, which has a density of 19.3 relative to water's density of 1, is mixed to perfection.[66] Albert describes the subtlety and high degree of interpenetration of the elements involved. The high luster of metals derives from the quantity and subtlety of water they contain, which renders them fusible; and gold, with the subtlest mixing of moisture, most fusible, shines brightest of all.[67] The elements within gold "pack firmly together" [*simul constabunt*], creating a subtle substance that has "a

---

[63] *DM* 4 (single tractatus), chap. 4; Wyckoff, 215; Borgnet, 5:87. His choice of the word derives from Aristotle. In its pure state, tin is actually very malleable: Wyckoff, 214 (editorial notes).

[64] ". . . non bene miscetur alii, et non bene continuabile propinquo sibi conjuncto": *DM* 4 (single tractatus), chap. 4; Wyckoff, 215; Borgnet, 5:87.

[65] "Vocatur autem *balbutiens mixtura*, quæ in aliquibus partibus mixtionis rationem attingit, et in quibusdam non, sed est compositio quasi minima, sicut homo balbutiens quædam verba attingit et quædam non": *DM* 3.2.1; Wyckoff, 187; Borgnet, 5:76.

[66] Wyckoff, 226 (editorial notes).

[67] *DM* 3.2.3; Wyckoff, 191; Borgnet, 5:77–78.

very large number of parts in a very small space" [*plurimæ partes in parvissimo loco*]. This is density or "solidity" [*consolidatio*], although Albert refers to it as gravid, for "the packing together of many parts in a small space or place causes the weight."[68] The elements are closely harmonized in a close union (*connexio*) that Plato calls "an agreement" [*fœdus*] and Empedocles "a gluing together of related things" [*collam germanorum*].[69] Unlike the other metals, which have sufficient pockets of air to be combustible, gold's "pores are tightly closed and cannot be opened" [*pori . . . arcti sunt et indissolubiles*].[70] Like a perfect number, so called because it is the sum of its divisors, gold's parts fit together perfectly, without spaces between, a whole that is the sum of its parts and no more. One might say that gold has integrity and loves itself. Representing a kind of ideal being, the minerally virtual made real, gold perfectly assimilates difference within. Its density arises from all its parts being packed together into a small space, because they love each other. This could not occur if there were not a fundamental resemblance, sympathy, or analogy between the differences. The different substances and elements have an affinity, a principle common to all that draws unlikely things together. Stuttering tin demonstrates the opposite of sympathy because of its discoherent parts. Sympathy or affinity overrides gravity as a concept. The sympathy of things makes all things connected, making the cosmos a metaphysical totality, a continuous whole and everything within it a continuous whole.

---

[68] ". . . constantia multarum partium simul in parvo loco et situ facit pondus." For this and the above cites, *DM* 4 (single tractatus), chap. 7; Wyckoff, 228; Borgnet, 5:92.

[69] *DM* 4 (single tractatus), chap. 7; Wyckoff, 228–29; Borgnet, 5:92.

[70] *DM* 4 (single tractatus), chap. 7; Wyckoff, 230; Borgnet, 5:93.

Continuous wholeness results in the fullness of things. The world is as full as an egg, for nature abhors a vacuum. Pumice might contain air in it because its ingredients have mixed badly, resulting in porosity (*porositas*), yet it holds no emptiness.[71] The cosmological thinking here is deeply anti-atomist, as elaborated in Aristotle's *Physics*.[72] It depicts the universe as a *plenum*, a fullness without void. Despite specific medieval arguments against *horror vacui*, it is worth retaining this idea of plenitude or fullness as a broadly conceived medieval mentalité.[73] The *plenum* names space that is intrinsically holy (whole and unbroken), positing substance as inside the temple of the sublunar world; the profane (*pro* + *fanum*) names everything else, which resides in front of and therefore outside the temple. The mechanization and secularization of space is an emptying of the *plenum*, a removal of matter outside the place of the temple. In the same way, scientific objections to teleology only make sense when present time is emptied of the promise of futurity. Medieval typological reading of history and the natural world—teleological to its core—holds past, present, and future in simultaneity; it reads nature in and as the fullness of time.

---

[71] *DM* 1.2.6; Wyckoff, 49–50; Borgnet, 5:20. When Albert earlier claims that the best mixed stones, compact and easily cut with flat sides, contain vapor that "approaches the subtlety and moisture of air" (*vergit ad subtilitatem æris et humiditatem*), he means that the earth and water have thoroughly interpenetrated, not that the stone is now light: *DM* 1.2.1; Wyckoff, 37; Borgnet, 5:14.

[72] For some late medieval atomist positions, and for vacuums, abhorred and otherwise, see Grant, *Source Book*, 312–60.

[73] Charles Taylor, *A Secular Age* (Cambridge: Belknap Press, 2007), uses the term "fullness" (6 et passim) to describe the "enchanted" world of cultures prior to early modernity. For "higher time," see 54–56.

Albert's metaphysical cosmos is a totality, internally connected by the congregation of similitudes and by analogies between polarities. Both analogy and natural place operate by the assembly of like things. Here numbers make friends, finding self in the aliquot parts of another. Amicable numbers (pairs of numbers the divisors of which add up to each other, e.g. 220 and 284) make (idealized) matter recognize self in difference. A mineral is the result of a celestial impulse to realize itself in subterranean rock. The elemental interconnection of things undermines any definitive schism in the kingdom of being between organic and inorganic.

Like Thomas Kuhn's paradigm shifts, Foucault's epistemic shifts give no final measure of scientific "progress," for they allow only periodic accumulation of knowledge, punctuated with convulsions—albeit only occasional—during which science has to wipe the slate clean and start over. To the extent that they show how observation is at least partially theory-laden those shifts enable a consideration of "pseudoscience" on its own terms, a reading of redundant scientific doctrines such as mineral virtue with a view to scientific self-understanding in the here and now, while bracketing the demarcatory questions of their truth-value or practical utility. Epistemic shifts make sense of unfamiliar Chinese encyclopedias even as they render familiar taxonomies as bizarre as Chinese encyclopedias.

In his consideration of postpositivist philosophy of science, in particular, the posthuman world animated by cyborgs and scallops-as-actors, Zammito speaks of having verged "on the realm of science fiction."[74] He means nothing complimentary by the comment, but in

---

[74] John H. Zammito, *A Nice Derangement of Epistemes: Post-Positivism in the Study of Science from Quine to Latour* (Chicago: University of Chicago Press, 2004), 225 [183–231].

the confines of this essay anyway, no offence is taken, for storytelling is one way to describe all accounting: by encyclopedia entries, syllogistic deductions, Euclidian proofs, arithmetic progressions, laundry lists, and descriptive models of scientific reality.[75] Eight centuries ago mineral virtue was cutting-edge theory, now pseudoscience. With a little modesty and imagination on our part, it helps us tell stories in which today's scientific givens (chemical elements, the in/organic divide) turn out to be tomorrow's fictions. Call it thought experiment, if you will.

---

[75] Mary S. Morgan, "Models, Stories, and the Economic World," *Journal of Economic Methodology* 8.3 (2001): 361–84.

YOU ARE HERE: A MANIFESTO

Eileen A. Joy

*for Aranye Fradenburg: the work is to keep moving,
but also to keep living*

> The poet produces the beautiful by fixing his attention on something real. It is the same with an act of love. . . . The authentic and pure values—truth, beauty and goodness—in the activity of a human being are the result of one and the same act, a certain application of the full attention to the object.
>
> Simone Weil, *Gravity and Grace*[1]

---

[1] Simone Weil, *Gravity and Grace*, trans. Emma Crawford and Mario von der Ruhr (London: Routledge, 1952), 119.

Animal, Vegetable, Mineral

Prolegomenon: A Mental Handout

Imagine a piece of paper, completely blank, except for a small black dot directly in the center. And then a small arrow pointing to the dot, and next to that, the phrase is written, "You Are Here." Strictly speaking, the dot is where you are. Paraphrasing Italo Calvino's short story, "All At One Point," which describes the time before the universe expanded, when all of matter was concentrated in a single point, and everyone and everything, in the words of the narrator, "was packed in there like sardines,"[2] every point of each of us coincides with every point of everyone else in a single point, which is where we all are. There is nowhere else. The idea of distance, or separation, or estrangement, is a dream. Which is not to say we should not mind the gaps.

Ideation Without Bodies / The Drowned World

> The strangest thing is that I am not at all inclined to call myself insane, I clearly see that I am not: all these changes concern objects. At least, that is what I'd like to be sure of.
>
> from the notebooks of Antoine Roquentin[3]

In J.G. Ballard's short story, "The Overloaded Man," the main character, Faulkner, is "slowly going insane."[4] In a nutshell, he's become dissatisfied with life in general, and having quit his job, he waits impatiently for his wife to leave every morning so that he can engage in a certain daily secret ritual. Living in a development called "the Bin"—a "sprawl of interlocking frosted glass,

---

[2] Italo Calvino, "All At One Point," in *Cosmicomics*, trans. William Weaver (New York: Harcourt Brace, 1968), 43 [43–47].
[3] Jean-Paul Sartre, *Nausea*, trans. Richard Howard (New York: New Directions, 2007), 2.
[4] J.G. Ballard, "The Overloaded Man," in *The Best Short Stories of J.G. Ballard* (New York: Picador, 1995), 112 [112–124].

white rectangles and curves, at first glance abstract and exciting . . . but to the people within formless and visually exhausting"[5]—Faulkner is eager to dematerialize his surroundings. Sitting on his veranda each day, he engages in a process of intense visualization, turning the entire field of recognizable "objects" in his view into "disembodied" forms, leading to a randomized, geometric "cubist landscape."[6] Unknowingly following some of the thing-logics laid out by Bill Brown in his 2001 essay, "Thing Theory," Faulkner reduces the world to thingness, where "things" denote both the "amorphousness out of which objects are materialized by the (ap)perceving subject" (things as the "anterior physicality of the physical world") and also the ways in which the world always exceeds our ability to apprehend it (things as "sensuous" and "metaphysical" presences that exceed their "materialization as objects or their mere utilization in objects").[7]

As in the bricolage technique of the Surrealists, which Brown refers to in his essay, Faulkner operates a variety of "cut-out switches" that sever objects from their always already "tenuous" hold on reality and thereby crafts what he believes is an "escape route" from a world he finds tedious and "intolerable." But Faulkner also believes, perhaps perversely, that "it was pleasant to see the world afresh again, to wallow in an endless panorama of brilliantly colored images. What did it matter if there was form but no content?"[8] Nevertheless, as the verbs of Ballard's story suggest—deleting, blotting, switching off, repressing, vanishing, obliterating, eliminating, erasing, stripping, reducing, demolishing, etc.—what Faulkner is really doing is

---

[5] Ballard, "The Overloaded Man," 114.
[6] Ballard, "The Overloaded Man," 115.
[7] Bill Brown, "Thing Theory," *Critical Inquiry* 28 (Autumn 2001): 5 [1–22].
[8] Ballard, "The Overloaded Man," 116.

deleting the world and all "traces of meaning" from that world, until even the cubist shapes he has reduced it to also begin to

> lose their meaning, the abstract masses of color dissolving, drawing Faulkner after them into a world of pure psychic sensation, where blocks of ideation hung like magnetic fields in a cloud chamber....[9]

Eventually, he also discovers that, in addition to his surroundings, his own body, which "seemed an extension of his mind," has vanished as well. That is, until his wife shows up and starts screaming at him and he decides to "dismantle" her as well, "erasing all his memories" of her "motion and energy," and turning her into "a bundle of obtrusive angles."[10] And yet, what he precisely *cannot erase* is the motion of her body fastening onto his, at which point he decides to "smooth and restrain her, molding her angular form into a softer and rounder one."[11] In other words, he strangles her to death.

As it turns out, even when you visually "dismantle" and erase the world and all of its "objects," including persons, they still retain their insistently sensuous and metaphysical thingness and demand your attention. Bodies continue to press in, even your own. And what Faulkner ultimately seeks is

> pure ideation, the undisturbed sensation of psychic being untransmuted by any physical medium. Only thus could he escape the nausea of the external world.

---

[9] Ballard, "The Overloaded Man," 118.
[10] Ballard, "The Overloaded Man," 123.
[11] Ballard, "The Overloaded Man," 124.

Joy—You Are Here: A Manifesto

And so, seeking "an absolute continuum of existence uncontaminated by material excrescences," he drowns himself in a shallow pond at the far end of his garden while looking up at the "blue disk" of the sky,[12] which he believes is somehow the only space freed of materiality. The sky is teeming with materiality, of course. The world remains, and Faulkner himself, even as a dead body, is still enmeshed with that world, and with his own body (he *is* his body), which cannot really be obliterated—at least, not by Faulkner *thinking* it away. Another way of putting this might be to say, even when you are dead, you are still *here*.

In another story by Ballard, "The Concentration City," Franz M., a physics student who lives at 3599719 West 783rd Street, is obsessed with trying to leave the City, which is comprised of seemingly endless buildings and streets and is "as old as time and continuous with it."[13] Although even just one sector of the City is "one hundred thousand cubic miles," Franz M. is convinced that somewhere beyond an outer boundary there is endless "free space" and he attempts to traverse the entire length of the City in one direction on a high-speed train in order to find a limitless Outside that he believes must exist. But through some trick of time-space curvature that is built into the train tracks he only ends up back where he started, with no time having elapsed, even though he was gone for three weeks. Although Franz M. continues to doggedly insist, even while being carted off to the psychiatrists, that the City must have "bounds," the City itself fills up all of time and space and cannot be traversed, or even imagined, as some sort of totality that could be crossed beyond. For the reader, as for Franz M., this is supposed to feel like a nightmare.

---

[12] Ballard, "The Overloaded Man," 124.
[13] J.G. Ballard, "The Concentration City," in *The Best Short Stories of J.G. Ballard*, 19 [1–20].

You Are Here/This Must Be the Place

> I guess that this must be the place,
> I can't tell one from another.
> Did I find you, or you find me?
> There was a time before we were born,
> If someone asks, this is where I'll be, where I'll be.
>
> The Talking Heads, "This Must be the Place"

In her book *Vibrant Matter: A Political Ecology of Things*, Jane Bennett mentions Hent de Vries's idea of the "absolute" as an "'intangible and imponderable recalcitrance" that points to

> a something that is not an object of knowledge, that is detached or radically free from representation, and thus nothing at all. Nothing but the force or the effectivity of the detachment, that is.[14]

Important to note here is that while this "absolute" may be radically detached from our world and systems of knowledge, it has also somehow come loose from that very same world and systems of knowledge, and therefore, it is both gone, yet also *still here*. In some systems this "absolute" could be God, but more importantly, for De Vries, it marks a place, or a *Thing*, which has "loosen[ed] its ties to existing contexts." Similar to the "thing-power" that Bennett articulates in her book, De Vries's notion of the absolute "seeks to acknowledge that which refuses to dissolve completely into the milieu of human knowledge," but whereas De Vries conceives of this absolute as an epistemological limit on *human* knowing that also *hovers*, recalcitrantly,

---

[14] Jane Bennett, *Vibrant Matter: A Political Ecology of Things* (Durham: Duke University Press, 2010), 3.

"between immanence and transcendence," Bennett wants to return matter ("things") to a more "earthy, not-quite human capaciousness" in which things would be released from their "long history of attachment to automatism or mechanism."[15]

Thinking of Ballard's two stories again, we might say that they both take up different forms of De Vries's version of the completely detached and *non*-earthy absolute (both characters are trying to literally *loosen* themselves from their respective worlds), and both stories also illustrate the anxiety and despair brought on by a desire to either inhabit the absolute position (which, ultimately, is never human, or let's say, liveable) or to somehow cross beyond it, to believe that there must be an Outside (an exterior) that would unfold or unfurl somehow from a more locally-positioned world contained by our mapping devices, which is to say, our minds, as well as our satellites. Without this Outside, we feel trapped, hemmed "in"—although strictly speaking, if there is no Outside, there is also no Inside. There is only here, and to quote the Talking Heads, "this must be the place."

With Timothy Morton, I believe that "there is no definite 'within' or 'outside' of beings"—for example, every time you breathe in oxygen you are inhaling "a by-product of the first Archæn beings (from 2.5 billion years ago back to an undefined limit after the origin of Earth 4.5 billion years ago)" and the "hills are teeming with the skeletal silence of dead life forms"—but as Morton also reminds us, we can't really "get along without these concepts [of inside and outside] either."[16]

Nevertheless, if we're going to formulate any sort of ethics that takes interdependence and coexistence (or what Morton terms "coexistentialism") seriously, as

---

[15] Bennett, *Vibrant Matter*, 3.
[16] Timothy Morton, *The Ecological Thought* (Cambridge: Harvard University Press, 2010), 39.

Morton argues, we're going to have to dissolve "the barrier between 'over here' and 'over there,' and more fundamentally, the metaphysical illusion of rigid, narrow boundaries between inside and outside."[17] And while we may certainly be *in something*—following the physicist David Bohm's idea of the "implicate order,"[18] everything might be *folded* into everything else—nevertheless, this is a something, or a *someplace*, "that has no center or edge," and there can never be "a background against which our thinking makes sense."[19]

There is still separation and difference, however, and this is an important point. As Morton puts it, "all beings are related to each other negatively and differentially," and while there is no authentic zero-point of origin or "specific flavor" for any one being (no absolute uniqueness)—"evolution jumbles bodies like a dream jumbles words and image"[20]—nor is there any way to hold the life and non-life distinction in place, nor can we hold the human and non-human distinction in place, nor is consciousness necessarily intentional or even "superior" ("sentience" may be the lowest, and not the highest, function implicit in evolu-

---

[17] Morton, *The Ecological Thought*, 39.

[18] On David Bohm's thinking on the implicate, enfolded order of the universe, see David Bohm, *Wholeness and the Implicate Order* (London: Routledge, 1980) and "The Enfolding-Unfolding Universe and Consciousness (1980)," in *The Essential David Bohm*, ed. Lee Nichol (London: Routledge, 2003), 78–138.

[19] Timothy Morton, "Materialism Expanded and Remixed," conference paper presented at "New Materialisms," Johns Hopkins University, April 13-14, 2010: 11 [1–17]; http://www.scribd.com/doc/25830212/Materialism-Expanded-and-Remixed.

[20] Morton, *The Ecological Thought*, 66, 65.

tion),²¹ and evolution itself may be pointless. Nevertheless, as Morton also asserts,

> We can't in good faith cancel the difference between humans and nonhumans. Nor can we preserve it. Doing both at the same time would be inconsistent. We're in a bind. But . . . . The bind is a sign of an emerging democracy of life forms.²²

Subjectivity may ultimately be a bottomless void, but saying that there is no coherent "something" there (with mappable contours and limits) is not the same thing as saying there is "nothing" there at all. Cadging from Morton, something is always "seeping through."²³ Further, every object I encounter, including persons (human and nonhuman), in Steven Shaviro's words, both draws me "into extended referential networks whose full ramifications I cannot trace" and also "bursts forth" in its singularity, "stun[ning] me in excess of anything that I can posit about it."²⁴ So, for me, the trick in going forward now, as regards an ethics of interdependence, or co-implicated dependence, also means becoming *more*, and not less, human. The

---

²¹ On this point regarding sentience as a possibly "lower" achievement of evolutionary biology, see Morton, *The Ecological Thought*, 72. I would also point those interested in this idea to the work of Rodney Brooks, who directs the Artificial Intelligence Laboratory at M.I.T., and to his influential paper, "Elephants Don't Play Chess," *Robotics and Autonomous Systems* 6 (1990): 3–15.
²² Morton, *The Ecological Thought*, 76.
²³ Morton, *The Ecological Thought*, 113.
²⁴ Steven Shaviro, "The Universe of Things," symposium paper presented at "Object-Oriented Ontology," Georgia Tech. University, April 3, 2010: 7 [1–18]; http://www.shaviro.com/Blog/?p=893.

human is also an inescapable *here*, a someplace, and not a no-place.

A Text is a Sentient Object/Objects in the Mirror are Closer Than They Appear/You Are Closer to Me Than It Appears/The Past Is Closer Than It Appears/You Do No Service To History By Keeping It Behind You/I Wish We Could Go On Talking Like This But I Have to Move Beyond the Title of This Section

> ... contrary to a deeply rooted belief, the book is not an image of the world. It forms a rhizome with the world, there is an aparallel evolution of the book and the world; the book assures the deterritorialization of the world, but the world effects a reterritorialization of the book, which in turn deterritorializes itself in the world (if it's capable, if it can).
>
> Gilles Deleuze and Félix Guatarri, *A Thousand Plateaus*[25]

I want to turn now to the question of how literature might have anything to do with any of this and, following the thought of Jane Bennett, I want to say something like: Texts are objects that possess vibrant materiality; they are "quasi forces" that possess something like "tendencies of their own."[26] They possess thing-power, and as much as they are able, they strive, in the words of Spinoza, to "persist in existing."

---

[25] Gilles Deleuze and Félix Guattari, *A Thousand Plateaus: Capitalism and Schizophrenia*, trans. Brian Massumi (Minneapolis: University of Minnesota Press, 1987), 11.

[26] Bennett describes "vibrant matter" as objects that are "active" and "earthy" and which possess a "not-quite-human capaciousness" (*Vibrant Matter*, 3). This is to ultimately think objects outside of their traditional roles "as passive stuff, as raw, brute, or inert" (vii) and to invent (dream?) for objects a lively ontology of "vital materiality" in which things "act as quasi agents or forces with trajectories, propensities, or tendencies of their own" outside of human will and human designs (viii).

JOY—YOU ARE HERE: A MANIFESTO

Texts are, in some sense, *alive*, while at the same time they are, even while produced by humans, utterly inhuman. No matter how many people—that is to say, characters—you put into a text, they still come out flat and dead. By which I mean, those aren't really people. Anna Karenina doesn't really exist and the only reason she feels alive to you when reading Tolstoy's novel is because you animated her through a technique we humans are particularly good at—I think of it as a felicitous form of "lying to ourselves." In addition, Michael Witmore reminds us that,

> Our work with narratives puts us in touch with forms of reduction or compression that are every bit as diagrammatic and so (potentially) inhuman as those who study the compression algorithms of physics or planetary biology. The key for us is the way in which narratives of human action introduce counterfactual ideals—impossible, limiting, but also operative and effectual—that are immanent in the objects we study, not simply projections of the creators or interpreters of those objects.[27]

So, literary characters are potentially inhuman (ciphers, even) although we often treat them as if they are fully human (they're more like symptoms, as well as

---

[27] Michael Witmore, "We Have Never Not Been Inhuman," in *When Did We Become Post/human?* ed. Eileen A. Joy and Craig Dionne, special issue of *postmedieval: a journal of medieval cultural studies* 1.1-2 (2010): 213 [208–214]. For a glimpse into Witmore's work with the forms of compression present in early modern literary texts, especially Shakespeare, see his weblog *Wine Dark Sea*: http://winedarksea.org/.

transitive signifiers, of the human[28]). They possess something of the qualities of Bruno Latour's *actant*—in Graham Harman's words, "a force utterly deployed in the world" which is on the same ontological footing as everything else, including us. As Harman writes of Latour's thinking on actants, if everything is on the same ontological footing, "this ends the tear-jerking modern rift between the knowing human subject and the unknowable outside world, since for Latour the isolated Kantian human is no more and no less an actor than are windmills, sunflowers, propane tanks, and Thailand."[29] Again: you are here. So is everything else. There is nowhere else to go.

I am recalled to the biennial meeting of the New Chaucer Society in Siena, Italy in July 2010, when Aranye Fradenburg delivered her moving plenary lecture, "Living Chaucer,"[30] where she argued that "the

---

[28] On the idea of traveling and transitive signifiers and their "living on"-ness within the corpus of medieval literature and in contemporary life, as well as the ways in which they enable intersubjective formations between various actors, alive and dead, located in the past and present (with some formations more psychologically unsettling and dangerous and historically damaging than others, and some more affectively sustaining and effectual for progressive change), the entire ouevre of Aranye Fradenurg is indispensable; see, most recently, Aranye Fradenburg, "(Dis)continuity: A History of Dreaming," in *The Post-Historical Middle Ages*, eds. Elizabeth Scala and Sylvia Frederico (New York: Palgrave Macmillan, 2009), 87–115, from whence I culled this essay's dedicatory line.

[29] Graham Harman, *Prince of Networks: Bruno Latour and Metaphysics* (Melbourne: re.press, 2009), 14.

[30] This lecture has since been published: L.O. Aranye Fradenburg, "Living Chaucer," *Studies in the Age of Chaucer* 33 (2011): 41–64. I cite here my (perhaps imperfect) notes from the Siena meeting in July 2010 in order to remain faithful, if just for the momentary purposes of this essay, to the bodily presence of Fradenburg and my memory of her words and

experience of narrative is a rapprochement with another mind," that we share with an author like Chaucer a kind of intersubjectivity in which it is not always easy to tell where the self (his, ours) ends and Otherness (Chaucer, us, his characters, language, signifiers, etc.) begins. Let's take this another step further and say that the experience of narrative is also a rapprochement with a "persisting object" that uses humans as an activation device, a sort of on-switch. We might tentatively qualify literature as a 'quasi-object' that is neither entirely an object nor either fully a subject but is nevertheless *in the world* as a 'constructer of intersubjectivity' in which the 'we' of any given moment is made in the "bursts and occultation's of the 'I'"[31] as texts are shuttled back and forth, over vast stretches of time, between shelves and tables and readers and other texts which may be, in Serres's terms, only "stations and relays." Who can tell when a text, or a reader, is 'it' and when it is an 'I' (or a 'we')? As Serres also writes, we don't know whether quasi-objects, which are also quasi-subjects, "are beings or relations, tatters of being or ends of relations. By them, the principle of individuation can be transmitted or can get stuck."[32] Put another way, we might say, following Latour, that a literary text, like the quasi-object, like ourselves, is "simultaneously real, discursive, and social," belonging "to nature, to the collective, and to discourse," and "bearing the traces of Being that are

---

arguments as she was delivering this lecture, and to the further thoughts she sparked in me at that time—a "shared mental experience," in Fradenburg's own terms ("Living Chaucer," 43).
[31] Michel Serres, *The Parasite*, trans. Larry R. Schehr (Baltimore: Johns Hopkins University Press, 1982), 227.
[32] Serres, *The Parasite*, 227–28.

distributed everywhere among beings."[33]

We might think, also, of literature as a kind of *living* and open signaling system, an endlessly looping reel-to-reel tape-feed (even when interrupted by static, worms chewing on the wires, bad translators, fire, and floods), that could also be described, as Fradenburg suggested in Siena, as a "territorial assemblage," one that enables an endless series of aparallel relations within and across various temporal zones that are, in some sense, always here with us now and also located in the Great Outdoors of a forest of textual data that may or may not always be accessible to us (or to our particular questions).[34] The human body is itself a time capsule of all previous bodies, just as texts are time capsules of all previous writing, and the "junk"—whether junk-DNA or spilled ink in the margins, is always with us. Nothing is ever lost, although if Harman is right, everything is always withdrawing from everything else. Again: you are here, but a part of you is also somewhere else. It is the same with texts. Although, strictly speaking, that "somewhere else" is also here. You can't get away from here, and the exits of the universe are locked.

According to Harman, all objects in the world—which can be armies, persons, ants, chalk, earthworms, raindrops, stones, etc.—are always in retreat from each other, always withdrawing, and every possible relation between any two objects is also an object. While Harman doesn't deny reciprocity and symbiosis and even celebrates them, he insists on a "weird realism" whereby no one real object could ever really "touch" any other real object. Nevertheless, there are sensual

---

[33] Bruno Latour, *We Have Never Been Modern*, trans. Catherine Porter (Cambridge: Harvard University Press, 1993), 64, 66.
[34] On this point, see Michael Witmore, "The Ancestral Text," *Wine Dark Sea*, May 9, 2011, http://winedarksea.org/?p=979.

relations, and he uses the term "allure" to describe the distance between any real object and the qualities that stream out of it, constituting the sensual object with which we engage. As he puts it, "Whereas real objects withdraw, sensual objects lie directly before us, frosted over with a swirling, superfluous outer shell."[35] Therefore, real objects can only "touch" other real objects by way of a sensual object, a "vicar of causation," as it were, that leads to ever more new objects being formed—in other words, new relations. Furthermore, and this is the really important implication of Harman's thought for me in thinking about how this might help us to formulate a speculative realist literary studies, "we do not perceive insofar as we merely exist, but only insofar as we are pieces of larger objects composed of us and other things." And it is in what Harman calls "the molten inner core" of these larger objects where sentience takes place, "as the perception of sensual objects."[36] For Harman sentience is happening all the time between all sorts of objects, and—who knows?—maybe even stalks of wheat and bricks "encounter" each other in some fashion in some sort of wheat-and-brick assemblage mediated by a sensuous vicar, which could be a person, or an ant, or a moonbeam.

In Harman's speculative realism, "the world is packed full of ghostly real objects signaling to each other from inscrutable depths, unable to touch one another fully." And yet, the "side-by-side proximity of real and sensual objects is the occasion for a connection between a real object inside an intention"—for example, *my* desire to be absorbed by these objects—

---

[35] Graham Harman, "On Vicarious Causation," *Collapse*, Vol. II: Speculative Realism (Oxford: Urbanomic, 2007), 179 [171–205].
[36] Graham Harman, "On Asymmetrical Causation: Influence Without Recompense," *Parallax* 16.1 (2010): 107 [96–109].

and another real object lying outside it. In this way, shafts or freight tunnels are constructed between objects that otherwise remain quarantined in private vacuums.[37]

Literary criticism, especially in medieval studies but really in any-studies of texts that are, in some sense, already-there (i.e., historical), might be reimagined as a networks of sensuous object relations within which a more capacious yet still bounded (feeling) sentience might take place—"bounded" in the sense of: everything was here, and then we arrived, and now we're all here. Start digging, but remember, we can't get out of here. Tunnel away all you want, for, as Harman says,

> We do not step beyond anything, but are more like moles tunneling through wind, water, and ideas no less than through speech-acts, texts, anxiety, wonder, and dirt. We do not transcend the world, but only descend or burrow towards its numberless underground cavities—each a sort of kaleidoscope where sensual objects spread their wings and colors. There is neither finitude nor negativity in the heart of objects.[38]

So, Here's This Plan I Have

> Those who care only to generate arguments almost never generate objects. New objects, however, are the sole and sacred fruit of writers, thinkers, politicians, travellers, lovers, and inventers.
>
> Graham Harman, "On Vicarious Causation"

---

[37] Harman, "On Vicarious Causation," 187, 201.
[38] Harman, "On Vicarious Causation," 193.

So, what now? As regards medieval studies, literary studies, the humanities under the aegis of new speculative realist, object-oriented, and post/humanist[39] work that encourages us to develop better and more ethical styles of collectivity?

Step One might be following Julian Yates's suggestion (and I think this is a step scholars such as Jane Bennett, Stacy Alaimo, Myra Hird, Noreen Giffney, Rosi Braidotti, Graham Harman, Levi Bryant, Sarah Franklin, Karen Barad, Donna Haraway, Freya Mathews, Timothy Morton, Cary Wolfe, Jeffrey Cohen, Karl Steel, and many others are mightily engaged in at present): to force the "solipsistic human *Dasein* . . . to idle and to listen or try to listen to the figurative chatter, songs or screams of the countless non-human actors whose manufactured declensions fund the networks that wrote the 'human' as self-identical being."[40] The human being, but also the humanist, as slow recording device. Think of the experimental artist Douglas Gordon who slowed down Hitchcock's *Psycho* to 24

---

[39] By placing the backward slash between 'post' and 'human' (post/human), I mean to denote a state of historical affairs by which, although we may have witnessed a certain dissolution of the liberal humanist subject as the world's sovereign meaning-maker, as well as the emergence of new non- and quasi-human 'intelligent' technologies, such as cybernetics, robotics, and bioinformatics that may supersede us, while we have also gained new insights into the fact that the 'human' has always been unstable, contingent, hybrid, accidental, other to itself, 'animal,' etc. ('we have never been human'), nevertheless, the human is always left open as a productive question, both *there* and *not-there* at once.

[40] Julian Yates, "It's (for) You; or, The Tele-t/r/opical Post-human," in *When Did We Become Post/human?* ed. Eileen A. Joy and Craig Dionne, special issue of *postmedieval: a journal of medieval cultural studies* 1.1-2 (2010): 225 [223–234].

hours.[41] Or the sound artist Lief Inge who stretched out Beethoven's Ninth Symphony for 24 hours.[42] Or Longplayer, a piece of music started in 1999 that is designed to go on playing for a thousand years, and whose chief "listening post" is a lighthouse in London?[43] Something like that, only tuned in to the nonhuman, while also recognizing that these endeavors would still constitute human follies. But these would be follies borne out of a love, and not a capricious and careless use, of the world.

Step Two would be to recognize that everything is a person of some sort and to start forming alliances and "personnel services committees" and special packet-switching stations with as many self-objects and literary-objects and other object-objects as possible in order to build a larger and more capacious and "stranger" sentience that could then form a sort of autopoetic system that might take better account of how, in Morton's words, "[e]verything is [already] intimate with everything else."[44]

This will require a Step Three as well, which probably really comes before Step One: self-donation, making ourselves hospitable so that things and events can take place in and with and around us, so that the world can happen *to us* for a change. The fact of the matter is, we're already "occupied," so let's make it official now with a sign posted out front that says,

---

[41] See Lee Ferguson, "Douglas Gordon's Stunning 24 Hour Psycho," CBC News, September 13, 2010, http://www.cbc.ca/news/tiff2010/2010/09/douglas-gordons-stunning-24-hour-psycho-update-screens-at-tiffs-lightbox.html.

[42] See Kyle Gann, "Norwegian Minimalist Raises Beethoven's Molto Adagio Bar," *The Village Voice*, 10 Feb. 2004, http://www.villagevoice.com/2004-02-10/music/norwegian-minamalist-raises-beethoven-molto-adagio-bar/.

[43] On Longplayer, see http://longplayer.org/what/overview.php.

[44] Morton, *The Ecological Thought*, 78.

JOY—YOU ARE HERE: A MANIFESTO

"*Hello*, Everybody!" Related to this: making room, like a broom of the system, for the initial starting conditions of spontaneous acts of combustive generosity and impossible unconditionalities. Making space, without liens, for the arrival of strangers whose trajectories are unmappable in advance.

Step Four: making new objects, giving birth to things, radical acts of coupling and natality and hetero-queer reproduction. Until you can't make things anymore. That's when you drop dead. But don't worry . . . you'll always be with us, by which I mean: with me. I'll never forget you and I trust you'll do the same for me. I'm talking to you but also to Sparkles, one of my many creaturely companions, the hawthorn outside my study window, the red berries budding on the hawthorn, the pebbled glass of the window itself, my favorite wine glass, all the random notes and letters rustling on my desk, and the imaginary pen I write my imaginary books with that will never get published, all the lives I'll never live but experience in literature, all the friends met and unmet, behind and up ahead in the future(s) we dream and play at together. We'll designate mourners and record their grieving, then play it on an endless feedback loop machine that has a one-thousand-year battery. In other words, we'll keep writing. Some call this literature. Or medieval studies. Or the humanities, which need to get more, and not less human.

But this will also entail, contra to but also with our tears and our ultimately frail efforts at projects of *memento mori*, better developing what Simon Critchley has called "the experience of an ever-divided humorous self-relation," where we would work to find ourselves "ridiculous," to see ourselves from the outside, and to "smile"—humor as "a powerful example of what we might call the human being's eccentricity with regard to itself."[45]

In the end, this what ethics is all about: Slowing down, paying better attention to what is close at hand and always already intimate with us—which is everything—welcoming the Other, not taking ourselves too seriously, and working together to add something of beauty to the world, which is always more than truth could ever calculate or bear.

---

[45] Simon Critchley, *Infinitely Demanding: Ethics of Commitment, Politics of Resistance* (London: Verso, 2007), 86.

JULIAN YATES

Sheep Tracks—A Multi-Species Impression

Moments of disorientation are vital.

Sara Ahmed, *Queer Phenomenology*[1]

By chance, I wrote these last words on the rim of Vesuvius, right near Pompeii, less that eight years ago. For more than

---

I should like to thank the audience of the "Animal, Vegetable, Mineral" conference for their questions; Jeffrey Jerome Cohen, Nedda Mehdizadeh, Lowell Duckert, and Jonathan Gil Harris for the invitation to participate and the inspiration their work affords. Special thanks go to Jeffrey Jerome Cohen whose gentle challenges to a draft led me to rethink things for the better and to Richard Burt for our conversations on Ginzburg and Derrida, which proved invaluable.

[1] Sara Ahmed, *Queer Phenomenology: Objects, Orientations, Others* (Durham: Duke University Press, 2006), 157.

> twenty years, each time I've returned to Naples, I've thought of her.
>
> Who better than the Gradiva, I said to myself this time, the Gradiva of Jensen and of Freud, could illustrate this outbidding in the *mal d'archive*?
>
> Jacques Derrida, *Archive Fever: A Freudian Impression*[2]

Here, in a postscript to *Archive Fever*, Jacques Derrida tells an autobiographical or pseudo-autobiographical story of how it is that he came to write these words. Covering his tracks as he appears to uncover them, back-tracking over the marks on paper that are now variously hosted in print and electronic media, he winks at us. Was he there on that rim, above that very volcano? Did his own *mal' d'archive* lead him to a supposed origin—an origin that reduces his Neapolitan jaunts to a repetition compulsion? As we read them, Derrida's tracks flicker in and out of being, and by that flickering they seem to speak for themselves, to be more curiously present, if only to the moment of encounter we name "reading."

Embarked on his own "outbidding" or rebidding of the archive that aims to discern the way Freud's archive fever, the fever that is psychoanalysis, comes into being, its constitutive metaphors caught in the mutual embrace of the substrates of handwriting and print, Derrida reads Freud's reading of Wilhelm Jensen's novel *Gradiva* (1907) [she who walks] as a signature. Freud competes with Jensen, in his view, 'claims again to bring to light a more originary origin than that of the specter . . . he wants to be an archivist, who is more an

---

[2] Jacques Derrida, *Archive Fever: A Freudian Impression*, trans. Eric Prenowitz (Chicago: University of Chicago Press, 1996), 97. Unless otherwise indicated, subsequent references appear parenthetically in the text.

archaeologist than the archaeologist (97) of the novel (Hanold), who falls in love with a Roman bas relief of this woman who walks. Outbidding Hanold and Jensen, Freud wants, writes Derrida,

> to exhume a more archaic *impression*, he wants to exhibit a more archaic *imprint* than the one the other archaeologists of all kinds bustle around, those of literature and those of classical objective science, an imprint that is singular each time, an impression that is almost no longer an archive but almost confuses itself with the pressure of the footstep that leaves its still living mark on a substrate, a surface, a place of origin. When the step is still one with the subjectile. (97)

Such an archive, he continues, which maintains no distinction between active and passive, between the touching and the touched, "would in sum confuse itself with the *arkhë*, with the origin of which it is only the *type*, the *typos*, iterable character or letter" (98). It would constitute

> an archive without an archive, where, suddenly indiscernible from the impression of its imprint, Gradiva's footstep speaks by itself! (98)

Derrida writes all this, apparently, on the rim of a volcano, a fossilized Pompeii, lively in its petrifaction, waiting below. And by this autobiographical or pseudo-autobiographical account he keeps his own tracks fresh, alive still, living on, even as they are variously remediated.

Derrida's rendering of Freud's rendering of Jensen's rendering of Hanold's rendering of the Gradiva, she who walks, herself a rendering or an impression, might be said to offer a particularly compelling enactment of the problem of the trace or the track as it is indexed to an ongoing set of relations between presence and absence, the organic and inorganic, the living and the dead. Posing a problem of translation to archaeologists and archivists or to readers of all kinds, the archive as sum of tracks or traces of things past / passed serves both as a repository that might be accessed and discarded 'as if' the "technical prosthesis [was] a secondary and accessory exteriority" (92) and as a restraint or condition on how we orient ourselves to these tracks. The substrate or material backing that constitutes the archive mediates, enabling certain orders of contact while disabling others. The substrate intrudes into the circuit that obtains between trace and archivist / archaeologist rendering each differently lively and inert, distributing life effects between them as the archive is put to use.

My aim in this essay is to respond to several sets of sheepy impressions or sheep tracks that I have been collecting as part of a larger project on what the likes of Donna Haraway might name the human / sheep / goat / dog (wolf) multi-species—a mutual capture of beings that constitutes a material-semiotic relay for making landscapes, human "persons" and animals.[3] In doing so, I am interested in what it means to treat such animal impressions as a "contact zone," a multi-species

---

[3] Donna Haraway, *When Species Meet* (Minneapolis: University of Minnesota Press, 2008). Relevant essays from this project include: Julian Yates, "What was Pastoral (Again)? More Versions," in *Early Modern English Literature and the Return of Theory*, eds. Paul Cefalu and Bryan Reynolds (New York: Palgrave, 2011), 93–118; "Humanist Habitats: 'Eating Well' with Thomas More's *Utopia*," in *Environment and Embodiment in Early Modern England*, eds. Garrett Sullivan and Mary Floyd Wilson (New York: Palgrave, 2007), 187–209; and "Counting Sheep: Or, Dolly does Utopia (Again)," *Rhizomes* 8 (2004): http://rhizomes.net/issue8/yates2.htm.

archive *qua* general or generative text out of which all manner of 'sheepy' and 'not-sheepy' or 'human' modes of being are generated. As my use of the term "archive" indicates, I remain interested in the orientation to the trace provided in deconstructive reading, finding therein a tariff or restraint on modes of reading or modeling the traces of things that have passed or which are "past" that treats this "contact zone" as a way of accessing other or occluded ways of being.[4] I share in the excitement felt by many in the humanities who explore the interpretive or ethical gains to be had in deploying the figure of an associative or additive model of a network, infrastructure, contexture, ecology, grid, knot, or mesh on offer in other disciplines in order to render the complexity we name "world." Such models enable us, for example, to question the primacy of human language as anything other than a subset of larger systems or codes of reaction and response (olfactory, visual, auditory, and so on), broadening access to the privilege accorded to humans by the order of finitude bestowed by language to include non-humans (animals, plants, fungus, stones, stars). Nevertheless, I am interested in what might be gained, still, even as we provincialize the "human," from maintaining, as Cary Wolfe suggests, that part of what it means to "be," for us, entails owning or being owned by

> the radically ahuman technicity and mechanicity of language (understood in the broadest sense as a semiotic system through

---

[4] Haraway uses Mary Louise Pratt's term to great effect in *When Species Meet*. The chapters of this book constitute in very different ways inquiries into nodes or knots of contact. See Haraway, *When Species Meet*, 214–16. See also Mary Louise Pratt, *Imperial Eyes: Travel, Writing, and Transculturation* (New York: Routledge, 1992).

which creatures 'react' and 'respond' to each other).[5]

For me, this issue plays out as a question of orientation. How do I orient myself to the tracks I have been following? What does it mean and what is at stake in that orientation?

In what follows then, I shall be aiming to tread carefully, to walk within a set of sheepy imprints, alive to the fact that as I do so the impressions that I leave do not quite belong to me even as they are my own. Such a deconstructive lingering or slowness to reading I take to be what Jane Bennett advises as she wonders how best we might respond to what she names "thing-power."[6] Such "idiocy" (an ungainly track) is what Isabelle Stengers recommends when she asks us to slow down and consider the cosmopolitical cast of our practices.[7] I begin with an iconic moment in the work of sociologist Bruno Latour that has led many scholars housed in the humanities to rethink or re-understand both their object and their expertise. I then offer a stenographic and highly partial inventory of sheep tracks, of impressions left by sheep in different media—sometimes all by themselves, sometimes with the help of human hosts. I then allow the sheep that have passed by to dog or worry me as I try to think about how best to orient myself to their tracks—a question I pursue by returning to a rich essay on clues, hoof-prints, symptoms, and gestures by Carlo Ginzburg read in concert with Derrida's *The Animal That Therefore I Am*

---

[5] Cary Wolfe, "Human, All Too Human: 'Animal Studies' and the Humanities," *PMLA* 124.2 (2009): 571 [564–75].
[6] Jane Bennett, *Vital Matter: A Political Ecology of Things* (Durham: Duke University Press, 2010), 17.
[7] Isabelle Stengers, "The Cosmopolitical Proposal," in *Making Things Public: Atmospheres of Democracy*, eds. Bruno Latour and Peter Weibel (Cambridge: MIT Press, 2005), 994.

(More to Follow) and Haraway's *When Species Meet*. I end by offering one example of a multi-species writing machine, a mode of inducting sheep into human discourses that attempts to own its zoo / auto / bio / bibliographic constitution.

A PARLIAMENT OF THINGS

Towards the end of *We Have Never Been Modern*, Bruno Latour imagines what he calls a "Parliament of Things," a step, perhaps, in the story of liberal democracy that would extend voting rights to those non-human entities or polities in our midst that our usual modes of thinking make nonsense of (the enduring example might be the way the fracture of nationhood renders the ozone layer essentially un-representable).[8] To do so, he embraces a mode of description that refuses any separation between nature and culture, subject and object, and embarks instead on an ecological modeling or rewriting of the world as a network or mobile knot of times, places, persons, animals, plants, and so on—all understood to be differently animated material-semiotic actants. The role of human persons in this project of reassembly would not be to speak merely on their own behalf or that of their fellows but to serve as mouthpieces or as some other variously sonifying, visualizing, or animating prosthesis for the non-human entities whose existence and whose concerns we hope to make present or knowable.

The sole task of this parliament, even as it speaks of other things, would be to inquire into the boundaries of its own collectivity, to inquire into what or who remains essentially or catastrophically underrepresented and so to ask what modes of translation, what impossible tasks of translation, or "speech impedi-

---

[8] Bruno Latour, *We Have Never Been Modern*, trans. Catherine Porter (Cambridge: Harvard University Press, 1993), 142–45.

menta," as Latour names then in *Politics of Nature*, still therefore need to be crafted.[9] Latour is after a mode of composition that collapses the distinction between acts of making (*poesis*) and acts of knowing or taking cognizance of what has been made and who and what has been unmade in the process (critique / deconstruction).[10] In order to cohere, the parliament needs to craft something on the order of a *Moebius* Strip between these two logically distinct categories—such that the black box of production can at least be monitored if not opened and the prospect or project of "hope" sponsored. All this labor is limited by the caveat, as Michel Serres maintains throughout *The Parasite*, that noise and death are necessary for the cascade of actants that we botch or screw up when we play the game of blindman's buff that is the modeling of the world as "system," "network," "assemblage," as "quasi-object" and "quasi-subject," all of which are, necessarily, catechreses or faulty references.[11]

The hope would be that by scaling the conversation so that the various metaphysics of non-human entities were not elided or reduced by what amounts to a failure of hospitality, we would create technically well modeled, which is to say, following Stengers, ethically well-modeled relations with other

---

[9] Bruno Latour, *Politics of Nature: How to Bring the Sciences into Democracy* (Cambridge: Harvard University Press, 2004), 63–64.

[10] For this modeling of deconstruction in relation to poesis as part of an ahuman system of communication, see Niklas Luhmann, "Deconstruction as Second-Order Observing System," in *Theories of Distinction: Redescribing the Descriptions of Modernity*, trans. William Rasch (Stanford: Stanford University Press, 2002), 94–112.

[11] Michel Serres, *The Parasite*, trans. Lawrence Schehr (1982; repr. Minneapolis: University of Minnesota Press, 2007), 1–14. As Serres points out, the figure of a "system" is an artifact of observation.

beings.[12] If we ever manage to do this, of course, we will have solved some very big ticket philosophical problems for we will know what and who belongs and also what and who does not belong, what and whom we may put to use, abuse, even kill—and righteously so—and also what and whom to love. I am, on the one hand, captivated by this parliament and, by that same hand, held hostage by the questions of sovereignty that the parliament seems to propose to answer. For in a different vocabulary, it might be said that Latour's parliament sponsors a further rationalization of those procedures for remarking more and more subdivisions of 'bare life,' as the state takes upon itself the permanent project of sorting those entities which may be judged to be potential citizen subjects and so embarked on the project of finding 'a way of living proper to the individual or the group' (*bios*) and those that are merely 'bare life,' which simply exist (*zoë*), and so may be put to use or to death.[13] I remain haunted then by the matter of tracks and traces and by the figure of a responsibility to which, no matter how sophisticated or brilliant our capture of the world, we will remain irresponsibly insufficient.

From the point of view of someone whose expertise is housed in the humanities, in the semiotic or rhetorical charnel house of the collective, and who's

---

[12] Isabelle Stengers, *Power and Invention: Situating Science* (Minneapolis: University of Minnesota Press, 1997), 216. For a Latourian-inspired attempt to "sensitize" human subjects in precisely this mode, see Emilee Hache, Bruno Latour, and Patrick Camiller, "Morality or Moralism? An Exercise in Sensitization," *Common Knowledge* 16.2 (2010): 311–30. Thanks to Jeffrey Cohen for drawing this essay to my attention.

[13] Giorgio Agamben, *Homo Sacer: Sovereign Power and Bare Life*, trans Daniel Heller-Roazen (Stanford: Stanford University Press, 1998). On the right to kill see Latour, *Politics of Nature*, 112–16.

trained to rake through the bones, to make the dead or the forgotten speak, to splice traces together in ways that produce effects of liveliness in our variously timed "presents"—the parliament of things might be said to represent a significant rewiring of our archive, overwriting our usual analytic terms, liquefying categories such as the social or the cultural, treating them as fractured remnants of a larger, irreducible process, and rejecting thereby the reduction of the shifting auratics of the multi-species to the aura of human exceptionalism bolstered by its great variety of memory devices and genres that enable it to forget. But, while the figure of the network, assemblage, or quasi-object offers us the appearance of a supped up regime of description that enables us to line up many more kinds of traces than we had previously imagined was possible—one can get pretty darned high doing a network-based reading—when the archive fever breaks, I find myself spat out and reterritorialized in a language object, in questions of rhetoric and genre—understood now as translational mechanisms by which we decline "things" so that they speak to and about ourselves.

Just when we seem primed to speed up, to refigure our archive and our expertise in the service of the past as a "contact zone" with other ways of being (which it is and which it may be), I want to remember the plodding slowness of "ANT" as Latour puts it, punning on the formic feel to the acronym for Actor Network Theory, and go slowly, inquiring into how our own practices are refigured by the arrival of new models.[14] For when the specter of the non-human presences and provincializes human exceptionalism, I would argue that what occurs amounts to a breakdown to our various protocols of

---

[14] Bruno Latour, *Reassembling the Social: An Introduction to Actor Network Theory* (Oxford: Oxford University Press, 2005), 23. Thanks go to Jeffrey Cohen for reminding me of the shared slowness of all flat ontologists.

reading and crafting stories by way of our orientation to an archive. There's a pause. Our ability to line up actants to tell stories about the "past" falters. And rather than mend this breakdown, I am interested instead in holding open this hiatus and exploring other ways of configuring traces and tracks and of orienting ourselves to them lest old and familiar routines merely assert themselves and we find ourselves blissfully transported into a series of blighted repetitions.

So, I do not want to seek out ways of agitating things, of getting the show back on the road as we return to business as usual and continue telling stories about what's "past" / "passed." I should like to avoid finding a rejuvenated historicist settlement by which we positivize this or that trace to stand as or for the "past." I should like not to find the new code, key or "transfer ticket" by which we may, to borrow Paul de Man's terms from his essay "Anthropomorphism and Trope in Lyric," "grammaticalize" the "rhetorical complexity" of all the things we now take as our subjects.[15] Let's remain, instead, ant-like, creeping our way within the paper, parchment, and variously "backed" or mediated trails that constitute the phenomena we analyze and inquire into the kinematics of our metaphors or forms, understanding that in the humanities we remain keyed to questions of the trace, of the impression, and so to a limiting / differently enabling question of media as that which may not be perfected or rendered instrumental. Such an insistence, I hope, may constitute a very soft, humanistic contribution to the conversations that take place in Latour's parliament.

In my case, a bit like the three shepherds at the beginning of the Wakefield Master's *Second Shepherd's Play* this means that I find myself counting sheep, but

---

[15] Paul de Man, *The Rhetoric of Romanticism* (New York: Columbia University Press, 1984), 239–62.

like Mak and Gill, I am not opposed to a little bit of sheep-stealing. The difference may lie in the fact that I do not actually know what a sheep, a singular, historical sheep, or a single, historical flock is, exactly—though by the end of that play, I think it's fair to say that they might not either. Instead, as primatologist-turned-sheep-farmer Thelma Rowell cautions me, I proceed on the basis that what we know of sheep derives almost completely from the way they have been rewritten. Rowell argues that the selective breeding of sheep, their modeling and manipulation as livestock or living capital has essentially rendered sheep "sheepish." The traditions of primatology and animal behavior studies have dictated that those animals who lead interesting lives (that is lives deemed interesting to us) have tended to serve as privileged experimental subjects—especially if they may be grouped as among the relatives of a certain *Homo Sapiens*.[16] Animals (and that is "most animals") who "spend the majority of their time doing nothing" tend to be neglected or asked only the most boring of questions. "Sheep behavior studies are mostly to do with what they eat, and sheep are not, generally, permitted to organize themselves," she writes.[17] Rowell's solution is to enable sheep to organize their own social structure and then to observe the results. She decides, in effect to "watch . . . sheep in the same way [she has] . . . been watching monkeys."[18]

---

[16] Thelma Rowell, "A Few Peculiar Primates," *Primate Encounters: Models of Science, Gender, and Society*, eds. Shirley C. Strum and Linda Fedigan (Chicago: University of Chicago Press, 2000), 65–66 [57–70]. The key cultural study, unparalleled in its scope, is Sarah Franklin, *Dolly Mixtures: The Remaking of Genealogy* (Durham: Duke University Press, 2007).
[17] Rowell, "A Few Peculiar Primates," 69.
[18] Rowell, "A Few Peculiar Primates," 65, 69.

What Rowell writes off as several thousand years of botched or abusive ethology amounts to the story whereby the human / sheep / dog / goat multi-species came to write the discourses of pastoral and pastoral care under whose rubric we still essentially make do. In effect, Rowell reads the long story of the bio-political capture of the living as an obstacle that a field science such as her own can short circuit by allowing sheep to decide which questions they find interesting and which they do not. One thing that Rowell's defamiliarizing of sheep makes legible is the way rhetorical routines we might figure as anthropomorphic play host to a mutually extensive zoomorphism. That is to say, the process that renders sheep "sheep," or "sheepish," and human persons "not sheep," or only sometimes sheep for a "not-sheep" shepherd or a "not-sheep" wolf, rebounds on us in all sorts of "sheepy" ways. The biopolitics of pastoral and the networks of pastoral care with which they are allied trade on a sheepy metaphorics in which all human persons oscillate between the roles of shepherds and their four-legged charges. Of what, then, consist their tracks—the tracks of this alliance?

SHEEP TRACKS

Tracks that I am learning to follow—always "more to follow," more and "more to follow"—to adopt the phraseology of the parenthesis to Derrida's "The Animal That Therefore I Am (More To Follow)"—a parenthesis which intrudes a second, more present, still more present, voice into the self predicating logic of the *Cogito*, tripping up therefore, thereby, the *ergo* that funds the ego, and unmooring the auto-reference of the "I," the *bêtise* of "ipseity" or selfness, hollowing it out, in advance of itself, by and in its exposure to an always "more to follow," an inexhaustible surplus of beings or tracks that one comes into being with, and which one finds oneself following just when one thought that there were no tracks, no more tracks, no tracks to follow.[19]

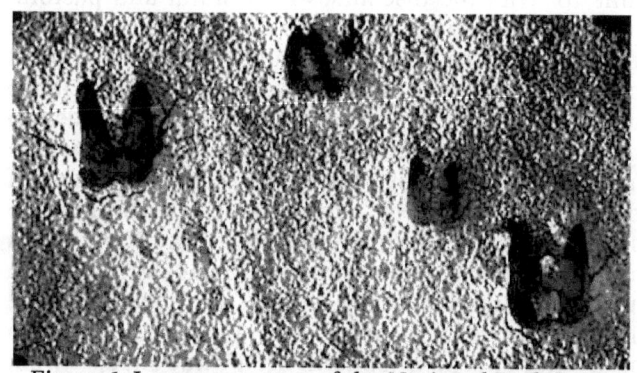

Figure 1. Image courtesy of the National Park Service. For a comparison of different mammal prints, see http://www.hunter-ed.com/wildlife/large_mammals.htm.

Sometimes hoof prints [Figure 1]—Dall and so not Romney, Big Horn, Texel, or Turki, to name just a few of what comprise nearly a thousand distinct breeds or kinds of sheep—it would take too long to name them all. Identify the print and you may, with practice, be able to summon an image of the sheep into existence, a single historical sheep standing for all, for the multiplicity of the flock, and disappearing into it just as soon as it appears.

---

[19] Jacques Derrida, "The Animal That Therefore I Am (More to Follow)," is the first chapter of the collected lectures *The Animal That Therefore I Am*, ed. Marie Louise-Mallet, trans. David Wills (New York: Fordham University Press, 2008), 1–51. See also Jacques Derrida, *The Beast and the Sovereign*, vol. 1, trans. Geoffrey Bennington (Chicago: University of Chicago Press, 2009).

No tracks [Figure 2]—no prints at least, just the image of a mountainside. The indentations become recognizable, if you are taught to see them, as a sheep track—the wear and tear of a multitude of hooves that obliterate their individual traces, carves a collective presence into the land. You may, as it turns out, be following sheep tracks even as you think you are not, etched into the sides of mountains, or through fields, coming into view or disappearing with the vagaries of weather or use. "Sheep tracks are never straight. The winding of trails allows sheep to observe their backside first with one eye, then the other," an online shepherd-friend informs. "Sheep can spot dogs or other perceived forms of danger from 1,200 to 1,500 yards away." Jogging left and right at intervals, you've been walking in step with the sheep.[20]

Figure 2. Image capture from the documentary *SweetGrass* (Harvard Ethnography Lab, 2009).

---

[20] See "Flee, not fight," *sheep101.info* [website], http://www.sheep101.info/bahavior.html.

Figure 3. Image capture from the documentary *SweetGrass* (Harvard Ethnography Lab, 2009).

Tracks that won't take [Figure 3]? Well—they're also, in this case, sheep tracks, though their mode has shifted—hooves make no impression on tarmac and so the photograph itself, once upon a time the chemical effect of light on silver halogens now gone digital, presents as fact / faux / simile of the sheep's track—the only indication to a human observer that they were there.

Figure 4. Image capture from the documentary *SweetGrass* (Harvard Ethnography Lab, 2009).

Figure 5. Image capture from the documentary *SweetGrass* (Harvard Ethnography Lab, 2009).

Covered tracks? A sheep in sheep's clothing [Figures 4 and 5]? Sheep, it seems, can, as is usually reserved to human animals, cover their tracks, deploy a feint, lie. With the help of a shepherd and the skin of a dead fellow lamb, one orphan attempts to fool the mother into allowing it to nurse.

ANIMAL, VEGETABLE, MINERAL

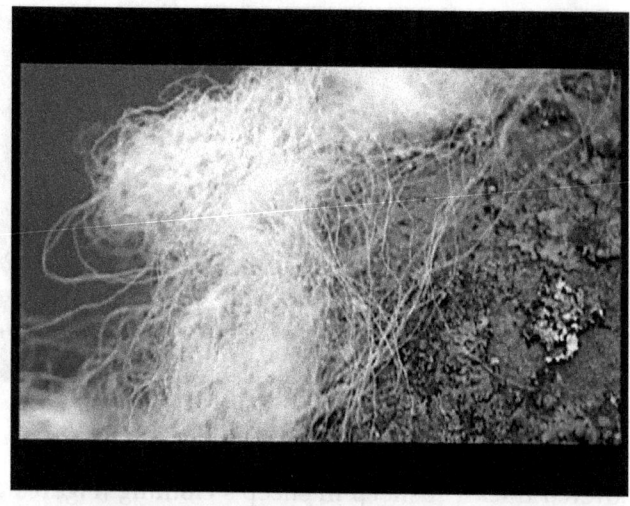

Figures 6-8. Image capture and quotations come from the documentary *Rivers and Tides: Working with Time* (Metropolis Film, 2001).

Woolly tracks [Figures 6, 7, and 8]—an installation by the artist Andy Goldsworthy in his native Scotland, where, among other time and space bound art he cards wool, trailing it atop stone walls (Figures 6 and 7), momentarily encasing stones in a woolly coat (Figure 8), all in order to do away with or to divest sheep, so he says, of their wooliness and so to deliver up what he terms their "power" to make the land take their impression.

His installations aim to make present what he calls "the absence in the landscape" occasioned by the introduction of sheep. Retasking the wooliness of sheep in his present and generating thereby all manner of uncanny, hairy stones, stones whose inorganic bulk knows no sympathy with the living, Goldsworthy aims to make the erasures (no trees; no people) of what he reads as a sheepy writing on the land presence. The sheep have passed on. Their presence remains as an aching absence, a writing deployed by English colonizers in order to unwrite particular human persons and a place.

And so Goldsworthy uncovers tracks that have been covered over, that the present no longer recalls. Creating faux-hybrid-stone-sheep and enlisting the labor of wool-making in order to delineate or rubricate the sheepy author of the stone walls that carve up the land, Goldsworthy takes the commodity value that attaches to a sheep's fleece and uses it to 'write,' to retrieve sheep tracks long since gone and so to remember a colonial past, people lost. Whatever relation obtains between wool and rock cannot be coded as sympathy. Instead, Goldsworthy's installations recode wool (and stone) by and in their relation not simply to one another but as actants caught within the impressions made by one corrosive iteration of the multi-species.

Following Goldsworthy, we might attempt something similar in our own libraries and archives, breaking in to the vault of the Folger Shakespeare Library, for example, under cover of night, with a list of differently bound and backed books, courtesy of its search tool, the porcinely named "Hamnet,"—and dress those books that have been backed in "sheep" and "goat," rendering them woolly once more.[21] The flickering presence of the animal that was would manifest here as a mode of commutative justice indexed to the sympathy between the substance of the book's binding (its skin) and the missing fleece of the sheep or skin of the goat. Hold your breath. Listen carefully. Is that a book bleating? As absurd as this putative archival reanimation or hallucination sounds, its value lies in the insistence that our collective writing machines by which the human remembers or remembers to forget this and that remains bound to other creaturely lives. Every writing machine remains always a multi-species impression.

Figure 9. Image capture from *Modern Times* (Charles Chaplin Productions, 1936).

---

[21] See "HAMNET: folger library catalog," *Folger Shakespeare Library* [online catalog], http://shakespeare.folger.edu/.

Whose tracks? Our tracks or sheep tracks? Courtesy of the time-image, a flock of sheep flicker into being within our being and then are gone [Figures 9 and 10]? Charlie Chaplin deploys the supposed sheepishness of sheep and the recalcitrance of a lone black sheep against the accelerated and attenuated temporality of the machine in *Modern Times* in a dissolve that makes the sheep in us presence on screen. The Little Tramp becomes a black sheep, who in human form, as you may recall, slows the capitalist machine right down. The film will enclose within itself pastoral vistas and utopian hiatus.

Figure 10. Image capture from *Modern Times* (Charles Chaplin Productions, 1936).

Wet Cement [Figures 11 and 12]. In an episode titled "Bitzer Puts His Foot in it," the animators of Nick Park's creation "Shaun the Sheep" imagine a scene in which sheep with their sheepdog turned co-conspirator run amok with a patch of wet cement, creating all manner of sheepy impressions that do not present on or by the hoof. In one frame, Shaun the Sheep and friends have drawn a Hollywood star in the cement. The anthropomorphism to Shaun and his flock that enables the iterative scheme of this really fun zoomorphic children's show overcompensates perhaps for the supposed sheepiness of sheep. When the farmer / owner turns his back, the otherwise fairly stereotypical sheep get up to all kinds of crazy writing games.

Figures 11-12. Image capture from *Shaun the Sheep: One Giant Leap for Lambkind* (Lyons / Hit Entertainment, 2010), Episode #4 "Bitzer Puts His Foot In It."

Does the name "Shaun," which emphatically presents a denuded self, a loss, a coerced removal, speak to a desire to write sheep differently, a desire that the likes of Thelma Rowell shares—a desire for differently articulated tracks?

ORIENTATIONS

How then should I orient myself to these tracks—to which you or I could add or substitute others that would pose the problem or the phenomenon of taking an impression differently?

"The footprint [though we might add scent, or any other trace] represents a real animal that has gone past," writes Carlo Ginzburg in his essay "Morelli, Freud, and Sherlock Holmes: Clues and Scientific Method."[22] Ginzburg is on the track of what he names a "conjectural model" or "semiotic paradigm" of reading and writing across the "borderline between natural sciences and human sciences" to its putative origins in hunter-gatherer societies. "For thousands of years," he writes,

> mankind lived by hunting. In the course of endless pursuits hunters learned to construct the appearance and movements of an unseen quarry through its tracks—prints in soft ground, snapped twigs, droppings, snagged hairs or feathers, smells, puddles, threads of saliva. They learnt to sniff, to observe, to give meaning and context to the slightest trace. They learnt to make complex calculations in

---

[22] Carlo Ginzburg, "Morelli, Freud, and Sherlock Holmes: Clues and Scientific Method," trans. Anna Davin, *History Workshop Journal* 9 (1980): 14 [5–36]. Unless otherwise indicated, subsequent references will appear parenthetically in the text.

an instant, in shadowy wood or treacherous clearing. (12)

Such skills find their like, he argues, in the tricks paleontologists use to summon dead creatures into being from their foot prints; in the protocols of fingerprinting which summon human presences into being from their paw prints; in the talking cure that Sigmund Freud uses to discern the workings of the unconscious from the marks it leaves on conscious behavior; in the minute inventorying of "characters" (aspects of the human form—ears, hands, etc.) by art historian Giovanni Morelli who claimed thereby to be able to identify the "hand" of certain Italian painters; and in the adductive methods that Conan Doyle's Sherlock Holmes uses to solve a crime. Moving across time and disciplinary boundaries, Ginzburg posits a cryptographical basis to reading, a model of reading that relies on what is not there to be read (any longer), on reading between the lines.

Ginzburg would like there to be every difference in the world between deciphering a track and a pictogram or a text composed after the transition to phonetic writing systems (14). He should like the "cloth" he's been "weaving," "the paradigm" or "common epistemological model," which "[he's] . . . summoned up from way back, out of various contexts—hunting, divining, conjectural, or semiotic" (23-24) to be marked by or to respect the difference between nature and culture—but he can't seem to catch an epistemological or discursive break. On the contrary, all his backtracking, his aligning of traces, performs the reverse. He is left with an epistemological quandary. "It is one thing," he continues,

> to analyse footprints, stars, feces (animal or human), colds, corneas, pulses, snow-covered fields or dropped cigarette ash; and another to

> analyse writing or painting or speech. The distinction between nature (inanimate or living) and culture is fundamental—certainly much more important than the far more superficial and changeable distinctions between disciplines. (24)

But by the end of his discussion, this distinction between nature and culture falls prey to the anti-anthropocentric turn to Ginzburg's own logic and to his answer to what he takes to be the key final question of analysis: "Is rigor [or what order of rigor is] compatible with the conjectural model" of tracking / tracing (28)? Ginzburg doubts that it is compatible—or that if it is, it must be an "elastic rigor"—one that is able to tolerate "factors in play which cannot be measured: a whiff, a glance, an intuition" (28). In short order, then, the project of weaving, as he calls it, of tracking and lining up this and that trace of the "conjectural paradigm" through Freud, Marx, Conan Doyle, medical semiotics, art history, cryptography, and so on, so that each trace constitutes a common track, turns into a question of magnitude and measure.

"Until now we have carefully avoided this tricky word, intuition," he confesses, as he moves to conclude,

> but if it is going to be used, as another way of describing the instantaneous running through of the thought process, then we must make a distinction between low intuition and high. (28)

Not surprisingly, it turns out, a paragraph or so later, that this distinction, this desire for a qualitative difference in mode if not model, also proves untenable. "This 'low intuition' is rooted in the senses," he continues, (though it goes beyond them). It exists everywhere in the world, without geographic, historical, ethnic, gender or class exception; and this means that it is very different from any form of 'superior' knowledge, which is always restricted to an elite. (29)

"Intuition," Ginzburg concludes, high and low, "forms a real link between the human animal and other animal species" (29).

We should be *impressed*. For, in a relatively short essay, Ginzburg arrives at the insight that may be said to found Derrida's *Of Grammatology*, that there exists a history of technology, of the machine, the plant, and the animal, of life, that is simultaneously and necessarily also a history of what has been called "human," and that telling that story, without the aura of human exceptionalism, will produce an order of archival vertigo at the proliferation of tracks and the leveling of ontological categories.[23] But what of Ginzburg's figure and phraseology of the "link," this "real link" (29) that forms between the human animal and other animal species? This figuring of a "link" prepares the way for an insight regarding the coarticulation or mutual genesis of the zoo- and anthropomorphic. It is the product of the "path" or pattern to be discerned from the tracks of Ginzburg's own conjectural wager in his essay. Ginzburg's careful anti-anthropocentric reweaving of traces, his back tracking through semiotic systems ends by positivizing the aligning of traces that a non-species centered modeling of the archive permits.

It seems key, however, to notice that what he positivizes, by way of an end to his tracking or tracing (there are no more tracks, no more tracks to follow) and

---

[23] Jacques Derrida, *Of Grammatology*, trans., Gayatri Chakravorty Spivak (Baltimore: Johns Hopkins University Press, 1974), 84–85.

what he will offer therefore as a beginning or founding truth to writing systems, is not exactly "a real link between the human animal and other animal species" so much as his inability to decide on a ratio by which one might judge intuition as low or high. The "link," the positing of, or provisional shaping of the form of an atemporal universal, constitutes instead the skin or fleece Ginzburg knits in order to cover over an epistemological quandary or nakedness that his composing of an archive entails—a quandary which might be understood to refer quite precisely to the difficulty that haunts Derrida throughout *The Animal That Therefore I Am* in deciding on the difference between what is termed "reaction" and that which is called "response" and which is said to be proper or reserved to the human.[24] It might be ventured that this question as to the threshold or internally divided and marked line between reaction and response, to what Derrida calls an "abyss" or "limitrophy,"[25] will tend to present to us and is perhaps allied to the question and composition of an archive, and that the question will, in one sense or another, be decided by the way in which we orient ourselves to it.

What are you following? How do you follow? What do you do if you think you might catch up with the being whose tracks you are following? Should you, as Latour invites but does not himself practice, catch up as quickly as you can and produce new orders of impression via the so very many "speech impedimenta" we will make in order to enable things to speak to and of us? I have been unraveling Ginzburg's cloth, worrying his tracks—threatening, so it may seem, to turn sheep-biter, because he converts the tracks into a trail. Instead, I wish to own the quandary that gets palmed in the process, the way the limit to his ability to decipher

---

[24] Derrida, *The Animal That Therefore I Am*, especially 119–40.
[25] Derrida, *The Animal That Therefore I Am*, 29.

traces that founds what he calls an historical method, installs a trans-species model of reading that defers and so does not address the question of non-human responsiveness and human reactivity.

I am left straddling or perhaps skipping between two readings, two orientations to Ginzburg's tracks and to the trace. On the one hand, that might, as before, be the same hand, we may read his conclusion (as I do) as an electrifying insight to the biomaterial-semiotic basis of our archive, adducing also the provincializing of human language to one semiotic, syntactical, and rhetorical system among many. All animals therefore read and write—not with ink but with urine, feces, and so very many other substances.[26] But it is hard to know whether or not Ginzburg's knitting of this "link," a link that might be said to cover over the nudity that he has uncovered, does not constitute a disavowal or arresting of the possibility that what passes as "response" in humans might be perfectly assimilated to a cadaverous order of reaction, not the chimerical multiplicity of the *animot*, so much as to what, in passing, Derrida names the *animort*, the "non-animal" or "non-living."[27]

As my skipping and straddling and the awkwardness of my feet signals, I have arrived at a parting of the ways, at a crossroads or crux. The instability to the relation between reaction and response might be said to fund Ginzburg's aligning of traces even as that alignment will come to settle the question, to provide a way beyond or around it. Maybe then I am simply stuck

---

[26] Such is a given for Michel Serres in *The Parasite*, *The Natural Contract*, trans. Elizabeth MacArthur and William Paulson (Ann Arbor: University of Michigan Press, 1998), and now in *Malfeasance: Appropriation through Pollution*, trans. Anne-Marie Feenberg-Dibon (Stanford: Stanford University Press, 2011).

[27] On the inert, see Derrida, *The Animal That Therefore I Am*, 62.

in the same old tracks, the flagging tracks of a dead horse I am still flogging. For from a certain perspective, it will be difficult not to read my response to Ginzburg's forming of "a real link between human animal and other non-human animals" (29) as a knee-jerk reaction, a parsimonious or ungenerous failure of imagination, a failure to escape a track that the speculatively realistic might say was really just a "correlationist two-step,"[28] a post-Kantian imprisonment that ensures that all that philosophy may interrogate is the means by which we know the world and so not the world itself. Where Derrida might locate in Ginzburg the same structure of disavowal regarding the question of the animal that he finds in Descartes, Lacan, Lévinas, Heidegger, the likes of Bruno Latour, Donna Haraway, Graham Harman, Quentin Meillassoux, among others, might locate a different orientation from which to begin—an alternate modality of the archive.

"Positive knowledge of and with animals might just be possible," writes Donna Haraway just as she parts company with Derrida's *The Animal that Therefore I Am* (nothing more to follow) in *When Species Meet*.[29] Up until now, Derrida presences in Haraway's book as he who "tracks down" "the whole anthropomorphic reinstitution of the superiority of the human order over the animal order, of the law over the living"—and so as "guide" to the western philosophical tradition. The problem, though, is that however caring and considerate, however open to being with, he may

---

[28] For this critique, see Quentin Meillasoux's astonishing *After Finitude: An Essay on the Necessity of Contingency*, trans. Ray Brassier (London: Continuum, 2008). On "the correlationist two-step" and the "archefossil" that silently surplants Derrida's "arche-writing," see especially 1–50. See also Graham Harman, *Prince of Networks: Bruno Latour and Metaphysics* (Melbourne: re.press, 2009).
[29] Haraway, *When Species Meet*, 21.

be, when confronted in the bathroom naked by his cat, and knowing full well that this historical cat could be said to respond to him, Derrida

> did not seriously consider an alternative form of engagement either, one that risked knowing something more about cats and *how to look back*, perhaps even scientifically, biologically, and *therefore* also philosophically and intimately. (20)

"He came right up to the edge of respect, of the move to *respecere*," writes Haraway,

> but he was sidetracked by the textual canon of Western philosophy and literature, and by his own linked worries about being naked in front of his cat. (20)

The wrong track.

> Derrida failed a simple obligation of companion species; he did not become curious about what the cat might actually be doing, feeling, thinking, or perhaps making available to him in looking back at him that morning. (20)

He did not inquire into the ethological literature on cats and so into what it may be that cats are already saying.

Parting ways is tough. Derrida, we learn, was a special kind of beast,

> among the most curious of men, among the most committed and able of philosophers to spot what arrests curiosity . . . relentlessly attentive and humble before what he does not know. (20)

And so what happens or fails to happen in that bathroom is all the more shocking. For Derrida, that most curious of men, was insufficiently curious. He was "incurious." We might even say therefore that, contrary to the adage, it was Derrida's incuriousness and not feline curiosity *per se* that killed this singular, historical cat.

Again, as with Ginzburg, I am not sure which way to turn—I am left straddling even as I might wish to skip ahead with Haraway to the prospect of "new possibilities" on offer from ethologists with regard to human / non-human animal interactions. Haraway knows enough about sheep, courtesy of Thelma Rowell, to know that their orientation to predation, their assumption of predation as a fact of their world, means that even on an island that's not seen a wolf in over a thousand years, they still check their rears every 1200-1500 feet.[30] What else could one expect Derrida to do—especially since he's on the track not of a sheep, a cat, the animal, or even of the *animot*—but of the autobiographical animal, that set of disavowals by which the story of the other is transposed into a reassuring story of the same—all in order to produce a shelter for one iteration of the "human"? "Autobiography," he writes,

> the writing of the self as living, the trace of the living for itself, being for itself, the auto-affection or auto-infection as memory or archive of the living, would be an immunizing movement (a movement of safety, of salvage, and salvation of the safe, the holy, the immune, the indemnified, of virginal and intact nudity), but an immunizing movement

---

[30] Haraway uses Rowell's work to excellent effect; see *When Species Meet*, 27–42.

> that is always threatened with becoming auto-immunizing ... Nothing risks becoming more poisonous than an autobiography.[31]

Here, as elsewhere in the course of *The Animal That (Therefore) I Am*, Derrida places his feet very carefully, enacting therein the shape of an autobiography or better, a "zoo-auto-bio-bibliographing," but always with an eye to his rear, lest that is the genre turns poisonous on him, gets the better of him, leads him down a path constituted by a disavowal.[32]

One emblematic moment of this care, this curious care not to kill (by mistake) regards the western philosophical tradition itself, all that Haraway would like to box up and leave behind, without trace. Casting himself as a wrestler, a hunter, or a fisherman, with the "nervous system of a single animal body"[33] (the system of disavowals whereby response becomes proper to the human in Descartes, Kant, Heidegger, Lévinas, and Lacan), he writes that his project

> is a little like someone who would claim to know which way to take hold of a cuttlefish or octopus, without hurting it too much, and especially without killing it, keeping it at a distance long enough to let it expel its ink. In order to displace its powers without doing anybody too much harm. Its ink or power would here be the 'I,' not necessarily *the power to say* 'I,' but the ipseity of being *able to be or able to do* 'I,' even before any auto-referential utterance in language.[34]

---

[31] Derrida, *The Animal That Therefore I Am*, 47.
[32] Derrida, *The Animal That Therefore I Am*, 34
[33] Derrida, *The Animal That Therefore I Am*, 91.
[34] Derrida, *The Animal That Therefore I Am*, 92.

Derrida is out to combat this tradition but also takes care "not to sacrifice to it any difference or alterity, the fold of any complication, the opening of the abyss to come."[35] Aiming to hold open the tradition to the traces it tries to forget and which may offer something entirely other, Derrida tries to walk within such tracks that there already are, taking care, if he may, to leave no impressions of his own.

Why such careful treading? Why such care to create no "new" tracks that might obliterate others? The difficulty lies, to reprise Ginzburg's "rigor," in understanding the ratio by which we will be able to know which "new or different possibilities" or "real links" do not themselves deploy the structure of disavowal that Derrida identifies, reacquiring all that inky power that he has been trying to expel from a philosophical cuttlefish that he wishes to keep a hold of? Haraway's disappointment with Derrida's in-curiousness regarding his cat, for example, represents one such crossroads, a moment when passing on to "new tracks" raises the possibility of a disavowal, a moment in which responsiveness, having acquired for so long an hypnotic scarcity value, is accorded to the living generally with such a surplus as to keep us all, human persons and not, responding for as long as we like. Such is the difficulty of the crux, the potential and the danger to the crossing.

HOSPITALITY

In this essay, I have been counting sheep tracks, tracks that lead me up to the crossroads or parting of the ways between two critical households. It is tempting, then to conclude by hallucinating both Derrida and Haraway hemmed in with their doggies and kitties by a flock of blithely indifferent sheep, sheep whom it may make no

---

[35] Derrida, *The Animal That Therefore I Am*, 92.

sense to differentiate from the larger entity, collectivity or polity that their flock constitutes—no more sense than it may for the animals we name "human." Not missing a b/l/eat, I end, therefore, by suggesting that in Derrida's tracking of a genre and its auto-immunizing, pro-life, agenda, I find a rubric for my orientation still to all the sheep tracks I amass—an orientation that I think may have some small value still in speaking back to those in the parliament of things who advocate for potentially more hospitable possibilities.

One such example might be that of Thelma Rowell and her Yorkshire sheep as she inducts them into the protocols of ethological research and they enjoin her to different gestures, thoughts, requirements, postures than those to which she is used, all in order for her to be what she considers a good scientist, which is to say, a good host. One such gesture that perhaps goes unnoticed or which simply puzzles most observers is the extra time Rowell appears to have on her hands. Visitors to Rowell's farm remark in their otherwise quite scholarly essays and books that, in addition to everything else, Rowell is a wonderful cook—and that there's always an impressive array of tea items on hand.[36] One of the reasons for this, I contend, as someone apt to appreciate a good cook and who aspires to deliver on this order of hospitality to others, is that to study the ruminating sheep with the equivalent protocols that one studies the sometimes hyperactive world of baboons, leaves the researcher

---

[36] In the Acknowledgements to *Dolly Mixtures*, Sarah Franklin comments warmly on the hospitality, conversation, and "homemade delicacies" that Thelma Rowell treated her to on visits to her farm [Franklin, *Dolly Mixtures*, ix]. My point in citing the cast of these comments is to discern the structure of politeness and hospitality that extends to humans and sheep alike on Rowell's farm. This politeness, this attentiveness to the other, seems the key addition to Rowell's experiments.

with a lot more time on her hands—empty time that might once upon a time, have been named *otium*—the privileged and recurring figure in Giorgio Agamben's *The Open*; the "malaise" of Derrida's "more to follow," the Heideggerian boredom or "*tiefe langweil*" in the last lecture of *The Animal That Therefore I Am* and the slowness of flat ontology.[37] The question for Agamben and Derrida will be whether anything of value persists or dwells in pastoral *otium*, in a deactivated, nontemporal *tempus*, something that may still be of interest to a common becoming, and vitally so.

As a reader tuned to pastoral motifs, I am inclined to read Rowell's research as the latest chapter in the genre of bucolic poetry, and to see her as opening a space or an archive for that which sheep might be said thus far to have lacked—an aura. She offers them, in other words, an opportunity to manifest as historical beings, there and then, here and now, and for the impressions that they make to count as writing worth keeping. By doing so, Rowell will have, I argue, in effect, been writing epic for sheep—though what that epic will be remains as yet to be seen. Why epic—even as sheep may refashion that genre? As fellow ethologist Vincianne Despret records, Rowell's

> observations usually start in the morning, with the same ritual: she takes each of her 22 sheep a bowl of its breakfast. But what puzzles any outside observer is that there are not 22 but 23 bowls, that is, always one too many.

---

[37] On *otium*, see Giorgio Agamben, *The Open: Man and Animal*, trans. Kevin Attell (Stanford: Stanford University Press, 2004), 63–70, 85–87. On melancholy and malaise, see Derrida, *The Animal That Therefore I Am*, 19–20. On Heideggerian boredom, see Agamben, *The Open*, 63–70 and Derrida, *The Animal That Therefore I Am*, 141–60.

"Why this extra bowl?" asks Despret, "Is the researcher practicing a kind of conviviality?"[38] For the reader of pastoral poetry it is tempting to suggest that Rowell is further transforming the *ekphrastic* wager of Theocritus's ivy-cup in the First Idyll, which in his hands, reader of epic that he was, became an ordinary bowl that his writing would adorn, extending thereby the forms of epic to everyday human life and concerns.[39] For Rowell, the ivy bowl materializes in even more humble garb as a feed bowl for a sheep, indeed as a feed bowl that is not used—somehow allowing these 22 historical sheep to refigure themselves and the *prosopopoeia* that once rendered them and us "sheepish." The 23rd bowl is, as Despret hints in what seems like misdirection, about politeness—about offering to "sheep" the chance to transform the protocols of the observation. The presence of the bowl and so the surplus of food transforms the questions that Rowell poses of her sheep, removing or suspending an automatic question concerning competition even as it registers that the findings are inflected by her presence. The bowl "is intended," Despret continues, "to expand the repertoire of hypotheses and questions proposed to the sheep . . . [but] to leave them the choice" of answering other questions than those posed to them. Like Theocritus, Rowell prepares the bowl, but it is her 22 sheep whose actions she records that co*write* the scene it depicts. For Despret, then, "this [now] emblematic," we might say [idyllic / *eidyllion*] twenty-

---

[38] Vinciane Despret, "Sheep Do Have Opinions," in *Making Things Public: Atmospheres of Democracy*, eds. Bruno Latour and Peter Weibel (Cambridge: MIT Press, 2005), 360. See also, Vinciane Despret, *Quand le loup habitera avec l'agneau* (Paris: Seuille, 2002).

[39] Here I rely on the revisionist reading of David Halperin in *Before Pastoral: Theocritus and the Ancient Tradition of Bucolic Poetry* (New Haven: Yale University Press, 1983), 211.

third bowl becomes a way of entering sheep into a human / non-human writing machine or "zoo-auto-bio-bibliographing," in a way which permits or requires the 'human' now merely to idle, to wait or attend.

The morphology of such figures as appear on the ivy cup, figures upon which that which was "human" now waits, remains to be seen, for the "human" has become an idling merely, a category held in abeyance, awaiting who knows what? If the project of common becoming that the parliament of things attempts to realize may be understood to require a cosmopolitan or cosmopolitical rewiring of abusive relays that disavow into joyful nodes of "becoming with," then I at least remain skipping and straddling the crux of reaction and response, clued into ethological invitations to "new possibilities," as best as I can, but also eyeing a cuttlefish which seems to have reserves of invisible ink. By now, all my straddling and skipping may have rendered me a figure of fun or an embarrassment, but such perhaps are the risks to be run by those who wish to tread within the double set of prints in one that constitute the mutual becoming of sheep and human person, our collective "sheep tracks." Bah!

THE RENAISSANCE *RES PUBLICA* OF FURNITURE

Julia Reinhard Lupton

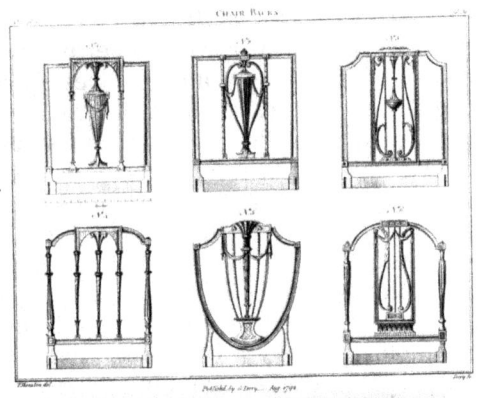

Is the Renaissance joint-stool *zany, interesting,* or *cute*? These are the categories put forward by Sianne Ngai in order to capture our contemporary experience of all things cultural, from ninja bunnies to crowdsourced dreams:

> The interesting, cute, and zany index—and are thus each in a historically concrete way about—capitalism's most socially binding processes: production, in the case of the zany (an aesthetic about performance as not just artful play but also affective labor); circulation, in the case of the interesting (a serial, recursive aesthetic of informational relays and communicative exchange); and

consumption, in the case of the cute (an aesthetic disclosing the surprisingly wide spectrum of feelings, ranging from tenderness to aggression, that we harbor towards ostensibly subordinate and unthreatening commodities).[1]

Zany pertains to the aestheticization of labor in the experience economy; *interesting* describes information and media in the age of TMI; and *cute* captures our relationship to objects in a world overrun by phones that look like their owners and puggles spiked with microchips. In this essay, I would like to suggest that the homely, ubiquitous Renaissance joint-stool participated in a version of the "zany" as new-minted by Ngai (supplemented by occasional encounters with Cute). Ngai links the zany to the performance of "affective labor," a phrase used by the Italian autonomists (including Michael Hardt, Antonio Negri, and Paolo Virno) to characterize those forms of work that curate the emotional envelope of social life, including caregiving and informal economies based on gift exchange and collective effort.[2] "Affective labor" refers

---

My thanks to the organizers and participants of the conference on "Animal, Vegetable, Mineral" that led to the creation of this volume. My account of affordances is adapted from my essay, "Making Room, Affording Hospitality: Environments of Entertainment in *Romeo and Juliet*," forthcoming in the *Journal of Medieval and Early Modern Studies*. My reading of *The Taming of the Shrew* is lightly adapted from my book, *Thinking with Shakespeare: Essays on Politics and Life* (Chicago: University of Chicago Press, 2011).

[1] Sianne Ngai, "Our Aesthetic Categories," *PMLA* 125.4 (2010): 948–49.
[2] Jack Bratich, "The Digital Touch: Craft-Work as Immaterial Labour and Ontological Accumulation," *Ephemera: Theory and Politics in Organization* 10.3-4 (2010): 308–9 [303–18];

to both the emotional work that often goes unmarked or uncompensated in domestic and social life as well as the sentimental expenditures carried by labor itself. In the information and experience economy, culture workers create and distribute affect as a product in its own right. Theater is a form of affective labor, and so is cooking; indeed, the traffic of stools between scenes of household management and stage management links these two zones of expressive performance. Generically, Ngai associates the zany with comedy (the cute belongs to romance, and the interesting to realism), and she recovers the resume of the zany in Renaissance theater: "Deriving from the character of the *zanni*, an itinerant servant in commedia dell'arte who is modeled after peasants seeking temporary work in Venetian households, zaniness has a history that stretches back to the sixteenth-century division of labor and the theater and marketplace culture of what is now Italy."[3] In Renaissance households, stools were highly mobile actors in the daily drama of artisanal work, domestic labor, and commensal pleasure in rooms that changed function over the course of the day as well as the week and the year. Closely linked to the butts they were designed to bear and imaginatively affiliated with beasts of burden, stools show up in the insult repertoire of Renaissance comedy as a handy extension of the lower body and its humor.

The stool belonged to what I call the Renaissance *res publica* of furniture. Bruno Latour poses the following challenge:

> Has the time not come to bring the *res* back to the res publica? . . . There has been an aesthetics of matters-of-fact, of objects, of

---

Michael Hardt, "Affective Labor," *boundary 2* 26.2 (1999): 89–100.
[3] Ngai, "Our Aesthetic Categories," 951.

Gegenstände. Can we devise an aesthetic of matters-of-concern, of Things?[4]

For Latour things are areas of public interest whose histories of production and patterns of use help shape the dimensions and directions of our shared spaces of verbal and economic exchange. Furnishings constitute a *res publica*, a public matter, in several senses. First, the hierarchy that places chairs above stools in the inventories of the period replicates the social order of the Renaissance household and the household-state; one *res publica* (the furniture system) mirrors and supports the other (the body politic) in its biopolitical and political-theological handling of limbs, spines, and butts. The furniture system is *biopolitical* insofar as distinct forms of seating afford specific styles and postures of human behavior, with stools belonging more to labor and task work and chairs obtaining more to the dignity of its inhabitant in scenes of public deliberation, audition, and spectatorship. This furniture system is *political-theological* insofar as the upright architecture of the noble chair bodies forth the second, official body of the king, while the zany stool, both mobile and multiple, scoots around in more low-lying and scatological service economies. Finally, in an age before mass production, furnishings of all sorts solicited care on the part of human users, who became the curators of things as much as their owners; here, *res publica* names a relationship of codependence and obligation among things, persons, and the locales in

---

[4] Bruno Latour, "From Realpolitik to Dingpolitik or How to Make Things Public," in Bruno Latour and Peter Weibel, eds., *Making Things Public: Atmospheres of Democracy* (Cambridge: MIT Press, 2005), 23 [14–43]. See also Latour, "Why Has Critique Run out of Steam? From Matters of Fact to Matters of Concern," *Critical Inquiry* 30 (Winter 2004): 225–40.

which they dwell. My examples for this essay include several scenes from Shakespeare, plus an inventory of home furnishings left by Bess of Hardwick to her son in 1601 and a pattern book written by cabinetmaker Thomas Sheraton in 1793, at the dawn of a new ordering of furniture. The scenes of use (and occasional abuse) disclosed by these texts grant us some access to the Renaissance *res publica* of furniture, a commons constituted by postures of craft, labor, conversation, and enjoyment distributed among chairs and stools, the persons who made, moved, and used them, and the environments in which they sat.

Much new work on objects in medieval and Renaissance studies draws on Latour's actor-network theater and on the adjoining but more speculative discourses of object-oriented ontology associated with Graham Harman, Levi Bryant, and Iain Hamilton Grant. Although I draw on Latour in particular, my own travels in the object world are guided by design and design discourse, including product design, graphic design, branding, and built environments, with special attention to the theory of affordances that runs through all of these practices of design. In design research, "affordances" designate those physical aspects of an object, including shape, color, layout, and position, that communicate to the human user how a particular thing, be it coffee cup or touch screen, is meant to be handled.[5] Affordances are thus directly related to interfaces: to the communicative points of contact between objects and users.[6] The term "affordance" was

---

[5] See Donald Norman's landmark study *The Design of Everyday Things* (New York: Basic Books, 2002), first published in 1988 under the title *The Psychology of Everyday Things*.
[6] See the classic study by Jef Raskin, *The Humane Interface: New Directions for Designing Interactive Systems* (Addison-Wesley, 2000), who uses "interface" as short-hand for

first coined by ecological psychologist James J. Gibson to describe the way in which animals perceive elements of their environment in relation to the possibilities for action born by specific features of their world. He begins with the flatness of the ground, which affords running and standing for quadrapeds, and he goes on to consider what he calls "the furniture of the earth," which encompasses *enclosures, convexities, concavities*, and *apertures*, each with their own distinct affordances for animal dwelling. Gibson groups human perception under animal perception, and thus considers humanity within a wider ecological scene. Although affordances in design research today often promote a reductive view of human-machine interaction (the hand on the doorknob, the finger on the button), affordance theory shares deep connections with phenomenology and pragmatism as well as ecology, as demonstrated by the work of environmental ecologist Harry Heft.[7] Many designers today are restoring an environmental perspective to usability studies, mining the history of affordances itself for new paradigms that might check the behaviorist and consumerist tendencies of their profession. "Environmental" carries here both its popu-

---

"human-machine interface," "human-computer interface," and "user interface." Raskin defines interface as "the way that you accomplish tasks with a product—what you do and how it responds" (2).

[7] Harry Heft emphasizes the affinities between affordance theory, phenomenology and pragmatism in order to explore human place-making and our navigation of parks and playgrounds. See "Affordances, Dynamic Experience, and the Challenge of Reification," *Environmental Ecology* 15.2 (2003): 149–80; and Heft's book-length study of Gibson, which approaches affordances from a genealogical, historical, and philosophical (humanistic) vantage: *Ecological Psychology in Context: James Gibson, Roger Barker, and the Legacy of William James's Radical Empiricism* (Mahwah: Lawrence Erlbaum Associates, 2001).

lar sense ("The Environment," as if there were such a thing), while also referring to the place of an object (such as a joint stool) or a practice (such as theater) in a set of nested and overlapping systems that might include urban, agrarian, monetary, climactic, craft-based, and informational networks.[8] These practical efforts echo Jane Bennett's call for a "political ecology of things" that maps human and non-human interaction from the view of the worm and the sardine can.[9]

Also relevant here is the idea of the assemblage, associated with the work of Giles Deleuze as reread by Manuel De Landa.[10] In new work on Renaissance melancholy, Andrew Daniel develops the assemblage as a way of tracking the life of resistant composites formed by things, ideas, persons, and environments.[11] Melan-

---

[8] A journal like *Design Ecologies* (published by Eniatype, a group of architects based in London) looks at "the complex relationship between human activity and the environment," examining "the totality or pattern of linkages between drawing and environment" (http://www.eniatype.com/index.php?/about-this-site/). Other designers committed to rethinking affordances from an environmental perspective include Tony Dunne and Fiona Raby, principals of Dunne & Raby Studio (www.dunneandrab.co.uk) and authors of *Design Noir: The Secret Life of Electronic Objects* (London: August Media Ltd., 2001). On affordance theory and the humanities, see Julka Almquist and Julia Lupton, "Affording Meaning: Design-Oriented Research from the Humanities and Social Sciences," *Design Issues* 26.1 (Winter 2010): 3–14. On affordances and Renaissance theater, see Evelyn B. Tribble, "Distributing Cognition in the Globe," *Shakespeare Quarterly* 56.2 (Summer 2005): 135–55.

[9] Jane Bennett, *Vibrant Matter: A Political Ecology of Things* (Baltimore: Johns Hopkins University Press, 2010).

[10] Manuel De Landa, *A New Philosophy of Society: Assemblage Theory and Social Complexity* (London: Continuum, 2006).

[11] Andrew Daniel, *The Melancholy Assemblage: Affect and Epistemology in the English Renaissance* (forthcoming from Fordham University Press).

choly is an assemblage, but so is Starbucks. The comparison tells us something not only about the ideational and thingly dimensions of disease, but also about the symptomatic morphology of marketing. The Cute, the Zany, and the Interesting are assemblages in this sense, since they are composed of objects, affects, and ideas distributed throughout environments that have been both wired and wall-papered by branding. Daniel's sources include avant-garde art practices (including his own) that body forth assemblage as technique and worldview.

Assemblage is so closely linked to *assembly* that their meanings often merge, but I will also distinguish the two terms. "Assemblage" involves the physical construction of experiential spaces out of objects, fabrics, and the haptic ingredients of ambience, as well as names, brands, and other myths. "Assembly" concerns the gathering of persons in those spaces for the purposes of deliberation, debate, celebration, or the exchange of bodily fluids. In distinguishing assemblage from assembly, I remain an Arendtian, and hence a humanist: I am concerned, that is, to cultivate the differences as well as the ongoing dependencies between human forms of appearing and the appearing of things. I read Arendt, however, for the productive interfaces between the oikos and the polis that surface throughout her work, and not for the supposed purity of their separation. In this task, I am guided by Patchen Markell's scanning of the landscapes of *The Human Condition* for scenes that reintegrate work, labor, and action in formations that can illuminate our contemporary cityscapes, retail zones, and housing arrangements.[12] Markell supplements what he calls the territorial strain in Arendt's writing—her desire to

---

[12] Patchen Markell, "Arendt's Work: On the Architecture of *The Human Condition*," *College Literature* 38.1 (Winter 2011): 15–44.

sequester engagement with things from human speech—by a "relational" reading of human action in built environments. In *The Human Condition*, for example, Arendt writes that self-disclosure accompanies all of our intercourse, not just privileged instances of public speech; whenever we work at something in concert with other people, we also talk, consider, negotiate, evaluate, plan, and decide.[13] The title of Markell's essay, "Arendt's Work: On the Architecture of *The Human Condition*," indicates his interests in world-building practices such as architecture and design that reconcile the utilitarian and aesthetic dimensions of human making in forms of dwelling and habitation that both require and support living together.

In *The Taming of the Shrew*, Kate calls Petruccio a joint-stool in an exchange that illuminates the networked character of Renaissance housing:

> KATHERINA: "Moved." In good time, let him that moved you hither
> Remove you hence. I knew you at the first
> You were a movable.
> PETRUCCIO: Why, what's a movable?
> KATHERINA: A joint-stool.
> PETRUCCIO: Thou hast hit it: come, sit on me.
> KATHERINA: Asses are made to bear, and so are you.
> PETRUCCIO: Women are made to bear, and so are you.

---

[13] "Even the most 'objective intercourse,' the physical, worldly, in-between along with its interests is overlaid and, as it were, overgrown with an altogether different in-between which consists of deeds and words and owes its origin exclusively to men's acting and speaking directly to one another": Hannah Arendt, *The Human Condition* (Chicago: University of Chicago Press, 1958), 182–83.

KATHERINA: No such jade as you, if me you mean.[14]

"Movable" means fickle, variable (as in the famous phrase, "La donna è mobile"), but Katharina swiftly fixes the adjective as the noun meaning furniture. As the Romance words *meuble*s, *mobilia*, and *muebles* indicate, furniture is defined by its status as movable property, and such movables were all the more in motion in a period when households frequently rezoned domestic spaces for purposes of work, eating, or rest.[15] Petruchio swiftly rejoins that he will happily bear her weight (disclosing a covert image of the woman on top); she in turn is quick to figure him as a mere beast of burden, whose language of "bearing" yields further bawdy potential for Petruchio.

The joint-stool [Figure 1] appears as an object in motion, an envoy from a reprogrammable space whose furnishings lend themselves to frequent rezoning.[16] The stool is inanimate in the sense that it does not move of its own accord, yet its design invites not only scooting under the table or filing against the wall, but also, under

---

[14] *The Taming of the Shrew*, ed. Barbara Hodgon (London: Methuen, 2010), II.i.194–202.

[15] On the migration of furniture (*meubles, mobilia*) between estates for aristocrats, and within public rooms in bourgeois homes, see Witold Rybczynsi, *Home: A Short History of an Idea* (London: Pocket Books, 1997), 26–27.

[16] On joining, joinery, and joint-stools in Shakespeare, see Patricia Parker, "'Rude Mechanicals': *A Midsummer Night's Dream* and Shakespearean Joinery," in Parker, *Shakespeare from the Margins: Language, Culture, Context* (Chicago: University of Chicago Press, 1996), 83–115; and Natasha Korda, *Shakespeare's Domestic Economies: Gender and Property in Early Modern England* (Philadelphia: University of Pennsylvania Press, 2002), 194–98. Neither account emphasizes affordances.

circumstances of rage or shame, hurling across the room.

Figure 1. Ellen Lupton, *A Joint Stool for Bottom*. Acrylic. 2009. Courtesy of the artist.

The stool is an actant in Latour's sense, which captures the way in which things "might authorize, allow, afford, encourage, permit, suggest, block, render possible, forbid, and so on."[17] The height of the joint-stool, the flatness of its upper surface, the stability and lift promised by its foot rail, and the elegance of the joint itself, in which mortise and tenon accomplish their own union without nails or glue, all invite sitting and in some cases standing by promising a measure of both convenience and security. Meanwhile, the stool's legs are also handles, easy to carry about for multiple uses.

We might say, following Sianne Ngai, that there is something "zany" about this scene and the imagined

---

[17] Bruno Latour, *Reassembling the Social: An Introduction to Actor-Network-Theory* (Oxford: Oxford University Press, 2005), 72. Latour uses the word affordance here, and footnotes Gibson.

movement of objects through it. Ngai links zaniness to the performance of labor: "Pointing to the intensely embodied affects and desires of an agent compelled to move, hustle, and perform in the presence of others," the zany bears "a special relation to affective or physical effort."[18] Stools are the workhorses of the household; like nags and jades, they are eminently assworthy, designed to support manual as well as skilled labor, tasks that help meet the biological and emotional needs of the household while sometimes generating their own affective surpluses (as gossip, reverie, or the pleasures of dexterity). Michael Hardt writes that,

> Caring labor is certainly entirely immersed in the corporeal, the somatic, but the affects it produces are nonetheless immaterial. What affective labor produces are social networks, forms of community, biopower.[19]

In this short exchange, Shakespeare allows us to glimpse the emergence of such immaterial networks out of the flow of objects among domestic, animal, and linguistic landscapes. Although objectification rules the speech—each speaker derides the other as thing and animal—the delirious mobility of these *mobilia* casts them into a metamorphic environment that houses humans alongside other forms of existence, including the inanimate life of objects, the laboring life of domestic animals, and the metaphoric life of language itself, as the busy, buzzing, prolix, punning medium through which these zany transformations are captured, transferred, and communicated.

The zany stool stands in some opposition here with the more stolid chair. Chairs were costly to make and uncomfortable to sit in; there might be one or two

---

[18] Ngai, "Our Aesthetic Categories," 950.
[19] Hardt, "Affective Labor," 96.

in a household, reserved for the patriarch, perhaps his wife, and honored guests. The chair may, like the stool, support the rump, but it also stretches upward to outline the higher elements of trunk, head, and arms. A political theology as well as a biopolitics shapes the life of chairs. The throne hosts the king's second, immortal body within an elaborate exoskeleton of carved wood and cloth of gold, since the ghostly *dignitas* of father, king, or bishop requires biotechnical support to maintain its fragile charisma. In the film *The King's Speech*, recall the scene with the coronation chair in Westminster Abbey: George finally finds his voice when he confronts his lowborn Aussie speech therapist brazenly lounging in the seat of kings. The throne, chair par excellence, is both the privilege of sovereignty and the response to a certain impotence, an inveterate stutter. The Renaissance "chair of ease," for example, was designed to cushion the buttocks of people suffering from anal fistulas (such a chair notoriously appeared on stage in Middleton's *Game of Chess*).

Sometimes stools seem to move all by themselves. In *A Midsummer Night's Dream*, Puck claims responsibility for the minor terror of tipped stools:

> The wisest aunt, telling the saddest tale,
> Sometime for three-foot stool mistaketh me;
> Then slip I from her bum, down topples she,
> And 'tailor' cries, and falls into a cough;
> And then the whole quire holds their hips and loffe
> And waxen in their mirth, and neeze, and sweat
> A merrier hour was never wasted there.[20]

---

[20] Shakespeare, *A Midsummer Night's Dream*, ed. Harold E. Brooks (London: Methuen, 1979), II.i.51–57.

Here Puck accounts for our sense that things conspire against us in the mishaps of everyday life, while also indicating the role of stools in the verbal life of women engaged in affective labor. We can take Puck's uncanny causality either as phenomenological, a stab at describing the way that we experience objects as animated (Merleau-Ponty), or as real, a means of asserting that objects actually do operate as causal agents or actants (Latour and Harman). In either scenario, Puck bids us to attend to the life of objects in an ecology composed of mixed goods and multiple systems in a scene that also records acts of human assembly and verbal display. Animating the zone of human accident and error, Puck is an emissary of assemblage who gives a name to interfaces that fail. He is moreover himself a fabrication of the folk intelligence shared by the women he mocks, authors of the premodern world of uncanny causality now revisited by Latour and others in search of richer paradigms for the life of things. Puck's antics allow us to address chairs and stools as what James Gibson called "value-rich ecological objects," dense composites of natural materials, artisanal skill, household labor, fantasy and folk tale, and the somatic music of the laugh, the cough, and the sneeze.[21] The stool rests its case in a play concerned with Bottoms of all kinds.

In *Macbeth*, the Renaissance *res publica* of furniture frames the famous banquet scene. Bidding his guests to sit down according their own degrees, Macbeth declares,

> Ourself will mingle with society,
> And play the humble host.

---

[21] Gibson, 140. On somatic music, see Daniel Albright, *Musicking Shakespeare: A Conflict of Theatres* (Rochester: University of Rochester Press, 2007), 109.

> Our hostess keeps her state; but, in best time,
> We will require her welcome.[22]

Her "state" is the chair of state that likely stood on a raised dais at one end of the great hall, upholstered and canopied with fine fabrics in order to set off the status of its occupant within the sovereign softscape. Visualizing the dignity of its occupant, this open pavilion also identified its sitters with their physical vulnerability, their need to be safeguarded from too much noxious air or unseemly mingling. Rather than sitting next to her on his own chair of state, Macbeth decides to "play the humble host" and "mingle with society"; engaging in the hospitable practice of "commoning," Macbeth taps the fiction of equality between guest and host by sitting at a long table south of the dais, likely furnished with stools or benches, not chairs.[23] Yet before he takes his seat, he must greet the murderers at the side doors, and their bloody message will, of course, prevent him from finding his place at the table after all: "*The Ghost of Banquo enters, and sits in Macbeth's place*" (stage directions at III.iv.40).

Simon Forman's 1611 account witnesses Banquo in a chair behind Macbeth[24]; putting Banquo on the chair of state next to Lady Macbeth would emphasize

---

[22] Shakespeare, *Macbeth*, ed. Kenneth Muir (London: Methuen, 1972), III.iv.3–6.

[23] On "commoning," see Astington, *Court Theater*, 37, and Michelle O'Callaghan, *The English Wits: Literature and Sociability in Early Modern England* (Cambridge: Cambridge University Press, 2007), 30–60.

[24] "The next night, being at supper with his noble men whom he had bid to a feaste to which Banquo should have com, he began to speake of Noble Banco, and to wish he wer there. And as he thus did, standing up to drincke a Carouse to him, the ghoste of Banco came and sate down in his cheir behind him": Simon Forman, cited in Kennth Muir, ed., *Macbeth*, xiv.

the hollowness of the new prince's claim to kingship.[25] Yet, as Dyson notes, Macbeth's existential complaint focuses on stools, not chairs:

> The time has been
> That, when the brains were out, the man would die,
> And there an end; but now they rise again,
> With twenty mortal murthers on their crowns,
> And push us from our stools. (III.vi.77–81)

So, too, Lady Macbeth mocks her husband's folly: "When all's done, / You look but on a stool" (III.iv.66–67). Given Forman's report and most staging practices, it seems most likely that Banquo's ghost occupies Macbeth's chair, and not the seat reserved for Banquo at the feast. If Banquo's ghost occupies Macbeth's chair, both Macbeth and Lady Macbeth nonetheless associate this haunted seat with the lowly stool. Perhaps the appearance of the ghost in the place of the king has symbolically demoted the royal dignity of the chair to the "commonness" of the stool. In any case, Macbeth's violations of hospitality have permanently cost him his place at life's great feast, and a haunted stool, not a haunted chair, may be the most appropriate seat to bear this void. It is interesting that Duncan, the parricide of the play, produces no ghost; it is Banquo's status as friendly stool-mate that makes his murder the one that haunts Macbeth the most. In *Macbeth*, the political theology of the king's two bodies, visualized by the throne as a kind of second skeleton and ideal form of the mortal monarch, makes room for the political theology of the stool, whose interchangeable intervals and butt-bearing affordances establish lower, more

---

[25] J. P. Dyson, "The Structural Function of the Banquet Scene in *Macbeth*," *Shakespeare Quarterly* 14.4 (Autumn 1963): 374 [369–78].

lateral, and more mobile forms of relationship and communion.

The voluminous inventory of Hardwick House, conducted for Bess of Hardwick in 1601, lists forms of seating in ordered clusters:[26]

> *A Chare of clothe of golde fringed with golde and black silk, a Table, a Carpet of darnix, a Joyned stoole, a Close stool, a stoole pan, a Chamberpot.* (34)
>
> *A Chare of Cloth of golde with golde and silke freeze, a stoole of Cloth of golde and grene and black velvet, a joined stoole inlayed* ... (34–35)
>
> *A Chare, a forme [bench], a square quition of needlework, a fier shovel, a payre of tonges, a Close stoole, a stoole pan* ... (36)
>
> *A Chare of red cloth fretted with grene & stitch with white & grene silk frenge, a lowe stoole of grene cloth fretted with red & stitch & fringed with white, a plane joyned stoole* ... (37)
>
> *Too wood Chares, tenn frames for Chares, three wood stooles, a Close stoole covered with lether, another close stole* ... (42)
>
> *a Chare of grene cloth stitch with yellowe silke, a stoole of grene cloth sticht with yellow silk, too Joyned stooles, a close stoole covered with Lether, a stool pan, a Chamber pot* ... (42)

---

[26] Santina M. Levey, ed., *Of Houshold Stuff: The 1601 Inventories of Bess of Hardwick* (London: The National Trust, 2001).

> *A Chare of cloth of tissue with golde fringe the frame guilt, a stoole of wrought cloth of golde and silver with yellowe and red silk fringe, a Joyned stoole... (44)*

> *A Chare of cloth of gold and cloth of tissue, the back needlework and wrought with golde, a little Chare of cloth of golde, a stoole of cloth of tissue and black wrought velvet, a Joyned stoole... (43)*

An implicit status landscape as well as a set of relationships organizes these lists. Chairs come first, then forms or benches, then upholstered stools, then joint stools, and finally close stools and their accoutrements (stool pans and chamber pots). This ordering draws on the deep relationship between chairs and buttocks as the list descends from chair to stool to close stool. These lists record orders of status across the lived and social bodies most certainly, but also relations of conservation and stewardship. In an era when furniture was made by hand and made to last, chairs and stools not only supported acts of labor and conviviality, but also solicited care. Bess of Hardwick instructed her son to keep her collection intact and in good health:

> the sayed plate Beddinge hanginges and other furniture so bequeathed or appoynted ... shall have speciall care and regard to preserve the same from all manner of wett mothe and other hurte or spoyle thereofe...[27]

These objects live in a domestic ecology of moisture, mold, and moths, of hurt and spoil: they inhabit Puck's world, a world of accident and happenstance at the

---

[27] *Of Household Stuff*, 10.

tempestuous fronts between clashing microclimates. The inheritor of Bess's collection is not their owner so much as their curator: in Roman law, the curator is the guardian of the estate and physical well being of his charge. Curation, unlike ownership, attributes something like rights to objects: the right to be cleaned and repaired, the right not to be thrown away. There is a burdensome side here as well: like God at Sinai with those weighty tablets of stone, Old Bess is entrusting her son with pages and pages of furniture, but she is also saddling him with it. In any case, curatorial exertions are more cute than zany, insofar as they concern "the tenderness. . . . we harbor. . . . towards . . . commodities."

It is not the wood so much as the fabric that requires conservation (and whose fringes and curves make furniture potentially cute in Ngai's sense). Ann Rosalind Jones and Peter Stallybrass have dubbed Renaissance England "a cloth culture," and indeed much wealth and design inventiveness as well as skilled labor went into tapestries, bed hangings, and upholstered furniture.[28] Bess's most valuable holdings were in fabric, not wood, and her inventory is stuffed with soft goods, from "a quition [cushion] of tapestry" and "tapestry Coverletts" to major cycles on themes like the planets, hunting, and the story of Abraham; her collection is especially famous for its holdings in appliqué and embroidery, including portraits of famous women pieced together from bits of ecclesiastical vestments.[29] Upholstery participated in the media architecture of the Renaissance not only through the

---

[28] Ann Rosalind Jones and Peter Stallybrass, *Renaissance Clothing and the Materials of Memory* (Cambridge University Press, 2000).
[29] *Of Houshold Stuff*, 25, 43. On Bess's fabric collection, see Santina M. Levey, *Elizabethan Treasres: The Hardwick Hall Textiles* (London: The National Trust, 1998).

images displayed on the woven and painted finishings of furniture, but also through the forms of framing, veiling, padding, enclosure, and partition that fabric afforded. I call the world shaped by moveable fabrics and furnishings the Renaissance softscape, a term borrowed from landscape architecture, where the hardscape encompasses permanent features such as paving, retaining walls, landforms, and gazebos, while the softscape gathers up the many plantings that arrange color, texture, smells, and shade according to diurnal, seasonal and life cycle habits of growth and decay.[30] A chair assembles hard and soft elements (frame and cushion) within its double body, but the chair's mobile architecture also contributes more broadly to the softscape of the Renaissance rooms that might house it, insofar as the chair is designed for reposititioning, transport, storage, and care in spaces shared by holiday and quotidian scripts.

The upholsterer, whose office emerges in the seventeenth century, is the artisan who made cushions for those chairs but also draped walls, bedsteads, and tables with "golde lace," "sarcenet Curtins," carpets of "tawnie cloth garded with velvet," "white fustian," and all the other woven goods that lent their ornamental, reflective, sound-absorbing, and light-blocking affordances to Renaissance chambers.[31] Thomas Sheraton's

---

[30] On the Renaissance softscape, see my essay, "Soft *Res Publica*: On the Assembly and Disassembly of Courtly Space," *Republics of Letters* 2.2 (June 2011): http://rofl.stanford.edu/node/96.

[31] Cloth words from *Of Houshold Stuff*, 24. On the profession of the upholsterer (from "upholder") as it emerged in the seventeenth century out of the earlier offices of fourriers and ushers, see Peter Thornton, "The Upholsterer's Task," in *Seventeenth-Century Interior Decoration in England, France, and Holland* (New Haven: Yale University Press, 1978), 97–129. See also Joan DeJean, *The Age of Comfort* (New York:

1793 manual, *The Cabinet Maker and Upholsterer's Drawing-Book*, which educates the artisans of the softscape in the science of perspective drawing, indicates the deep alliance between furniture makers and upholsterers as well as their desire to gain credibility from the more established design profession of architecture [Figure 2].[32]

Sheraton draws a visual analogy between the structure of the chair and the framing of the house in order to merge the softer work of the upholsterer and the cabinetmaker with the harder arts of formal building. Sheraton's assertion of professionalization reflects the increasing immobility of furniture in a world in which floor plans and room functions had become firmly fixed.[33] At the same time, by releasing upholsterers and cabinetmakers into forms of space organized by perspective drawing and thus attached to the technology of the image and the society of spectacle, Sheraton's book anticipates the rise of the interior decorator and later the interior designer. These masters and mistresses of the modern softscape were the first fabricators of the experience economy, whose tools in our new century include not only mass-produced wall coverings, Pantone colors, and a maze of carpeting options, but also computer-generated building forms, sound gardens, smart walls, and ambient projections.[34]

Bloomsbury, 2009), on the expansion of upholstery in the eighteenth-century interior designer (121–23).

[32] Thomas Sheraton, *The Cabinet-Maker and Upholsterer's Drawing Book* (London: T. Bensley, 1793).

[33] DeJean, *Age of Comfort*, 103–4.

[34] On the experience economy as the shape of our contemporary *theatrum mundi*, see B. Joseph Pine II and James H. Gilmore, *The Experience Economy: Work Is Theatre and Every Business a Stage* (Boston: Harvard Business School Press, 1999). On the architecture of the experience economy, see Anna Klingman, *Brandscapes: Architecture in the Experience Economy* (Cambridge: MIT Press, 2007).

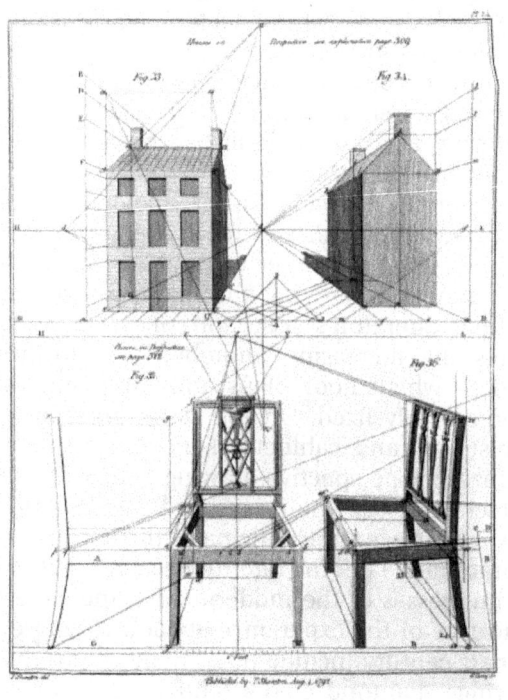

Figure 2. from Thomas Sheraton, *The CabinetMaker and Upholsterer's Drawing-Book, in Three Parts,* 1793. Figure 36: "How to Represent a Chair Having its Front Perpendicular to the Picture."

"Liquid architecture," incorporating flexible floor plans and multiple traffic patterns into spaces whose functions fluctuate with the market, is the new softscape.[35]

---

[35] Klingman, *Brandscapes*, 130.

In each of these scenes of assembly, chairs and stools in various states of dress constitute a *res publica* of furniture. Latour reminds us that Heidegger used the word "gathering" to "account for the 'thingness of the thing,'" and he goes on to write that "A gathering, that is, a thing, an issue, inside a Thing, an arena, can be very sturdy, too, on the condition that the number of its participants, its ingredients, nonhumans as well as humans, not be limited in advance."[36] Chairs and stools are "public things," furnishings moved about in order to zone and rezone the environments of entertainment; themselves gatherings of distinct materials and skills as well as whole zoologies and anthropologies, they invite acts of human gathering through the affordances of their shapes and their organizational contributions to the shifting softscape of work, conversation, and conviviality. (We all know the difference between chairs in a circle and chairs in rows.) If chairs are composites of materials and systems—assemblages in a physical sense—they are also tools that support assembly in the sense of public gathering and convening, whether for a state dinner, a gossip fest, or a flyte of insults.

Establishing the importance of affective labor for the Italian autonomists, Michael Hardt writes that

> Affective labor is itself and directly the constitution of communities and collective subjectivities. The productive circuit of affect and value has thus seemed in many respects as an autonomous circuit for the constitutions of subjectivity, alternative to the processes of capitalist valorization.

Whereas affective labor dominated the productive practices of pre- and early modern cottage industries, it dwindled into mere women's work during the great age

---

[36] Latour, "Matters of Fact, Matters of Concern," 246.

of manufacturing. In our moment, Hardt notes, the experience and knowledge economies have "incorporated and exalted" service work, making affective labor into "one of the highest value-producing forms of labor" in today's software sweatshops and retail theaters.[37] Yet affective labor, through D.I.Y., localvore, and slow food movements as well as through daily exchanges of social capital at the verges of consumerism, has the capacity to resist total cooption by creating forms of "biopower from below" that cable-stitch corporeal expenditures and somatic satisfactions into new ideational and social networks, as Jack Bratich has argued forcefully.[38]

The zany Renaissance stool is a cipher of the creative capacities of affective labor, its compact architecture plugged into artisanal practice, household work, commensal pleasure, and the informal arts of conversation and performance that accompany all of these. Stool-anchored labor is seated but not secured, poised for changes in task, posture, and spatial rearrangement as the occasion calls for; as such, stools afford though by no means insure styles of sociability that are themselves responsive, fluid, and egalitarian. In the heyday of manufacture, the assembly line replaced sitting work with standing labor, while the mass-produced chairs pumped out by modern industry and design incorporated the proletarian pragmatism of stools into their stacked, portable, factory-built frames. Today, sitting—not on stools but on desk chairs, couches and the tyrannous buckets and benches of the minivan—has become an emblem of the forms of physical and ethical inertia built into a world in which

---

[37] Hardt, "Affective Labor," 89, 90.

[38] On biopower from below and its link to gendered labor, see Hardt, "Affective Labor," 98–100. On D.I.Y., affective labor, and the Italian autonomists (including Hardt), see Bratich, "The Digital Touch."

both work and play seem designed to keep us on our asses. The standing desk and WiiGolf promise to restore the mobility once afforded by *mobilia,* but without questioning the conditions of our new situation. Rearranging your furniture into knitting circles, rezoning the kitchen table for the business of crafting, or claiming the tools of marketing and design for community yard sales or underground music may lead to some of that short-circuiting of capital that Hardt and Bratich associate with the gift-giving virtues of affective labor, even if the surplus such efforts deliver is more sugar rush than velvet revolution. Still, if some fresh wrinkles can be furrowed into the botoxed brandscape by acts of design, ethical and economic channels just might open up for several kinds of actors, whether it's craftivist mothers, do-their-share dads, free range children, AIDS quilters, urban gardeners, food pornographers, three-legged rescue dogs, tofu turkeys, analogue toasters, object-oriented cookery,[39] Steam Punk office furniture,[40] Helvetica hoodies,[41] or pillows shaped like Zoloft.[42] When you rezone the experience economy, don't forget to make room for a few stools. The stool below [Figure 3], hewn from hazel branches,

---

[39] See the essay by scholar-chef John Cochran, "Object Oriented Cookery," *Collapse*, Vol. VII: Culinary Materialism (July 2011): 299–330. The volume also includes an interview with object-oriented ontologist Iain Hamilton Grant (3–38).

[40] See "Stunning Steampunk Office Furniture for Hiding Corporate Secrets," *Co.Design*, http://www.fastcodesign.com/1663635/stunning-steampunk-office-furniture-for-hiding-corporate-secrets?partner =co_newsletter.

[41] See "Helvetica Neue Descending a Zippered Hoodie," *typographshop.com*, http://typographyshop.com/helvetica-unisex-hoodie.html.

[42] See "Zoloft Pillow," Longstocking Design, *Etsy.com*, http://www.etsy.com/shop/longstockingdesign.

is just right for a prosumer Goldilocks seeking a new perch in the forest of affordances.[43]

Figure 3. "Fall/winter stool," oak slab and hazel branches, designed by Valentin Loellmann for Galerie Gosserez. The construction is similar to the mortise-and-tenon joints used in the making of Renaissance joint stools. Courtesy of the artist.

---

[43] See "Valentin Loellman: Fall/Winter," *designboom.com*, http://www.designboom.com/weblog/cat/8/view/13832/valentin-loellman-fall-winter.html.

POWERS OF THE HOARD: FURTHER NOTES ON MATERIAL AGENCY

Jane Bennett

THE CALL OF THINGS

There exists a rich metaphysical tradition in the West that engages stuff—animal, vegetable, and mineral—as lively intensity, as vital force.[1] Take, for example,

---

I am grateful to Dorothy Kwek, Jennifer Culbert, Nathan Gies, Drew Walker, Jennifer Lin, Chad Shumura, Martin Coward, Anand Pandian, Jairus Grove, Constance Bennett, Rebecca Brown, Katrin Pahl, Christine Sylvestre, William Connolly, Christine Hentschel, Debbie Lisle, William Galperin, Derek

Spinoza's belief that every body (person, fly, stone) comes with a *conatus* or impetus to seek alliances that enhance its vitality; or Diderot's materialist depiction of the universe as a spiderweb of vibrating threads; or Thoreau's account of The Wild within human and nonhuman nature; or Lucretius's physics of atoms that swerve, which Michel Serres spun into an ontology of fluctuating ado or *noise*.

I wrote a book called *Vibrant Matter* that positioned itself within this tradition, which Althusser termed "aleatory materialism."[2] But my book was not just a response to other books. It was also, quite literally, a reply to a call from matter that had congealing into "things." In particular, some items of trash had collected in the gutter of a street in Baltimore—one large black workglove, one dense mat of oak pollen, one unblemished dead rat, one white plastic bottle cap, one smooth stick of wood—and one sunny day as I walked by, they called me over to them. I stood enchanted by

---

McCormack, Eileen Joy, Jeffrey Cohen, Jonathan Gil Harris, the members of the 2011 seminar of the Rutgers Center for Cultural Analysis, the 2011 Fellows of the Institute for Cultural Inquiry in Berlin, the participants in the workshop on The Political Life of Things at the Imperial War Museum in London, the 2011 fellows of the Institute for Cultural Inquiry in Berlin, and the participants of the Political and Moral Thought 2010 seminar at Johns Hopkins University for their contributions to this essay.

[1] This is so despite Kant's claim that the concept of lively matter "involves a contradiction, since the essential character of matter is lifelessness, *inertia*": Immanuel Kant, *Critique of Judgment*, trans. Werner S. Pluhar (Indianapolis: Hackett, 1987), sec. 73.394, 276.

[2] Louis Althusser, "The Underground Current of the Materialism of the Encounter," in *Philosophy of the Encounter: Later Writings, 1978-87*, trans. G.M. Goshgarian, ed. Francois Matheron (London: Verso, 2006), 163–207.

the tableau they formed, and for a few surreal moments thought I caught a glimpse into a parallel world of vibrant, powerful things. Sullen objects revealed themselves to be expressive "actants," to use Latour's term, or, to quote one hoarder attempting to justify his collecting, "The things speak out."[3]

The uncanny task that I and other "new materialists" in a wide variety of disciplines[4] are pursuing is to

---

[3] Alvin, a hoarder, is quoted in Randy O. Frost and Gail Steketee, *Stuff: Compulsive Hoarding and the Meaning of Things* (New York: Houghton Mifflin Harcourt, 2011), 211. For Latour, an actant is a source of non-mechanical action, either human or nonhuman, that has sufficient coherence to produce effects or alter the course of history; 'actant' names a participant in a world swarming with multiple modes and degrees of agency. See Bruno Latour, *The Politics of Nature: How to Bring the Sciences into Democracy*, trans. Catherine Porter (Cambridge: Harvard University Press), 2004. My encounter with the trash was an instance of those times when, in Sarah J. Whatmore's words, "the material fabric of our everyday lives becomes molten": "Mapping Knowledge Controversies: Science, Democracy and the Redistribution of Expertise," *Progress in Human Geography* 33.5 (October 2009): 587–98; or what Kathleen Stewart describes as "the unexpected discovery of something moving within the ordinary": "The Perfectly Ordinary Life," *S&F Online* 2.1 (Summer 2003): 7; http://barnard.edu/sfonline/ps/stewart.htm. See also Kathleen Stewart's "Cultural Poesis: The Generativity of Emergent Things," in *The SAGE Handbook of Qualitative Research*, eds. Norman Denzin and Yvonna Lincoln (London: Sage, 2005), 1027–42: ". . . ordinary things were beginning to seem a little 'off', and that was what drew [my] . . . attention to them. Or, maybe the ordinary things had always seemed a little off if you stopped to think about them" (1021).

[4] See, to cite just some examples, Michelle Bastian, "Inventing Nature: Re-writing Time and Agency in a More-than-Human-World," *Australian Humanities Reviews* 47 (2010): 99–116; Nicky Gregson, H. Watkins and M. Calestant, "Inextinguishable Fibres: Demolition and the Vital Materialisms of

see what happens—to our writing, our bodies, our research designs, our consumption practices, our sympathies—if this "call" from things is taken seriously, taken, that is, as more than a figure of speech, more than a projection of voice onto some inanimate stuff, more than an instance of the pathetic fallacy.[5] What if things really can (in an under-determined way) hail us and offer a glimpse, through a window that opens, of lively bodies unparsed into subjects and objects? How does that work?

Asbestos," *Environment and Planning A* 42.5 (2010): 1065–83; Steven Shaviro, "The Universe of Things," *Steven Shaviro* [website], http://www.shaviro.com/Othertexts/Things.pdf; Graham Harman, "The Assemblage Theory of Society," in *Towards Speculative Realism: Essays and Lectures* (Winchester: Zero Books, 2010), 170–98; Aaron Goodfellow, "Pharmaceutical Intimacy: Sex, Death, and Methamphetamine," *Home Cultures* 5.3 (2008): 271–300; Eileen A. Joy and Craig Dionne, eds., "*When* Did we Become Post/human?", special issue of *postmedieval: a journal of medieval cultural studies* 1.1-2 (Spring/Summer 2010); Jussi Parikka, *Insect Media: An Archaeology of Animals and Technology* (Minneapolis: University of Minnesota Press, 2010); and Bruce Braun and Sarah Whatmore, "The Stuff of Politics: An Introduction," in Bruce Braun and Sarah Whatmore, eds., *Political Matter: Technoscience, Democracy, and Public Life* (Minneapolis: University of Minnesota, 2010), ix–xl.

[5] I think that the notions of "pathetic fallacy" and "prosopopeia," even if stretched creatively, are not right for my project. Satoshi Nishimura defines the former as the "ascription of human characteristic to inanimate objects, which takes place when reason comes under the influence of intense emotion" (Nishimura, Satoshi, "Thomas Hardy and the Language of the Inanimate," *Studies in English Literature: 1500-1900* 43.4 [Autumn 2003]: 897 [897–912]). This notion, like "prosopopoeia" (the trope that confers a human voice on a dead thing), assumes and insinuates that only humans (or God) can indeed participate in speech. The pathetic fallacy and prosopopeia remain too closely aligned with Kant's categorical distinction between life and matter.

At best, this window has a rickety sash liable to slam shut without warning. And after it did that morning in Baltimore and I regained my composure as a subject among objects, I tried to narrate what I saw, to enunciate this thing-power, to translate the non-linguistic emissions of glove-pollen-rat-cap-wood. In this essay, I will again pursue this quixotic task, even as Zarathustra's dwarf, who sits on my shoulder dripping lead into my ear, whispers this: "Attempts to cross the ontological divide between people and things leads only to incoherence, animism, romanticism, vitalism, or worse." The plan is to refine the accounts of thing-power and distributive agency that I pursued in *Vibrant Matter*, again by engaging some trash, this time a whole hoard. My primary tactic will be to listen to how hoarders—people who are, one could say, preternaturally attuned to the call from things—talk about their things.[6]

---

[6] It might seem that the most reasonable approach would have been to follow the path of Merleau-Ponty's phenomenology. And it is true that even though his *Phenomenology of Perception* tended to reduce the expressivity of things to a projection of the bodily structure of *human* depth-perception, his later work pursued a less anthropocentric approach. If *Phenomenology of Perception* focused on the perceptual field in which subject and object appear simultaneously (Merleau-Ponty as perhaps the quintessential "correlationist" of Quentin Meillassoux's *After Finitude*), the unfinished text *The Visible and the Invisible* invokes the notion of "flesh" precisely in order to give things more of their due. He says there that "when we speak of the flesh of the visible, we do not mean to do anthropology, to describe a world covered over with all our own projections, leaving aside what can be under the human mask": Maurice Merleau-Ponty, *The Visible and the Invisible*, trans. Alfonso Lingis (Evanston: Northwestern University Press, 1968), 136. Merleau-Ponty now presents the power of things as the very impetus or generative force *behind* the formation of projections, and thus as having a certain independence from

I'll experimentally theorize their insights. A less verbose practice (performance art, photography, painting, music, dance) is probably better suited to the task of acknowledging the call of things. Word-workers can best keep faith with things, I think, if they approach language as rhetoric, as word-sounds for tuning the human body, for rendering it more susceptible to the frequencies of the material agencies inside and around it. The goal: to use words to make whatever communications already at work between vibrant bodies more audible, more detectable, more *senseable*.

I am hardly the first to try to address the uncanny agency—the capacity to impress—of things. Heidegger, to name one influential strand of thinking, considered the topic in several of his late essays, where he emphasizes the *incalculability* of the thing and its persistent *withdrawal* from our attempts to use, represent, or know it.[7] In a similar vein, the natural

---

them. Still, by definition, there are limits to how much independence is thinkable within the frame of phenomenology, as is evidenced in the way, in the following quotation, things "exist only" as tethered to "my flesh": "What makes the weight, the thickness, the flesh of each color, of each sound, of each tactile texture of the present . . . is the fact that he who grasps them feels himself emerge from them by a sort ot coiling up or redoubling, fundamentally homogeneous with them, he feels that he is the sensible itself coming to itself and that in return the sensible is in his eyes ... his double or an extension of his own flesh. . . . The things—here, there, now, then—are no longer themselves, in their own place, in their own time; they exist only at the end of those rays of spatiality and of temporality emitted in the secrecy of my flesh" (114).

[7] But note that this flight is not merely a postulation that Heidegger makes as a philosopher. It is for him also something that we can *sense*: the thing's act of seeking cover is, he says, a "draft" from the "Open"—or that slight breeze made as the window slams shut.[7] Thus even for Heidegger, the withdrawal is a beckoning *call* (as well as the Thing's refusal to acknowledge that anyone has received its call). See

historian Stephen Jay Gould spoke of the utter "*intractability* of actual organisms in real places."[8] In Adorno's *Negative Dialectics*, the use of exclusively privative descriptors (incalculability, intractability, unknowability) rises to the level of an ethical virtue: thing-power ought only be described in relief, as "nonidentity" or the object's adamant refusal to coincide with our concepts—to say any more would be to perpetuate the violent hubris of man upon a world not designed for him.

I agree with Gould, Heidegger, Adorno, and others that any list of thing-powers should include recalcitrance, elusiveness, and the ability to impede (and thus perhaps to chasten) the will to truth.[9] But while such terms direct attention to the capacity of materialities to humble us as thinkers, these terms also tend to elide the power that things have to draw us near and provoke our deep attachments to them. Just how is it that bonding between human selves and "inanimate"

Martin Heidegger, "The Age of the World Picture," *The Question Concerning Technology, and Other Essays*, trans. William Lovitt (New York: Harper, 1982), Appendix 13: "Everyday opinion sees in the shadow only the lack of light, if not light's complete denial. In truth, however, the shadow is a manifest, though impenetrable, testimony to the concealed emitting of light. In keeping with this concept of shadow, we experience the incalculable as that which, withdrawn from representation, is nevertheless manifest in whatever is, pointing to Being, which remains concealed." Related to this is Graham Harman's notion of the "allure" of the object's mysterious withdrawal from the realm of our knowing; see his *Guerrilla Metaphysics: Phenomenology and the Carpentry of Things* (Chicago: Open Court, 2005).

[8] Stephen Jay Gould, *The Structure of Evolutionary Theory* (Cambridge: Harvard University Press, 2002), 1338; my emphasis.

[9] Thing-power as the ability to remind us to mind the limits of human knowing. Or, as a bumper sticker puts it: "Don't believe everything you think."

objects is possible? In order to explore *this* dimension of thing-power, we are going to have to risk hubris and ignore the dwarf, and experiment with a speculative account of the active, expressive, "calling" capacity of the thing. Foucault said that his main concern in the *History of Sexuality* was to trace the outlines of a strange new kind of power he vaguely discerned around him, a *productive* power that did not operate by repressing or "refusal, blockage, and invalidation." Extending Foucault's method, I want to keep my eyes, ears, and words focused on the *productive* power of things. Yes, nonhuman things are recalcitrant and never fully calculable. But let's try to sharpen our perception of their powers by thickening our description of their activeness, their vitality. For help, I turn to hoarders and their hoards.

INSTEAD OF THE PATHOLOGICAL

First, two maxims to guide our encounters:

1. Keep returning the focus to the nonhuman bodies of the hoard, considered as actants. The human practice of hoarding, as a psychosocial phenomenon, is fascinating, but aim to put the things in the foreground and the people in the background.

2. Meet the people, the hoarders, not as bearers of mental illness but as differently-abled bodies that might have special sensory access to the call of things. In examining hoarders' self-reports of their relationship to their stuff, resist the frame of psychopathology, in order to better hear what the hoarder might have discerned about her objects' thing-powers.

If the hoarder is a human body positioned at one end of a continuum whose points mark degrees of positive attraction between human and nonhuman bodies (owner, connoisseur, collector, archivist, pack-rat, "chronically disorganized," hoarder), then because the hoarder's body forms unusually resilient, intense, and intimate bonds with nonhuman bodies, she may have broader access to thing-power, access from the inside out, so to speak.

Hoarders display what one researcher called "extreme perception."[10] They seem to notice *too* much about their things, are struck *too* hard by them. "When most of us look at an object like a bottle cap, we think, 'This is useless,' but a hoarder sees the shape and the color and the texture and the form. All these details give it value. Hoarding may not be a deficiency at all—it may be a special gift or a special ability."[11] Henri Bergson's thoughts about the physiology of normal perception are relevant here. He modeled perception as an essentially *subtractive* process: most of the swirl of activities around us are screened off or allowed simply to "pass through" our bodies; only a few are isolated for attention and "become 'perceptions' by their very isolation."[12] The principle of selection is pragmatic: we

---

[10] Corinne May Botz, as quoted in Penelope Green, "Documenting Accumulation and Its Discontents," *New York Times*, November 3, 2010, http://www.nytimescom/2010/11-/04/garden/04botz.html.

[11] Randy O. Frost, author (with Gail Steketee) of *Stuff: Compulsive Hoarding and the Meaning of Things*, as interviewed by Thomas Rogers in "'Stuff': The Psychology of Hoarding," *Salon.com*, April 25, 2010, http://www.salon.com/books/feature/2010/04/25/hoarding_interview_stuff.

[12] Henri Bergson, *Matter and Memory*, trans. Nancy Margaret Paul and W. Scott Palmer (London: George Allen and Unwin, 1911), 28–29. To perceive is to "attain" *only* to "certain parts and to certain aspects of those parts" of all the "influences" of matter; there is a "necessary poverty" to perceiving (31). Mark Hansen puts the point this way: for Bergson, "the body functions as a kind of filter that selects, from among the universe of images circulating around it and according to its

typically discard those vibrant materialities that have "no interest for our needs" and what we do detect "is the measure of our possible action upon bodies."[13] Normal perception is biased toward instrumentality rather than vibrancy, simplification rather than subtle reception.

A working hypothesis: the hoarder is bad at subtraction / good at reception: his perceptual filter is unusually porous.[14] ("I was born with an overwhelming curiosity about everything and anything," says Ron of California, one of the people featured on the "Hoarders" television show, produced by A&E.) If so, then this would help to make sense of the initially implausible claim of some hoarders to be *artists*. These people do not make works of art in the same deliberate way that, say, Jean-Simeon Chardin composed his 1766 "Still life with Attributes of the Arts" or Song Dong arranged his 2009 MOMA installation "Waste Not," but perhaps they can be said to be "artistic" in their exquisite sensitivity to the somatic effectivity of objects. "Visual art bounces my electrons," says one hoarder.[15]

---

own embodied capacities, precisely those that are relevant to it": Mark B.N. Hansen, *New Philosophy for New Media* (Cambridge: MIT Press, 2004), 3.

[13] Bergson, *Matter and Memory*, 31. Bergson acknowledges that perception cannot be described in purely physiological terms: "In fact, there is no perception which is not full of memories. With the immediate and present data of our senses we mingle a thousand details out of our past experience. In most cases these memories supplant our actual perceptions, of which we then retain only a few hints, thus using them merely as 'signs' that recall to us former images" (*Matter and Memory*, 28–29).

[14] Hoarders are often depressed (one estimate is 40%) and if we think of a depressed body as a slower and less energetic one, then the balance of power in the human-thing relationship will be shifted in favor of the latter.

[15] Cited in Frost and Steketee, *Stuff*, 211.

Hoarders participate in the found-art assemblage not by creating it but by conjoining their sensuous bodies with it (which is why they cannot bear to part with an item of the hoard—more on this below). Let's at least consider the possibility that the person who hoards and the artist who creates share something of a perceptual comportment, one unusually aware of or susceptible to the enchantment-powers of things.[16] Hoarders and artists hear more of the call of things—to conjoin with them, play with them, respond to them.

Of course, nonhoarders and nonartists are not wholly deaf to the call. Ours is, after all, a consumer culture fueled by sensuous responsiveness to things, things whose power does not seem to be exhausted by the cultural meanings invested in them. Though I want to avoid a pathological reading of the individual hoarder in order to focus on the nonhuman powers of the hoard, before I do so, let me say a few words about

---

[16] The Deleuze of *Difference and Repetition* (New York: Columbia University Press, 1995) might describe the external lure for this greater-than-average receptivity as a realm of "virtual intensities"; see also James Williams, *Deleuze's Difference and Repetition: A Critical Introduction and Guide* (Edinburgh: Edinburgh University Press, 2004), 8. Virtual intensities, like the related notion of "powers of the false," are forces that are real enough to exert multiple effects under variable conditions (many of which may never occur—hence, their 'falseness') but are often too vague to qualify as a definite actuality, or even a preformed possibility: "The *power* of the false is the potentia of that which is merely simmering in a formation; it is not implicit in the sense of tending on its own to become only one thing. The powers of the false refers to that which quivers with a potential that can be defined authoritatively only after the fact of its emergence and evolution." See Jane Bennett and William Connolly, "The Crumpled Handkerchief," in *Time and History in Deleuze and Serres*, ed. Bernd Herzogenrath (London: Continuum Press, 2012).

hoarding as a symptom of a hyperconsumptive body politic.

Consumptive Culture

In *Mad Travelers: Reflections on the Reality of Transient Mental Illnesses*, Ian Hacking makes a persuasive argument that some forms of mental illness arise "only at certain times and places," and are semantically located between a virtue celebrated in the culture and its accompanying vice.[17] Hacking examines the strange epidemic of *fugueurs* (compulsive walkers) in 1887 in France and shows how it arose in the space between the culture's *celebration* of travelling abroad and its *pathologization* of vagrancy. What this particular virtue-vice pair expressed was the thematization of physical mobility as an area of ethical and political concern. If the fugueur was the madman for his time and place, as hysteria has been called the prototypical psychopathology of Victorian England, then perhaps hoarding is the madness appropriate to a political economy devoted to over-consumption, planned obsolescence, relentless extraction of natural resources ("Drill Baby Drill"), and vast mountains of disavowed waste.[18]

---

[17] Ian Hacking, *Mad Travelers: Reflections on the Reality of Mental Illnesses* (University Press of Virginia, 1988), 2.

[18] Jairus Grove explores the fascinating connection between "domestic" consumption practices and international affairs: American e-waste, after it is dumped in sites in Africa and the Middle East provides the raw material for the Improvised Explosive Devices that at the time of this writing account for an estimated 50% of the casualties in Afghanistan (see http://www.afghanconflictmonitor.org/2011/01/us-casualties-from-ieds-skyrocket-from-2009-to-2010.html): Jairus Grove, "Becoming War: Ecology, Ethics, and the Globalization of Violence" (PhD diss., Johns Hopkins University, 2011), 96.

Americans seem especially obsessed with things today: we stockpile canned goods, weapons, shoes, cats, junk mail, email, pdfs, music files, light bulbs, books, data, paper, car parts, you name it. In the U.S., the most famous hoard is that of the Collyer brothers, Homer and Langley,

> wealthy, reclusive Manhattan pack rats who lived for decades in squalor in a Fifth Avenue brownstone and died within a labyrinth of trash . . . [including] human organs in brine, pianos, a Model T Ford . . . After their deaths, in 1947, investigators had to break an upstairs window to gain entrance. Burrowing through walls of clutter, they soon found Homer's body, but it took weeks to locate Langley's, which lay within 10 feet of his brother's, crushed beneath a booby trap he'd set for prowlers. After both Collyers were extracted, more than 100 tons of refuse was removed from the building.[19]

An example of a more collective hoard is the Great Pacific Garbage Patch, a continent of plastic debris roughly the size of Texas. (There is now also an Atlantic version.) This 21st-century "commons" is a creation of the conjoined actions of water currents, capitalist accumulation, a fervent ideology of economic growth and "free markets," and the trillions of plastic bags, toys, packagings, machines, tools, bottles that humans manufacture, use, and discard daily. The U.S. military and domestic extremists hoard weapons, governments and corporations hoard cell phone and web browsing

---

[19] Liesl Schillinger, "The Odd Couple," review of *Homer and Langley* by E. L. Doctorow, *New York Times Sunday Book Review*, September 8, 2009, http://www.nytimes.com/2009/09/13/books/review/Schillinger-t.html.

histories, in quantities that exceed even their use-value. We collect objects in museums, which, according to Patrick Moran, enact "the impossible project of containing time," of "accumulating everything . . . in one place."[20] We try to immortalize our data with backups on disks and drives and clouds. "The urge to store up information . . . is analogous to the imperatives felt by compulsive hoarders."[21] The worldwide web is one gigantic hoard.

So, yes, hoarding expresses a pathology of capitalist accumulation. Or, as Felix Guattari said,

> Of course, capitalism was and remains a formidable desiring-machine. The monetary flux, the means of production, of manpower, of new markets, all that is the flow of desire.[22]

The affectivity of political economy is a point that deserves further attention. But for now, I want to return the focus to things, and to what the subjects of the A&E reality TV show "Hoarders" say about them.

"HOARDERS"

Each episode of A&E TV's "Hoarders" examines two stuffed households and the humans who get pleasure and pain from the hoard. The format of the show is this: First, a screen with the text of the scientific definition:

> Compulsive hoarding is a mental disorder marked by an obsessive need to acquire and

---

[20] Patrick W. Moran, "An Obsession with Plenitude: The Aesthetics of Hoarding in *Finnegan's Wake*," *James Joyce Quarterly* 46.2 (Winter 2009): 287 [285–304].
[21] Moran, "An Obsession with Plenitude," 295.
[22] Felix Guattari, *Chaosophy* (Cambridge: Semiotext(e), 1995), 63.

keep things, even if the items are worthless, hazardous, or unsanitary.

Second, an account of the impending doom that prompted the hoarder finally to agree to (televised) help (child protective services will remove the children, the city has condemned the property, health officials detect deadly "black mold"); then the hoarded house is surveyed on camera in all its shocking glory while the hoarder offers an incongruously flat description of the "clutter"; after which, family and friends testify to the untenability of the situation; and finally, the hoarder meets with a "support team," consisting of a professional therapist or psychologist, family members who return to the scene of the hoard after many years away, "extreme cleaning" entrepreneurs, and a small army of men who haul junk and women who sweep, wipe, and disinfect. The hoarder is regularly accused of caring more about things than people, of choosing her stuff over her human family.

The therapeutic accounts offered on the show are insightful, but they are premised on a strong dichotomy between subjects and objects, where agency is located in subjects with complex, intersubjective relations and not at all in things. But the hoarders themselves regularly contest this framing: almost every one of them denies "responsibility" for the hoard. They do not occupy the position of sovereign agent. A typical scene goes like this: standing on a tiny clearing in a room filled floor to ceiling with housewares, rotting food, bags and bags and bags, opened and unopened boxes, and many unidentifiables, the hoarder picks up one particular item and speaks bitterly about how her son / daughter / husband dropped this and that's why the place is such a mess. Or the hoarder uses elocutions that leave the agent or genesis of the hoard unspecified: "The pile just accumulated . . . No answer for it," says Lloyd.

A good answer to the question—how did this hoard happen?—would be to name the hoard-assemblage, to name, that is, the *joint* agency of people and things. The hoarder, of course, does not speak of thing-power or material agency or of the efficacy of assemblages; within the framework of psychopathology that the show employs, to say anything close to "the things did it" would only bring down upon the hoarder the full, punitive weight of normalizing power. In this sense, hoarders retain elements of normal subjectivity: they find themselves *imperiously called* to buy, to collect, to amass stuff, and yet they obey the (supreme) taboo against animistic thinking when describing what attracts them to things.

Obliquely, however, hoarders do affirm the existence of a *material* agency at work. They repeatedly say that "things just took over," got out of hand, and "overwhelmed" them; they experience the hoard as having its own momentum or drive to persist and grow; they offer rich and impassioned descriptions of the insistent allure of objects in thrift shops and dumpsters—how the items demanded to be taken home.

How do mere things manage to do this? Let me turn now to three insights about the operation of material agency that hoarders seemed to me to offer.

POWERS OF THE HOARD

§ Slowness

One way to explain the ability of paper, plastic, wood, stone, glass to "overwhelm" humans is in terms of their comparative advantage over human flesh when it comes to endurance, patience, waiting it out. This is the first of the insights about thing-power made possible by a close encounter with various hoards. It concerns the "speed" of the thing, the relative slowness of its rate of change.

A common observation made by the therapists on the show is that hoarding is triggered by the death of a parent, child, or marriage, or even by an "empty nest," (especially in the case of women hoarders). The mounds of trash, stacks of paper, collections of jars, etc. somehow compensate, in an unhealthy but not unsatisfying way, for that loss. Hoarding, in other words, is a coping response to human mortality. I find this explanation, that hoarding is all bound up with the fear of death and pain of loss, plausible. Especially if a materialist element is added to the psychological analysis: the hoarder desperately clings to things because metal / plastic / glass / ceramic / wooden objects (what one hoarder terms his "miscellaneous") *last longer* than human flesh. Their relatively slow rate of decay presents the reassuring illusion that at least *something* doesn't die.[23] When asked why her house is filled with thousands of rocks, the hoarder Tami replies: "Well, I like rocks, I love rocks. They are peaceful."

If the volume of the hoard is large enough, it can provide a veritable cocoon of matter—the ingroup term is "comfort clutter," that may be shielding the hoarder from a world in which becomings happen all to quickly. A sociologist of hoarding writes: "There are . . . [homes] where I've walked in and there were papers all the way up to the ceiling, and I wondered whether something was going to come crashing down on me. When I first started going into these homes, I was struck by their darkness, and wondered if people who hoard have this tendency to want to be encased in a protective shell."[24] The daughter of Ron, featured on one episode, agrees:

---

[23] I am suggesting that the love of stuff is a love of immortality. In *Archive Fever* (Chicago: University of Chicago Press, 1998), Derrida associates it with the death-drive or the desire to return to inorganic indeterminacy.

[24] Randy O. Frost, cited in Rogers, "'Stuff': The Psychology of Hoarding."

her father, she says, "wants to just stay there in his little cocoon...."

The hoard is protective by its sheer volume and heft, but also by the familiarity of its sensuous affects or distinctive smells, colors, textures. Hypothesis: the slowness of objects is preferred to the faster and more visible rate of decay that characterizes human bodies and relationships. "I like rocks, I love rocks. They are peaceful." Thing-power as a power of slowness; its efficacy is in part a function of its examplary patience, stability, duration.

§ Porosity and Contagion

The second insight about material agency yielded by hoarding is that thing-power works by exploiting a certain porosity that is intrinsic to any material body, be it fleshy, metallic, plastic, etc. I use the verb "exploit" in a non-purposive sense, as in the way the bodies of ground water "exploit" openings in (find their way into) basement foundations. It is in the nature of bodies, Spinoza said, to be susceptible to infusion / invasion / collaboration by or with other bodies.[25] Any extant contour or boundary of entitihood is always subject to change; bodies are essentially intercorporeal. This applies to the hoarded object as well as to the hoarder's body: each bears the imprints of the others.

---

[25] This is akin to Goethe's notion of metamorphosis, which became for Emerson and Thoreau the "master symbol for *all* natural process. Before the ideas of evolution and natural selection become our catchall explanation of natural change—and our all-but-universal and therefore invisible metaphor for social change—the Romantic generation, from Goethe to Whitman, expressed its conception of the role of change in nature, quite detached from any notion of progress, in the idea of metamorphosis": Robert D. Richardson, Jr., *Henry Thoreau: A Life of the Mind* (Berkeley: University of California Press, 1986), 30.

Hoarders are acutely aware of these connections, and articulate a keen sense of themselves as permeable and aggregate formations that have become integrated into their hoard. The things with which they live, and which live with them in close physical proximity, are less "possessions" (a term rarely used by hoarders) than pieces of self. "I can't even imagine getting rid of my tapes. They are a part of me," says Beverly of Kansas, whose house is filled with thousands of videocassette recordings of the television shows that were broadcast on each day of her life since the 1980's.

Family members and viewers may recoil at other hoarder's nonchalant embrace of the cat-urine, black mold, rat feces, and rotting food in their cocoon. But if the hoarded house emits strong odors of decay, excrement, filth, the hoarder does not smell it any more than I can smell my own flesh. "I don't mind it," says Ingrid. Ingrid's acceptance of what others find disgusting seems to be linked to her extreme sense of connectedness to her place and space. A friend of Jill explained to the cleaners why Jill resisted discarding the rotten food packed into her filthy fridge: "to her it felt like you removed layers of skin." The hoarded object is like one's arm, not a tool but an organ, a vital member. When a therapist has to leave the kitchen of another hoarder, Karen, because the smell is too revolting, Karen becomes upset and insulted. When the therapist explains, "This is not a personal reflection of you," Karen is adamant in a way that is both ashamed and proud: "Of course it is." "But this isn't you," the therapist says soothingly. "Of course it is," Karen repeats with annoyance.[26]

---

[26] This could be an example of what the geographer Derek McCormack calls "thinking-spaces," as opposed to thinking-about spaces. See his "Thinking-Spaces for Research-Creation," *Inflexions* 1.1 (May 2008): http://www.senselab.ca/inflexions/volume_4/n1_mccormack.html.

I speculated above, with reference to Bergson's model of perception as subtraction, that the hoarder might have a relatively non-action-selective perceptual style compared to the nonhoarder, which might allow hoarders to take pleasure in what nonhoarders see as filthy junk. This same distinctive sensibility might also account for why hoarders experience the bodies of their junk and their own biological body as fused, as forming a *working whole*.

A therapeutic discourse would say that hoarders have lost the ability to distinguish between person and thing. A vibrant materialist would say that hoarders have an exceptional awareness of the extent to which *all* bodies can intertwine, infuse, ally, undermine, and compete with those in its vicinity. Biochemistry has lately focused on the nonhuman contributions to human agency: when *any* human (hoarder, connoisseur, minimalist) acts, she is not exercising exclusively human powers, but is expressing and inflecting the powers of a large variety of indispensable "foreign" bodies within the human body. These include microbiomes in the human gut and on the skin,[27] heavy

---

[27] The crook of my elbow alone is "a special ecosystem [of] . . . no fewer than six tribes of bacteria. . . . [which] moisturize the skin by processing the raw fats it produces." Overall, the its outnumber the mes: "The bacteria in the human microbiome collectively possess at least 100 times as many genes as the mere 20,000 or so in the human genome": Nicholas Wade, "Bacteria Thrive in Inner Elbow; No Harm Done," *The New York Times*, May 23, 2008, http://www.nytimes.com/2008/05/23/science/23gene.html. Cancer researchers now note that "some 90 percent of the protein-encoding cells in our body are microbes. We evolved with them in a symbiotic relationship, which raises the question of just who is occupying whom. 'We are massively outnumbered,' said Jeremy K. Nicholson, chairman of biological chemistry and head of the department of surgery and cancer at Imperial College London. Altogether, he said, 99 percent of the

metals such as mercury or chemicals such as dioxin absorbed into flesh, foods metabolized in this or that way, not to mention the sounds imbibed from natural and cultural environments, our reliance upon prosthetic technologies, etc. What is more, the 'I,' as a compound of human and nonhuman parts, is continually entering and leaving larger assemblages (ideologies, diets, cultures, technological regimes) made up of other sets of composite or compound bodies. A full acknowledgement of the porosity and contagion between bodies would entail a dramatic revision of the role of "will" and "intentionality" in human agency.[28]

---

functional genes in the body are microbial": George Johnson, "Cancer's Secrets Come Into Sharper Focus," *The New York Times*, August 15, 2011, http://www.nytimes.com/2011/08/16/health/16cancer.html?_r=1&ref=science.

[28] Other findings from microbiology and from the biochemistry of addiction, schizophrenia and other forms of atypical brain conditions also reveal the limits of the common sense assumption that the default locus of action is the willing or intentional human individual. Once we admit to the nonhuman members of self, "intentionality' and "will" are better translated into terms that allow their distribution and dissemination across various species of nested bodies engaging in something like what John Dewey, in *The Public and Its Problems* (New York: Henry Holt and Co., 1927), termed "conjoint action." Many of us now believe that the *locus* of action is probably better figured as an assemblage of human and nonhuman bodies, each of which emits quanta of thing-power. If you think of materiality as vibratory (Deleuze), or prone to swerves and flukes (Lucretius), or expressing a conative drive to ally itself with other bodies in order to enhance its power (Spinoza), then it becomes harder to believe that humans are anything other than participants composed of many actants with variable degrees of agency. Human bodies have their distinctive powers—both humans and apes have mirror neurons, for example, but ours can resonate with intransitive or abstract movements in our sensory field and theirs cannot (thanks to Rom Coles for that

But the point I want to emphasize now is this: the difficult task of enunciating the ingression or call of things is made possible at all by the fact that the ethnographic translator is already herself a thing with thing-power.[29] Which brings me to my third point.

§ Inorganic Sympathy

In addition to bringing the efficacy of slowness and porosity to light, hoarding allows us to specify a third quality of thing-power: things work on us by tapping into what (for lack of a better term) I'll call the human inorganic. Hoarders (again more acutely than ethnographers or theorists) feel the force of the "its" that scientists increasingly find at work inside us, for good and ill. In an act of sympathy and self-recognition, the

---

point)—but *all* material configurations have their specialties. The notion that the effective locus of agency is a collective rather than any individual is not news to my home discipline political science, which regularly examines the agency of crowds, bureaucracies, nation-states, international and transnational systems. But what social scientists have tended to ignore is the active participation of ordinary objects inside these collectives, and inside the collective called the I. The thought of a *material* and *essentially distributed* agency is hard to retain and pursue even for scholars of the new materialist or posthumanist persuasions, a point which I take up in at the end of this essay.

[29] In a world of vibrant materialities, the agency of a self appears not only as radically *entangled* with nonhuman things, but as partially composed of such stuff. That's why I think that the notion of our "embodiment" is insufficient; we are, through and through, an array of bodies, many different kinds of them in nested sets. For a good discussion of this point, and of microbiomes and their implications for thinking about sovereignty at the personal, state, and international levels, see Stefanie Fishel, "New Metaphors for Global Living" (PhD diss., Johns Hopkins University, 2011), especially the chapter "I have all lives: Metagenomics as Paradigm."

hoard accesses the it-stuff within the hoarder herself and forms bonds therein. This bond can be as adamantine as rock, as durable as teeth or bones, as becomes clear in the pain and violence hoarders experience when they are wrenched from their things. As it flies through the air toward the 1-800-Got-Junk? truck, the vibrant matter morphs into useless trash. What I am calling an act of "inorganic sympathy" may be akin to what Freud was getting at with the "death drive." The human body, he says, longs to return to the indeterminacy of the inorganic:

> Starting from speculations on the beginning of life and from biological parallels, I drew the conclusion that, besides the instinct to preserve living substance and to join it into ever larger units, there must exist another, contrary instinct seeking to dissolve those units and to bring them back to their primaeval, inorganic state. That is to say, as well as Eros there was an instinct of death.[30]

The so-called death drive could also be described as a distinctive form of *relationality*, a peculiar associational logic, a subterranean "sympathy" between bodies that we normally segregate: life / matter, person / thing, animal / vegetable / mineral. Sympathy, as a mode of relationality or encounter, is different from both relations of instrumentalitiy and relations of aesthetic appreciation. One the one hand, the hoard-hoarder relationship has little to do with utility or instrumentality—items of the hoard are rusted, broken, rotten, or simply inaccessible, and I'm not willing to go so far as to project purposiveness onto things and say

---

[30] See Freud's *Civilization and Its Discontents*, trans. James Strachey (New York: W.W. Norton, 1989).

that *they* are using the hoarder.[31] On the other hand, neither is the relationship aptly described in terms of the usual alternative to utility, i.e., aesthetics.

I'll try to make clear why not by reference to Walter Benjamin's analysis of the relationality operative in the connoisseur and his collection. The connoisseur, says Benjamin, does not "use" his collection but rather makes "the glorification of things his concern." Benjamin explains the irrelevance of utility to the collector-body's longing to escape the oppressive world of marketed goods, as a desire to engage with bodies other than those of the commodified type:

> The collector . . . made the glorification of things his concern. To him fell the task of Sisyphus which consisted of stripping things of their commodity character by means of his possession of them. . . . The collector dreamed

---

[31] Here the question of panpsychism arises, and I think there is promise in the version that finds "mind" as existing in all things, in the sense that "all objects, or system of objects, possess a singular inner experience of the world around them." This panpsychism "asks us to see the 'mentality' of other objects not in terms of *human* consciousness but as a subject of a certain *universal quality* of physical things, in which both inanimate mentality and human consciousness are taken as particular manifestations": David Skrbina, *Panpsychism in the West* (Boston: MIT Press, 2007), 16–17. For a related discussion, focusing on the implications of the concept of material agency for a philosophy of mind, see Lambros Malafouris's brave analysis in "Knapping Intentions and the Marks of the Mental," in *The Cognitive Life of Things: Recasting the Boundaries of the Mind*, eds. Lambros Malafouris and Colin Renfrew (Cambridge: McDonal Institute Monographs, 2010), 13–22.

that he was in a world . . . in which things were freed from the bondage of being useful.[32]

Like the collector, the hoarder often reports feeling a high or a surge of pleasure when she is called by and becomes bonded to a new item for the hoard. And perhaps Benjamin is right that part of what is happening there is a human body taking pleasure in the useless, sheer thereness of other bodies.[33] But from the point of view of a vital materialist, Benjamin falls too quickly down the slide from thing-power to human power when he speak of the collector's "glorification" of things, especially if "glorification" is something that the self-possessed human beholder *bestows* upon dull things. (Maxim 1: keep the focus on what things do and resist the all-too-human tendency to reduce thing-power to a projection of human agency.) It may be Benjamin's focus on the connoisseur and his *deliberate* aestheticism, rather than the more extreme case of the hoarder and hoard, that lends itself to this anthropocentrism. The overwhelming volume and often wholly non-discriminatory quality of the hoarder's collection jars with the idea of artistry. The hoarder and artist may share, compared to the average person, a sensibility, but they are not identical.

As a description of a relationality that is neither utilitarian nor quite aesthetic, Roland Barthes's term "advenience" has some advantages over "glorification."

---

[32] Walter Benjamin, *Charles Baudelaire: A Lyric Poet in the Era of High Capitalism* (London: Verso, 1997), 168-69.
[33] Benjamin early on voiced the lament, even more common today, that opportunities for non-commodified encounters are vanishing, though as I look around Baltimore and the life of the streets, I'm not so sure about that. See Jane Bennett and Alex Livingston, "Philosophy in the Wild: Listening to Things in Baltimore," *Scapegoat* 02, special issue on "Materialism" (January 2012): (n.p.).

In the wake of a particularly vivid encounter with a photograph, Barthes wonders just what "is in it that sets me off." He describes the peculiar calling-out of the thing as "*advenience* or even *adventure*"— "This picture *advenes*, that one doesn't." Davide Panagia explicates Barthes's term of art, emphasizing the way the process of advenience is indifferent to the normal logic of cause and effect and to the human interest in knowledge-production: "For something to advene means that it . . . strikes without designating. An advenience is at once wholly present and always partial," an "incomplete becoming." An advenience marks a presence that we can sense but not know.[34]

Advenience is a making-present to human sense-perception, a jutting or intruding into the "regime of the sensible."[35] It is a standing up and standing out that the ancient Greeks called *ekstasis* ("to stand outside

---

[34] Panagia *includes* advenience *within* the realm of the aesthetic, which he defines as that sphere of vitality and appearance that is unstructured by the human interest in knowledge, where things indicate their presence without designating an object: "This is what aesthetic disinterest ultimately means: the absence of a structure of interest that would guarantee a causal relation between an advenience and a referent, between a cause and an effect. The advenience of an appearance . . . [resists] the *a priori* of interest, cognitve or otherwise. Whereas an armature of interest is such that it assigns a privilege to the knowing of things, the advenience of an appearance resists the privileges of . . . assignation and designation. We might state the matter this way: an object becomes a commodity (i.e., instrumental and useable) if—and only if—it exists within a structure of interest. The moment that interest is dislocated, the commodity-status of the object is discontinued" (Davide Panagia, *Ten Theses for an Aesthetics of Politics*: http://trentu.academia.edu/Davide Panagia/Papers/406813/Ten_Theses_for_an_Aesthetics_of_Politics).

[35] See Jacques Ranciere, *The Politics of Aesthetics*, trans. Gabriel Rockhill (London: Continuum, 2004).

oneself, a removal to elsewhere"). These are some attempts to mark the thing's role as the *impetus* that sets in motion the sympathy or strange relationality described above.

STICKY WORDS

It is not normal today to think of "inanimate objects" as possessing a lively capacity to do things to us and with us, although it is quite normal to experience them as such. Every day we encounter the power of possessions, tools, clutter, toys, commodities, keepsakes, trash. Why this tendency to forget thing-power, to overlook the creative contributions of nonhumans and underhear their calls? One source of the tendency is a philosophical canon based on the presumption that man is the measure of all things (and, as noted already, even the dissenters have tended to focus on the negative power of things). Another source is a default grammar that diligently assigns activity to subjects and passivity to objects.[36] (Here an antidote might be to develop the "middle voice," which is not formally marked off in English but is present nonetheless, as in such phrases as "The pie cooked in the oven," where "cooked" is syntactically active but semantically passive; or "Shit happens," where the happening is not an quite an active endeavor and the shit is not quite a passive object.)

Another impediment to detecting thing-power is what Bergson identified as the action-bias built right into human perception. Sensory attention is continually directed pragmatically toward the potential *utility* of external bodies, rather than toward their non-instrumentalizable aspects or thing-powers. Jacques

---

[36] Related here is an onto-theology according to which creativity and agency belong only to God and, to a lesser extent, to the beings made in His image.

Ranciere makes a related point in the context of a theory of political power: political power operates, he notes, by imposing a set of aesthetic-affective habits that restrict the range of what it is possible to perceive at all: they erect a "partition of the sensible."[37] An example here might be the way the figure of matter as nonlife (passive stuff) supports the irrational pursuit of limitless economic growth and consumption. And vice versa: the pursuit deepens the attachment to the figure.[38]

But here we've again reverted to making a point about how things "refuse, block, invalidate" our framing efforts, when the task is to find ways of talking that select for the active powers of things and expose a material agency in which human perception and conceptualization participate but do not exhaust.

Poets have explored with more grace than I this enunciative project. (Paul de Man said that "poetic language seems to originate in the desire to draw closer and closer to the ontological status of the object."[39]) Listen, for example, to James Joyce's bobbing description of the living space of Shem the hoarder in *Finnegan's Wake*:

---

[37] Jacques Ranciere, *Disagreement*, trans. Julie Rose (Minneapolis: University of Minnesota Press, 1998).

[38] There are lots of green thinkers in philosophy, geography, history, and biology who today are making the call for more sustainable, less noxious modes of production and consumption in the name of a world swarming with lively materials rather than for the sake of "the environment" which serves only as a context for human action. They include Freya Mathews, Donna Haraway, Gay Hawkins, Jamie Lorimer, and Timothy Morton, to name just a few.

[39] This project was for de Man "essentially paradoxical and condemned in advance to failure." He thus might be added, alongside Gould, Heidegger, and Adorno, to the list of those who focus on the privative.

> The warped flooring of the lair and soundconducting walls thereof, to say nothing of the uprights and imposts, were persianly literatured with burst loveletters, telltale stories, stickyback snaps, doubtful eggshells, bouchers, flints, borers, puffers, amygdaloid almonds, rindless raisins, alphybettyformed verbage, vivlical viasses, ompiter dictas, visus umbique, ahems and ahahs, imeffible tries at speech unasyllabled, you owe mes, eyoldhyms, fluefoul smut, fallen lucifers, vestas which had served, showered ornaments, borrowed brogues, reversible jackets, blackeye lenses, family jars, falsehair shirts, Godforsaken scapulars, neverworn breeches, cutthroat ties, counterfeit franks, best intentions, curried notes, upset latten tintacks, unused mill and stumpling stones, twisted quills, painful digests, magnifying wineglasses, solid objects cast at goblins, once current puns, quashed quotatoes, messes of mottage.[40]

Or to the contemporary poet of lively matter, Kevin Davies in *The Golden Age of Paraphernalia*:

> Any surface at all, inside or out, you touch it
>   and a scrolled menu appears, listing
>   recent history,
> chemical makeup, distance to the sun in
>   millimetres,
>   distance to the Vatican in inches, famous
>   people
> who have previously touched this spot, fat
>   content,

---

[40] *Finnegan's Wake*, quoted in Moran, "An Obsession with Plenitude," 288.

> will to power, adjacencies, and further articulations.
> And each category has dozens of subcategories
> and each subcategory scores of its own, all
> meticulously cross-referenced, *linked*, so that each square
> centimetre of surface everywhere, pole to pole,
> from the top of the mightiest Portuguese bell tower to
> the intestinal lining of a sea turtle off Ecuador, has
> billions of words and images attached, and a special area,
> *a little rectangle*, for you to add your own comments.
> It is the great work of a young-adult global civilization, a metaliterate culture with time on its
> prosthetic tentacles, at this point slightly more silicon
> than carbon, blinking vulnerably in the light of its o
> *radiant connectedness.*[41]

---

[41] Kevin Davies, *The Golden Age of Paraphernalia* (Washington, DC: Aerial/Edge Books, 2008), 58. Christopher Nealon says that Davies, like Lisa Robertson, does a wonderful job of "describing what it feels like to live now—... among both the effluvia of the object-world and the liquidity that is constantly building it up and casting it aside" (Christopher Nealon, "What is Bennett's Materiality?", conference paper presented at "New Materialisms," Johns Hopkins University, Baltimore, Maryland, April 13-14, 2010).

Thing-power, "blinking vulnerably in the light of its own radiant connectedness," is intermittent at best. It continually darts behind the utility screens of perception and the anthropocentric figures of speech that insistently rise up with it. Still, sometimes it manages to advene.

Hoarding is of interest to me because it is one site where the appearance of the call of things seems particularly insistent, and I've turned to hoarders for help in the admittedly paradoxical task of trying to enunciate the nonlinguistic expressivity of things. Perhaps words can be deployed as sticky substances to slow the perceptual transformation of thing-powers (slowness, inter-corporeal infusion, strange attraction) into human powers (imaginative projection, artistic production, use- or aesthetic-value). Hoarding is, of course, not the only site of thing-power. Insight into nonhuman agency might also be pursued via poetry, or a study of religious orders (the Franciscan friars, the Poor Clares) whose practices of voluntary poverty are counter-attacks against the allure of material possessions.[42] Much could also be learned from archaeological digs, where exquisite attention is paid to the smallest material shard.[43] The project of listening to the call

---

[42] Thanks to Jennifer Culbert for this point.
[43] Chris Gosden, Chair of European Archaeology at Oxford University, makes explicit his object-centered approach to the agency of prehistorical European artifacts: "It is often assumed that society is created and reproduced through the actions of human agents who are shaped and constrained by the broader society in which they live. For the prehistorian, the active human subject is a problematical entity, but artifacts are often abundant. . . . There are a number of strands of thought within archaeology and outside which explore the effects that things have on people and I would like to use these to start thinking about the obligations objects place upon us when they are operating as a group." Gosden uses the incorporation of Britain into the Roman Empire as a case

from things might also engage the experience of "attention deficit disorder," refigured as a preference for the punctuated time of lively things over the smooth linearity of intentional motion. Or one could explore the world of paranoia—again considered less as a psychological disorder than as an over-extended receptivity to the activeness of material bodies. On this point, the media theorist Jussi Parikka notes how the recent new materialist interest in the thing "is parallel to the observational power of the paranoid schizophrenic, who believes in thing-power—or that things have agency, connected to wider networks."[44] Or one might revisit the "fetish" objects of museum curators and art lovers, or examine the uncanny persistence in popular culture of lucky charms. Additions to the lexicon of inorganic agency might even be gleaned from examining the web-marketer's sensitivity to the call from the data of web-page hits, as that data morphs from useless thing to commodified object.[45]

Each of these sites might shed light on the role that a not-quite-human form of effectivity might be playing

---

study in "What Do Objects Want?" *Journal of Archaeological Method and Theory* 12.3 (September 2005): 193–211.

[44] Jussi Parikka, "Object-oriented Madness" [weblog post], *Machinology*, July 10, 2011, http://jussiparikka.net/2011/07/10/525/.

[45] Relevant here is Paul Caplan's study of the way the jpeg protocol, used, for example, when one posts a photo on Facebook, acts to conceal both its own agency and that of "machine vision systems," where computers 'see', 'file' and 'analyse' with no human intervention." Caplan notes that this masking action might be described as a "photo object connecting with face-recognition object within a surveillance-image-evidence object." See Paul Caplan, "Jpeg: more than accidents, relations and qualities" [weblog post], *The Internationale*, April 2011, http://theinternationale.com/blog/2011/04/jpeg-more-than-accidents-relations-and-qualities/.

in maintaining the over-consumptive, ecologically disastrous society that I inhabit. This concern is really at the heart of my project and it reveals the fact that, despite my interest in material agency, mine is not a *post*-human project. Quite to the contrary: it is my conviction that to really understand social practices it is necessary to acknowledge the non-human components that are always at work inside them. Ultimately, I am looking for a road that leads toward more sustainable consumption practices; things might have something to say about how to forge such a path.

Response Essays

Speaking Stones, John Muir, and a Slower (Non)humanities

Lowell Duckert

> There's no question that ANT prefers to travel slowly, on small roads, on foot....
>
> Bruno Latour, *Reassembling the Social*[1]

By the time you arrive at this point in the collection, you will have realized that the essays herein demand a

---

[1] Bruno Latour, *Reassembling the Social: An Introduction to Actor-Network-Theory* (Oxford: Oxford University Press, 2005), 23.

slow reading. Perfect: the practice of tracing connections between actors, slowly, as Bruno Latour's ant (or ANT, short for Actor Network Theory) would tell us, is the way to go. According to Latour's self-defined "slowciology," we are to follow the actors themselves—examining the relationships they assemble, interrupt, or disturb. Latour's process is "agonizingly slow" by necessity.[2] Yet in writing my response, I find myself running down a fast lane. The time when these authors first presented their work at the conference, "Animal, Vegetable, Mineral: Ethics and Objects in the Medieval and Early Modern Periods," coincided with one of the most accelerated points in my doctoral career. Then as now, I was deep in my dissertation topic of eco-materialism: reconceiving early modern waterscapes as vibrant, living, actor-networks of (non)human desires and assemblages. Ecocriticism is a vast road to travel. And six months later, I was racing onto the job market. Do academics move too hastily? So let us *slow* down. My response will pick up on Eileen Joy's idea of the humanist as a "slow recording device," a being involved in a world of *complication* who also describes a world of *co-implication*, of sentience, becomings, and desires shared between actors inanimate and animate. What happens when we slow down, when we take the time to take these ethical steps seriously?

Slowness, the ant tells me, is all. Could composing new relations actually bring us some composure? The contributors to this volume suggest that the ontological questions we ask—we need to ask—about humans and nonhumans are beginning to get more speculative. Eileen Joy, for example, references Timothy Morton's work on the binary bind between human and nonhuman, inside and outside. According to Morton's dark ecology, we cannot cancel or preserve this binary, just accept it, and should furthermore delve deeper into it

---

[2] Latour, *Reassembling the Social*, 25.

than deep ecology allows. His "melancholy ethics" means "loving the thing *as* thing," even if it means staying in "this poisoned ground."[3] Graham Harman is another interlocutor in many of these essays. Harman's object-oriented ontology argues that objects and their relationships recede from us; never really touching, objects relate to one another only in the presence of a third (the vicar) in what he calls "vicarious causation."[4] Questions abound and *complications* emerge. The "ethics of interdependence" that Joy ardently speaks of suddenly feels necessary. Ethics is, in Joy's words, a "slowing down," a welcoming of the other, an addition of beauty. We should listen to the countless inhuman actors in the world, start forming alliances for more sentience (and keep doing it!), and make room for hospitality and its possibilities. Peggy McCracken's emphasis on the "giving and taking" of hosts is a significant case in point. To paraphrase two (or four?) of Joy's alerts, *you are here* and *there are relations. Hello, everything*—we are *co-implicated*.

I will try to trace a solid example. "Track," actually, might be more useful when talking about steps left behind for us, borrowing from Julian Yates's woolly essay. Not surprisingly, I turn to an object [Figure 1]: the stone I retrieved from Valerie Allen's lapidary grab bag that passed through the audience during her presentation of "Mineral Virtue." There *is* a surprise to this object, after all. In its very method, Allen's lecture

---

[3] Timothy Morton, *Ecology without Nature: Rethinking Environmental Aesthetics* (Cambridge: Harvard University Press, 2007), especially 181–205.
[4] See, for instance, Graham Harman, "Time, Space, Essence, and Eidos: A New Theory of Causation," in *Cosmos and History: The Journal of Natural and Social Philosophy* 6.1 (2010): http://www.cosmosandhistory.org/index.php/journal/article/view/133/276.

performed the stony agency her essay (of the same name) examines.

Figure 1. stone dispensed from Valerie Allen's lapidary grab bag at the conference; photograph by author.

The randomness of the bag—why did I receive an *alluring* light blue rock that now cohabits my apartment?—underscores what Yates elsewhere has called "agentive drift." For Yates, drift represents agency itself: when/how one becomes an actor, what these varying actors will become across their endlessly variable networks, into what aleatory directions they might go, "a dispersed or distributed process in which we participate rather than as a property which we are said to own."[5] This process importantly produces. Becoming light-blue stone, perhaps, is the slowest thing imaginable. But drifting with the random stone connected me at that moment, and connects me still, to others with their mutifarious rocks. This form of

---

[5] Julian Yates, "Towards a Theory of Agentive Drift; Or, A Particular Fondness for Oranges circa 1597," *parallax* 8.1 (2002): 48 [47–58].

audience participation (or *petrification*?) conveys one of Julia Reinhard Lupton's points neatly: how the proximity of *assembly* and *assemblage* relates the essential (inter)dependence between persons and things. Is not this collection, at its heart, as *event*, this very thing?

But wait! Slow down. There is an additional thing out of the bag (at least for now). I am speaking about the rock as part of a "domestic ecology" (Julia's phrase). Or, should I say, I am speaking *to* it? Or, should I say, it is speaking *to* me? As I write this, *it* is "over there" on my desk. For some critics, minding place poses the very problem of contact and how things relate. Yet in my conversation with the stone—and I use "conversation" deliberately: stressing the *con-* (with) and the *verse* (to turn)—my very writing (right now!) is an alliance, a thing that exists *because* it is a relation and produces relations. These continuous connections—stone, keyboard, rain, you the reader—should not primarily lead to the complications of causality, origin, and distance, for they fundamentally take us to the weird joys, strange horizons, and new modes of being that co-implicated assemblages afford. And they should at least drift us away from the bullying terms of anthropocentrism and anthropomorphism that too often mire ecocriticism. The speaking-writing-stone-subject-object that I am does not dissolve the human / nonhuman border in an act of prosopopoeia, but in fact challenges this border's ontological existence. In turn, an "ethics of interdependence" involves the "humanist recording device" tracing these tracks of (non)human connections, all the while making new ones *slowly* across time. Composing my response with a rock "over there" would be one (ecopoetical) example. What else?

Like speaking stones. Like stooping to stone. I think we have a lot to learn from the zany ethics of someone like John Muir, the nineteenth-century Scottish naturalist known for, in addition to his tireless preservationism, his eccentric habits and perambulations in the Yosemite Valley. Muir, in other words, was a consummate *drifter*; he drifted with the world. Coincidentally, he was ridiculed for the strange habit of "stone sermons," moments when he dialogued with rock he believed to be alive. Like a good ant, he recorded the lessons learned—and on foot, no less:

> I drifted about from rock to rock, from stream to stream, from grove to grove. Where night found me, there I camped. When I discovered a new plant, I sat down beside it for a minute or a day, to make its acquaintance and try to hear what it had to say. When I came to moraines, or ice-scratches upon the rocks, I traced them, learning what I could of the glacier that made them. I asked the boulders I met whence they came and whither they were going. I followed....[6]

Muir stoops to listen, not to conquer. His methodology beautifully encapsulates what Jane Bennett invokes in her piece about hoarders: hearing "the call of things." As such, Muir risks the same pathologization that hoarders incur for being "preternaturally attuned to the call from things." As I have been suggesting in this response, an ethics of interdependence is just Muir's method: an ethics attuned to the voices of things (like rocks) spoken *to* ("I asked") and heard *from* ("to hear what it had to say"). The humanist recording device translates these voices into a body of work, thereby inventing an assemblage of (non)human traces. By *drifting* "from rock to rock" with a living landscape, by following the boulders' physical tracks ("whence they

---

[6] *John of the Mountains: The Unpublished Journals of John Muir*, ed. Linnie Marsh Wolfe (Madison: University of Wisconsin Press, 1979), 69.

came and whither they were going"), Muir's "traced" (or written) experiences emerge. Nevertheless, although hearing the call of things is a powerful moment of interdependence for Muir, Jane reminds us that this call is not devoid of complications. Kellie Robertson, in her exemplary essay on Chaucer as "human-rock assemblage," notes how rocks are often "walled off from the animate." Karl Steel's and Sharon Kinoshita's essays put pressure on animal / human boundaries but also expose the fears that perpetuate them: the precarious "living, lupine home" (Steel), the "apparent religious and cultural divides" that Muslim-Christian animal exchanges cross (Kinoshita).

In others words, *things* are *complicated.* Slowing down means taking the time to record the complicated relationships between things—and, at times, to address their grievances. *There is no question*: we must continue drifting—even if slowly, even if the road is small, even if the delays pile up—to truly reach an ethics of interdependence. Ultimately, what is crucial to remember is *that there are relations*, and that hearing the calls of animals, vegetables, and minerals—*hello, everything*—leads us into places unknown, both dark and beautiful, and into *co-implicated* conversations, Muir-like, that we "follow" and "follow" and "follow" some more.

'RUINOUS MONUMENT': TRANSPORTING OBJECTS IN HERBERT'S PERSEPOLIS

Nedda Mehdizadeh

> The Characters are of a strange and unusual shape; neither like Letters nor Hieroglyphicks; yea, so far from our deciphering, that we could not so much as make any positive judgment whether they were Words or Characters . . . Nor indeed could we judge whether the writing were from the right hand to the left, according to the Chaldee and usual manner of these Oriental Countreys; or from the left hand to the right, as the *Greeks*, *Romans*, and other Nations. . . .
>
> Thomas Herbert, *Some Yeares Travels* (1664)

As part of his journey to Persia in 1626,[1] travel writer Sir Thomas Herbert visits the ruins of the ancient political center of the Persian Empire, Persepolis. Rather than narrating the customs, dress, or histories of the inhabitants as he does elsewhere in his travelogue, *A Relation of Some Yeares Travaile*, Herbert gives a detailed account of the size, structure, and material of the palace. He sifts through the stones of the rubble and imagines what they would have looked like when the structure was intact before Alexander the Great's conquest. Herbert's account describes an encounter with Persia's past, and is defined by the objects that remain after its fall. In a narrative primarily concerned with the inhabitants of a foreign place—whether the natives of the early modern period or the ghosts of the ancient past—why does Herbert dwell on the stones that once made up the palace of Persepolis?

This moment in Herbert's narrative is one he cannot escape. In fact, he goes back to the section "Persepolis" with each successive edition of his travelogue, reimagining it by linguistically reconstructing it through narrative. The fragments, then, continue to call to him long after its first publication in 1634. As the contributors to this volume suggest in their essays about non-human literature and culture, these seemingly mundane objects are in fact full of potential and power. Like the objects that called to Jane Bennett, inspiring her book *Vibrant Matter* and resurfacing in her essay "Powers of the Hoard," Herbert's stones beckon to him to return to Persia and to dwell in its past. Persepolis—as a term, concept, space—withstands the test of time, carrying with it a layered story that resides in the stones which "draw us near and provoke our deep attachments to them."

---

[1] Herbert acted as an attendant to English ambassador Sir Dodemore Cotton on an embassy to Persia begun in 1626 sanctioned by King Charles I and the East India Company.

The essays of this volume underscore the animal, mineral, and vegetal agents of literary and cultural texts; of particular interest to me are the agentic objects that reorient the subject in a foreign encounter. The animals of Sharon Kinoshita's essay are facilitators of exchange between the Christian and Islamic worlds, often associated with a variety of movements brought about by gifting or bartering. Her description of "the medieval culture of empire: a set of shared courtly forms and practices signifying imperial power" underscores the mutuality of exchange that can exist among cultures. Peggy McCracken explores an episode from *Roman d'Alexandre* in which Alexander the Great, during his tour in India, encounters a forest filled with "flower maidens" who offer their bodies to the warriors in a mutual exchange of desire. The forest, which can restore virginity to its maidens, acts as the one place Alexander cannot successfully conquer; though a forest of women offering themselves to their male visitors suggests the potential for conquest, that the space can transform the maidens back into virgins makes it impossible for Alexander to truly hold power over the forest or the virgin territory.

Kinoshita's animals and McCracken's flower maidens demonstrate the ways in which space determines identity. This concept extends to Valerie Allen's discussion of the earthiness of fossils and minerals in her essay, "Mineral Virtue," where the stones take on properties of the space from which they come. This is particularly relevant to Herbert's narrative where he explains that the "ruinous monument" of Persepolis "was extracted and cut out" of "whole mountains of excellent blacke Marble."[2] According to Herbert, Persepolis is literally extracted from the Persian

---

[2] Thomas Herbert, *A Relation of Some Yeares Travaile* (London, 1634), fol. H4v.

landscape, which is where he believes the stones inherit their virtue.

"The Persian qualities of the stones transport Herbert to a different place and time in much the same way that Kellie Robertson's "Exemplary Rocks" travel through space. She explains that

> the mineral suggests something about the human relationship to the world that a human being cannot, unprompted comprehend by itself . . . . Stones allow for a projection into the space of the other, a conscious leap made through the medium of an ostensibly unconscious instrument.

Though the objects of Persepolis seem stationary, moments such as the one cited in the epigraph that begins this essay underscore the effect and power that reside in the relics themselves as they move Herbert between temporalities. In fact, Herbert moves back and forth between the characters inscribed on the marble table on which the writing is etched to determine how to place Persia on the timeline of civilization by determining the direction in which the script should be read. To draw his conclusion, Herbert must rely on what he knows of the languages of the East (many of whose scripts, by moving from right to left, model for him a "backward" tendency) and the West (whose scripts he sees as moving temporally as much as lexically forward, literally in the "right" direction). For Herbert, the meaning of the Persian writing is insignificant. Rather than wonder at the engraver's message, Herbert questions the characteristics of the Persian language: he relies, in other words, on the stone to tell a story about the Persian Empire.

Herbert's desire to "read" the stone—or, rather, decipher its visual components—comes from his initial interactions with Persepolis in the 1634 edition of his narrative. He opens "Persepolis" with the moment of conquest when Alexander the Great

> more easily gaue a Period to this glorious Citie, by one blaze, at the whoorish councell of the *Athenian Thais*, so that, through his riot and her villany, this Imperiall Citie felt the flames of Warre, which *Alexander* afterwards deplored with teares, but helpless.[3]

He continues the description of Persepolis, however, as though the ancient site still stands in all its splendor:

> ... the wals are rarely engrauen with Images of huge stature, and haue beene illustrated with Gold, which in some places is visible, the stone in many parts so well polisht, that they equall for brightnesse a steele mirrour: this Chamber has its wals of best lustre. But Age and Warres, two great consumers of rare monuments, has turned topsie-turuie, this, as many other things, and left nought but wals to testifie the greatnesse of that glory and triumph it has enioyed.[4]

The Persia Herbert shows us is one he imagines before its destruction: The engraved walls have not yet eroded, their images have not yet the absence of their illustrious gold, and the marble of which the palace is made has not yet lost its luster. Similar to the forest of Alexander's flower maidens, Persepolis is a site that, though historically devastated by Alexander's conquest, refuses to yield to its destruction. In fact, even Alexander, according to Herbert, "deplored" his act "with teares, but helpless." Herbert imagines this moment as though

---

[3] Herbert, *A Relation of Some Yeares Travaile*, fol. H4v.
[4] Herbert, *A Relation of Some Yeares Travaile*, fol. I2r.

it is unfolding before him, a moment he is brought to by the power of an encounter with the non-human. That his passage reads within the present tense further underscores Herbert's insistence to remember a moment of history during its time of greatness. I use the term "remember" deliberately here, because it is through *remembering* that Herbert is able to *exist* within this ancient time. Indeed, only a few pages before, he describes seeing his reflection in the marble in an act that quite literally remembers his body into the Persian past.

Herbert has to remember not to get carried away, though. As Jeffrey J. Cohen states in his short essay from the inaugural edition of *postmedieval*, "Stories of Stone," "stone loves nothing more than story" and that

> all stone is possessed of hydrous motion, and that mobility might even be said to constitute an agency, a desire, posing a blunt challenge to anthropocentric histories.[5]

Were Herbert to fully embrace the power of the stones, he would lose his own sense of agency, and his sense of self. The conjunction, "but" in the middle of the passage—only one example of the many rhetorical reroutings in the section—is indicative of a compulsive need to bring himself back to the present, to what really lies before him. "Age and Warres," he tells us, "two great consumers of rare monuments, has turned topsie-turuie, this, as many other things." To remind himself that Persepolis exists to be consumed—by age, by war, by travelers' voracious eyes—is to fight against Persepolis' ability to consume him. Keeping the inanimate lifeless, the dead buried and gone, Herbert

---

[5] Jeffrey J. Cohen, "Stories of Stone," *postmedieval: a journal of medieval cultural studies* 1.1-2 (2010): 56–63.

freezes Persepolis in time as a place to which he can return, and on which he can continue to act.

But the stone continues to act on Herbert as well. Over the next fifty years, he returns the call of the Persian stones by revisiting and revising "Persepolis;" the epigraph to this essay, in fact, is excerpted from just such a revision in the 1664 edition of his travelogue. Turning to the Persian writing of the marble table, Herbert attempts to reorient himself by using the script to offer his own narrative about the story of the stone. Having previously asserted his inability to tell whether the Persian script moves from right to left in the manner of "Oriental" writing or from left to right like "Greek" or "Roman" scripts, he then ventures a firmer speculation, saying "by the posture and tendency of some of the characters . . . it may be supposed that this writing was rather from the left hand to the right, as the *Armenian* and *Indian* doe at this day."[6] For Herbert, the Persian script demonstrates a Persia that is eastern yet like the west, antique yet moving forward. The objects of this ancient past not only represent the multiple temporalities of Persia, but also transport Herbert between these temporalities with each encounter of "Persepolis."

Even as he moves away from Persia, and eventually towards England, he will never exist in a world in which he has not been touched by the ancient stones. By succumbing to their power with every return, Herbert can continue to travel back and forth to a Persepolis that is both other and familiar; it straddles a middle space that facilitates a mutual exchange between cultures that Herbert hopes will place England within the realm of cultural empire that Kinoshita has outlined. The essays of this volume, with their focus on the animal, mineral, and vegetable, encourage a more expansive dialogue between subject and object, human

---

[6] Herbert, *A Relation of Some Yeares Travels*, fol. v.4r.

and non-human. By considering an aspect of literature and culture that has been largely ignored, these essays have encouraged me to approach Herbert's Persepolis with a new perspective, one that attends to a variety of voices that transcends place and time.

ANIMAL, VEGETABLE, MINERAL: TWENTY QUESTIONS

Jonathan Gil Harris

Animal, Vegetable, Mineral. If this volume's theme sounds like a premodern version of the parlor game "Twenty Questions," it is perhaps only appropriate that my response should also take the form of twenty questions. The parlor game's questions seek to arrive through processes of elimination and guesswork at a positive individual entity; but I hope my questions will do the opposite—that is, resist the allure of any singular or final answer. So here goes.

1. What do we mean by the "nonhuman" in medieval and early modern culture?

2. Are we dealing (as the "Animal, Vegetable, Mineral" parlor game does) with taxonomies of the natural world

that presume, as did Linnaeus in his *Systema Naturae* of 1735,[1] the exteriority of the nonhuman to the human?

3. Is the nonhuman itself subdivided according to this principle of absolute exteriority, which would make of animal, vegetable, and mineral entirely discrete entities?

4. Or did medieval and early modern writers see the nonhuman as always already in the human—and, by logical extension, the mineral in the vegetable, the vegetable in the animal, and so on?

5. What do we mean by the "life" of animals, vegetables, and minerals in the medieval and early modern worlds?

6. Writers in the Middle Ages and the Renaissance tend not to speak of "life" but of "lives." This plural form certainly appeals to those of us who wish to resist making of "life" a universal abstract exchange value. But what exactly do we pluralize when we speak of "lives" rather than "life"—singular living entities, individual conceptions of "life," otherwise homogeneous taxonomic categories?

7. How might the phrase "nonhuman lives" potentially reify even as it admirably pluralizes the "nonhuman"?

8. What critical idiolects do we invoke when we refer to "nonhuman lives"?

9. "Nonhuman lives" might tap into the language of biopolitics, famously codified by Xavier Bichat, who in

---

[1] Carolus Linnaeus, *Systema Naturae per regna tria naturae: secundum classes, ordines, genera, species, cum characteribus, differentiis, synonymis, locis* (Stockholm, 1735).

1800 characterized life as "a habitual succession of assimilation and excretion."[2] Bichat's conception of life draws loosely on Aristotle's conception of nutritive life as diminished in relation to higher forms of animal and human life. And this distinction itself resonates with the well-known Greek hierarchy of *zoe*—or bare life—and *bios*—or life proper to the *polis*, an ordering that Giorgio Agamben sees as crucial to the crypto-theological constitution of modernity.[3] How may "lives" in the plural implicitly presume a distinction between the meaningful and the negligible life—as in the political theological distinction Julia Lupton traces between the upright chair that bodies forth the king and the low-lying stool that participates in meaner forms of labor?

10. "Nonhuman lives" might also suggest Arjun Appadurai and Igor Kopytoff's influential conceptions of object biographies as they move from one arena of valuation to another.[4] Are "lives," then, diachronic extensions through space and time of individual entities—like Eleanor of Aquitaine's vase and Emperor Frederick's exotic animals, discussed by Sharon Kinoshita?

---

[2] Marie François Xavier Bichat, *Recherches physiologiques sur la vie et la mort* (1800); cited in Giorgio Agamben, *The Open: Man and Animal* (Stanford: Stanford University Press, 2004), 14.
[3] See in particular Giorgio Agamben's *Homo Sacer: Sovereign Power and Bare Life*, trans. Daniel Heller-Roazen (Stanford: Stanford University Press, 1998).
[4] Arjun Appadurai, ed., *The Social Life of Things: Commodities in Cultural Perspective* (Cambridge: Cambridge University Press, 1986), especially Arjun Appadurai, "Introduction: Commodities and the Politics of Value" (3–63) and Igor Kopytoff, "The Cultural Biography of Things: Commoditization as Process" (64–91).

11. "Nonhuman lives" might presume less diachronic extension through time than forms of agency. Drawing on Jane Bennett's accounts of vibrant matter and the hoard, we can think (as does Bruno Latour) of non-human things as participants in the course of action waiting to be given a figuration, communicating with other actants, including humans.[5] Things, in Bennett's words, call us. But (to rework Hotspur's retort to Owen Glendower in Shakespeare's *Henry 4, Part 1*), if things call, will we come?

12. What do all these understandings of nonhuman lives do to our conceptions of time, chronology and period, including the very terms "medieval" and "early modern"?

13. Diamonds are forever, the saying goes. The geological time that compresses carbon into adamant and eventually a diamond crystal is almost inconceivably long; the millions of years that it takes to produce a diamond make our conception of period, or even Fernand Braudel's *longue duree*, seem impossibly short. As Manuel De Landa notes in his discussion of non-organic life in *A Thousand Years of NonLinear History*, periods are simply local strata in larger "glacial" temporalities that include the flows of lava, biomass, genes, memes, norms.[6] And yet our restratifications of those flows do possess a historicity according to specific logics of production. Diamonds

---

[5] See Jane Bennett, *Vibrant Matter: A Political Ecology of Things* (Durham: Duke University Press, 2010). Bennett's account of agency owes an express debt to Bruno Latour's *Politics of Nature: How to Bring the Sciences into Democracy*, trans. Catherine Porter (Cambridge: Harvard University Press, 2004).

[6] Manuel De Landa, *A Thousand Years of Nonlinear History* (New York: Swerve/Zone, 1997).

are forever, but the social life of the blood diamond that comes from modern Sierra Leone differs from that of the bloody diamond that comes from Sir John Mandeville's medieval India, retrieved by a swooping eagle from the bottom of a canyon on a slab of animal meat thrown by the eagle's handler. Each presumes different modes of supply, labor, exchange, and even imaginative possibility. How, then, do nonhuman lives ask us both to dispense with human history and to recognize the impossibility of doing so?

14. How do the terms "nonhuman" and "lives" invite us to think of their nominal opposites?

15. Death may seem to be the opposite of, and excluded from, life. Yet in medieval and early modern theology all living matter was potentially considered dead. This wholesale mortification was resisted in various vitalist traditions, which understood seemingly dead matter as heterodox forms of sublunary life possessed of "virtue," as Valerie Allen's discussion of Albertus Magnus reminds us. And, as Karl Steel pointed out in one of the question-and-answer periods at the conference that inspired this volume, the phrase "dead matter" presumes that it must have once been alive for it to die. How, then, should we understand death in relation to nonhuman lives?

16. The nonhuman would seem to presume the human. What is the status of the human once the nonhuman becomes an object of analysis?

17. Thomas Nagel advocates that humans should imaginatively attempt to become the bat they cannot be;[7] the Renaissance poet Henry Vaughan asks his

---

[7] Thomas Nagel, "What Is it Like to Be a Bat?", *Philosophical Review* 53 (1974): 435–50.

readers to acknowledge the vital vegetal life that we all possess;[8] Geoffrey Chaucer, as Kellie Robertson reminds us, imagined himself as iron between two magnets. Are such imaginative acts of becoming-nonhuman antihumanist, posthumanist, neohumanist?

18. Lupine / sylvan children (Karl Steel); petromorphic prosopopoeia (Kellie Robertson); anthropo-floral hospitality (Peggy McCracken); co-implicated interdependence (Eileen A. Joy); sheepish sidetracks (Julian Yates). What are the ethics of such nonhuman becomings, and how much might they be in thrall to a salvationist impulse—the hope that things will redeem us?

19. The early modern German hermeticist Heinrich Nolle suggests that "humans ape plants."[9] More specifically, we have seen maidens ape flowers in Peggy McCracken's essay. What happens—as the syntax of Nolle's phrase invites us to do—when we start thinking of humans and nonhumans in terms of networks that conjoin multiple actants?

20. Take the Bezoar stone. Edmund Scott certainly did. In his 1606 treatise *An Exact Discourse . . . of the East Indians*, Scott refers to the Bezoar stone as one of the most hotly coveted commodities in Java.[10] This seeming mineral was of unusual provenance: it was a carbuncle excised from the intestine of an animal, usually a goat, and was believed to be caused by eating

---

[8] Henry Vaughan, *Silex Scintillans: Sacred Poems and Private Ejaculations* (London, 1650).
[9] Heinrich Nolle, *Physica Hermetica* (Frankfurt, 1616).
[10] Edmund Scott, *An exact discourse of the subtilties, fashishions [sic], pollicies, religion, and ceremonies of the East Indians* (London, 1606), sig. G2. I thank Theodora Danylevich for bringing this passage to my attention.

too much persimmon fruit. The Bezoar stone was believed also to possess miraculous medicinal powers: it was traditionally ingested by the European traveler to combat the noxious effects of the pathogenic vapors she inhaled in the hot and humid climate of Java. So what is the Bezoar stone, and what are its lives—Animal, Vegetable, Mineral . . . Human?

oliphaunt

Oliphaunt Books aims to create and sustain lively scholarly conversations on topics of wide interest across time periods and specialties. In these conversations, we hope, the best traditional methods for understanding historical and literary texts meet innovative modes of analysis, argumentation, and publication. Oliphaunt strives to develop what the poet Wallace Stevens called a *lingua franca et jocundissima*. We are against the partitions that would separate the study of the past from an understanding of the present, the lines that cordon disciplines from each other needlessly, the ghettos that unnecessarily compartmentalize cultures, and the separations that attempt to obviate the hybridities that arise when differences meet. We are proponents of collaboration, risk-taking, diligence and creativity. We attempt a capacious exchange of ideas which, while attentive to the violence and injustices through which history has been shaped, remains affirmative, provocative and experimental.

<www.oliphauntbooks.com>

www.ingramcontent.com/pod-product-compliance
Lightning Source LLC
Chambersburg PA
CBHW050103170426
43198CB00014B/2439